THIRTEEN SECONDS

CONFRONTATION AT
KENT STATE

The Original Narrative of Events that Shook the Nation

JOE ESZTERHAS
MICHAEL D. ROBERTS

GRAY & COMPANY, PUBLISHERS
CLEVELAND

Gray & Company, Publishers
www.grayco.com

ISBN 978-1-938441-63-9

Printed in U.S.A.
v1

Contents

Preface to the Paperback Edition
by Joe Eszterhas

Nearly a half century after its publication, I'm still proud of the fact that *Thirteen Seconds* dared to speak the unspeakable: That Richard Nixon, allied with Ohio Governor James Rhodes and Ohio National Guard Director Sylvester Del Corso, helped cause the deaths of four innocent young people.

Through the use of inflammatory and demagogic words, President Nixon and his Ohio allies created a national climate of division and hatred, culminating in murder. Nixon and his allies didn't actually pull the triggers of the Guardsmen's weapons, but they might as well have.

The official history of the events at Kent State—James A. Michener's *Kent State: What Happened and Why*—was the Nixon's administration's whitewash, written by a man with close ties to the Republican Party and the Nixon administration. The book was an obscene attempt to put the blame for the deaths on the victims themselves: the dead kids. I am proud that thanks to the very existence of Thirteen Seconds, that attempt failed. In a one-hour interview on the *Today Show*, Michael D. Roberts and I (with the legendary political pundit I. F. Stone) confronted James Michener and decimated him.

One of the great lessons of the horror at Kent State is that inflammatory political rhetoric, divisive and polarizing propaganda, can lead to violence and death.

I think it is worthwhile to keep that lesson in mind.

— Joe Eszterhas, August 2012

Preface to the Paperback Edition
by Michael D. Roberts

The killing of four students at Kent State University on May 4, 1970 by the Ohio National Guard was in a way the final, awful act of a tumultuous decade. Not since the Civil War, a hundred years before, had America found itself so torn and divided as it was in the 1960s, a decade full of acrimony, one generation pitted against another over civil rights and the war in Vietnam. It was the incursion into Cambodia in the spring of 1970 by U.S. forces that caused a demonstration that lead to the violence at Kent State. The deaths of those four students stunned a nation that never thought its youth to be at risk at home.

This book was written in the four months following the shootings and published that fall. Joe Eszterhas and I arrived on campus shortly after the shootings, and then spent days covering the tragedy for *The Plain Dealer*, the Cleveland newspaper for which we both were reporters.

It was an unpleasant task in many ways. First, the newspaper had failed to cover the story over the previous weekend when the tension was mounting in the city of Kent and a confrontation with the Ohio National Guard was forming. This meant that the paper was unprepared to cover what would be one of the tragic moments in history. (This was one of the factors that motivated us to stick with the story and write it as a book.)

Second, the emotion and agony surrounding the event gave one pause as to the course of the nation.

One could draw many parallels between America today and the polarization of the nation in 1970. The big difference would be the degree and the direction of that polarization. The Vietnam War divided the country not only politically, but also generationally. The draft would send thousands of young men to their deaths, and the contempt young people felt for older and conservative leaders was matched only by the bewilderment of older adults toward what they saw as a growing unruly and undisciplined element undermining society. These attitudes were noticeable as we set out to document what had happened over those few days in Kent. Neither side trusted our intentions in telling this story.

The collective experience Joe and I possessed played an important role in how we approached the story. Joe, only 25 years old, had a deep understanding of the youth culture of the time, and I—by virtue of covering the Vietnam War for a year—had some insights into the National Guard's actions that day.

We divided the book between us, each responsible for certain chapters and personae. The hardest thing was spending hours with the parents of those killed and feeling their loss and pain. They could not understand why their children died on a campus seemingly remote from the turmoil that gripped the county. It was precisely that, the middle-class nature of the school, that added to the national shock.

Over the years, that fateful day has been revisited in seminars, articles, memorials, investigations, and government inquiries. In that time, no major revelation has come to light that would alter the facts in this book. True, many theories abound, some conspiratorial in nature, but nothing has been proven to support these theories of exactly what caused the Guard to shoot.

I believe that the first guardsman who fired from the hill on that day knows what caused him to shoot. Only he can answer why he chose to do so, and it is unlikely we will ever have that answer.

Over the years, Kent State remained with me in one way or another, too. The most ironic was my discovery, years later, that my father's cousin, Major General Elvy B. Roberts, was the commander of the Cambodian Incursion in 1970 that indirectly resulted in the shootings at Kent.

President Nixon personally asked Roberts to lead the assault after a Vietnamese general, chosen to lead the operation as a symbol of the "Vietnamization" of the war, refused the assignment because his fortune teller predicted his death.

— Michael D. Roberts, July 2012

Thirteen Seconds

1

What Will Happen Now?

Dusk, Monday, May 4, 1970: Black flags flutter from students' windows. The big dormitories are dark. The campus has been evacuated. There is an eerie silence. A sheriff's deputy's red light ricochets off the walls. The streets, littered with trash, are nearly empty. Telephones are still out. The beginning of a fog moves in on the Commons. Townsfolk sit on porches, fingering shotguns. Children are kept inside darkened houses—armed escorts guided them home from their classrooms. The stores are closed and their windows boarded.

What will happen now?

Talk: Nothing like this has ever happened in America. The volley has been heard around the world. Volunteer policemen have come from all over Ohio in souped-up cars with trunks filled with weapons. The news media talk about it every hour.

What will happen now?

Armies of revenge? Long-haired, hazy-eyed, hollowcheeked, drug-crazed Weathermen with New Red Army bandoliers and new weapons? The roads are being watched. They must not get here. All long-hairs on nearby roads are being spread-eagled against cars and searched. A sign on a fraternity house says:

"FOUR KILLED-AN EYE FOR AN EYE."

A city sanitation truck hoses down the parking lot behind Taylor Hall. The first hosing doesn't do much good. One bloodspot won't go away. The hosing begins again. The bloodspot fades.

Guardsmen unload big boxes of tear-gas canisters from a truck.

A group gathers around. Inside the semicircle a guardsman demonstrates a new kind of tear-gas sprayer. A limited supply is available and guardsmen jockey for position to get their hands on the new sprayer.

What will happen now?

The bloodstains are faded and yet the rumors of apocalypse become shriller: Snipers are coming in from out of state to even the score. They will be led by Jerry Rubin. The reason Jerry Rubin spoke here two weeks ago was to get a good layout of the place. Didn't he say it was time for everyone to kill parents? There is LSD in the water supply; drink as little water as possible. The revolution is scheduled to begin at Kent. Army paratroopers are on their way. So are two hundred students from Akron who will overrun the town. They are armed with grenades. All of Ohio is under martial law. The police radio warns: "Be on the lookout for four Weathermen believed to be disguised as National Guardsmen." Guardsmen look at each other suspiciously.

Helicopters with searchlights roam over the big farms nearby. Farmers run to their fields with shotguns. Weathermen will invade in platoons coming through the fields. A helicopter reports a sighting! Two other helicopters are dispatched, one of them armed with a machine-gun. The glare of their spotlights shows, hiding behind a tree . . . a cow, lost, wandering, afraid of the lights.

On campus two hundred students huddle together in front of a television set. They are all foreign students. This, they say, is America.

No, one says, this is Amerika. They talk about Franz Kafka. They talk about the tanks they have seen in Prague and in Chicago, and the armored personnel carrier not far from them, by the campus gate, under the arch. They talk about going home.

The Commons is surrounded by troops. Two firecrackers explode. Nervous, red-eyed guardsmen call for help. They take cover behind trees, rifles pointed at the darkness. They wait. The big helicopters hover overhead for twenty minutes. Nothing happens.

A chubby guardsman in fatigues stands in the safety of the shadows, protecting the university president's home. The house is dark. There is a pistol in the guardsman's hands. He leans against a tree. His hands shake.

"Hey," someone yells to him, "can you come down a minute?"

He leans away from the tree, pistol pointed rigidly at a figure in front of him. The pistol's safety is off. The figure says he is a reporter. The guardsman looks at his identification. It is dark and the guardsman can't make it out. The reporter motions to a light.

"You're not getting me to go out there," the guardsman says. "There are snipers out there."

He gets on his radio and calls for the helicopters. The reporter is told to stand still. The helicopters cast bright lights on the scene. The reporter is a man in his early forties, wearing a dark gray suit and a red striped tie. He has his hands in the air. "Freeze," a microphone booms from the helicopter. The reporter does not move.

A jeep is summoned. The guardsmen in the jeep point pistols at the reporter, put him in the back seat, and take him away. At a command center an officer examines the reporter's identification. He finds it to be proper. Nevertheless, the reporter is told to leave town as fast as he can. He does not argue.

A policeman assures a buddy over the police radio there is nothing to fear: a specially trained army anti-sniper team is flying in from Fort Bragg, North Carolina.

Late that night a barn near campus burns to the ground. The sky lights up. Townsfolk clutch their weapons. The fire in the sky means the Weathermen have begun their attack. Nothing happens.

When the sun rises, some of the men are asleep on their porches, shotguns dangling from their laps.

Tuesday, May 5: A fifty-two-year-old man in an Uncle Sam suit, wearing horn-rimmed glasses and carrying a flag, is arrested near campus by guardsmen. He identifies himself as an all-American citizen, a poet, an entertainer, a Christian, and a barber. He drove from Connellsville, Pennsylvania, 136 miles away. He says he is known as Mr. Rainbow. He says he sometimes makes appearances in a prison convict's uniform. "As an American citizen, I am interested in the American way of government," he says. Uncle Sam is put in a jeep and given an armed escort out of town.

Wednesday, May 6: Three guardsmen are taken to Robinson Memorial Hospital suffering from acute stomach cramps. They have suffered food poisoning. Two hours earlier, they say, they ate three donuts given to them by Red Cross volunteers in a bright red 1970

Mustang. The police radio advises all officers to be on the alert for four Weathermen disguised as Red Cross volunteers. The Guard, meanwhile, begins to move out.

Thursday, May 7: An advertisement appears in the Kent *Record Courier*, owned by Robert C. Dix, a chairman of the board of trustees of Kent State University. It says, in bold print, "THANK YOU GENERAL DEL CORSO AND THE NATIONAL GUARD." It is signed by a prominent town businessman.

Mayor LeRoy Satrom, first full-time mayor in city history, makes his first statement after the shooting: "I cannot speak with enough praise when I speak of the protection of the City of Kent offered by the Ohio National Guard while they were on our streets. All of these men deserve a great deal of credit for preventing further damage and injury." The Guard continues to move out.

Friday, May 8: Bob Carpenter, news director of Kent's radio station, WKNT, airs an editorial urging everyone to maintain reason in an atmosphere charged with emotion. He receives a call from Roger DiPaolo, head of the Portage County Democratic Party and Hubert Humphrey's area campaign chairman in 1968, attacking him for running the editorial. DiPaolo says it is critical of the Guard. Carpenter asks DiPaolo if he has carefully listened to the editorial. DiPaolo says he hasn't heard the editorial himself, but has heard from others who have.

DiPaolo calls Robert C. Dix, who owns the radio station. Within the hour Dix calls Carpenter and tells him to take the editorial off the air. Carpenter complies. The Guard, meanwhile, has totally withdrawn.

Saturday, May 9: A guardsman's mother writes the Kent *Record Courier*: "I'm asking you, all of you, do you want protection or do you want the guards to sit at the armory and disregard your situation? My son is a citizen of the United States and he is protecting your country. What are you doing?" That same day a prominent local attorney says, "I feel the Guard did its job, which was to uphold law and order.

I'll tell you something honestly. If I'd been faced with the same situation and I had a submachine-gun, I'm afraid there wouldn't have been four killed, there probably would have been 140 of them dead. And that's what they need."

Sunday, May 10: In the predawn hours of the morning a Portage County sheriff's deputy sees a car run a red light and attempts to chase it. The car speeds away. The deputy calls for help. Four sheriff's cars join the chase. Shots are fired at the fleeing auto and, deputies think, some may have struck the car. The car gets away. In their report the deputies list the car occupants as "possible Weathermen."

Monday, May 11, one week after the shooting: The day is clear and pleasant, remarkably like last Monday. The four dead have been buried. The faculty is back on campus, but university president Robert I. White says the university must remain closed due to "lack of protection." Town businessmen complain about the missing student trade.

Dusk, Monday: The town is quiet. The black flags are gone. Stars and stripes flutter from the windows.

2

The University

On Campus Day at Kent State paunchy alumni come back in their best business suits to ogle the lithe coed queen candidates and sit with their wives in a big tent near the center of campus, off the Commons, and listen to the university president theorize. They eat hot dogs and their kids get free balloons to pop. They trek across the lush, sloping knolls near the western edge of the campus and reminisce.

Of forty-three thousand Kent State University alumni, thirty thousand still live in Ohio, most of them employed in middle-management posts in state industries. They don't have to come from far away. Campus Day is always a happy time. Mock orange, elm, hawthorne, and Chinese-chestnut trees are in bloom everywhere. The chimney swift, a charcoal-colored fair-weather bird, comes to celebrate and signals the arrival of spring.

A little knoll near Taylor Hall, the journalism-architecture building, is crowded at this time of year, a melange of blankets, coeds, books, and young men.

Known as Blanket Hill to both alumni and students, the knoll has a small concrete pagoda at its crest. Through the generations the knoll has been a place of joy and, sometimes, of responsibility. Many alumni met their wives here. Several generations of Kent State University graduates like to think they lost, or at least began to lose, their innocence here on warm, humid nights. In the nearby dormitories men have amused themselves by training binoculars on Blanket Hill and placing bets on various bouts.

Here on this knoll, 19.6 feet higher than a parking lot 230 feet away, at 12:22 p.m. on May 4, 1970, twenty-six Ohio National Guardsmen from the 145th Infantry and 107th Armored Cavalry Regiments fired fifty-nine shots at a group of student demonstrators and, in thirteen seconds of gunfire, killed four and wounded nine.

The shooting took place exactly five days before the first Kent State University Campus Day in the Age of Aquarius was to have been held. A victory bell, used to signal gridiron prowess, tolled as the shots rang out. The sky was blue. The temperature was seventy degrees. There was a gusty wind. The rifles were M-1s of World War II vintage with a range of more than half a mile. Most of the victims were dressed in bell-bottoms and flowered Apache shirts, and most had Rolling Stone haircuts. Some carried books. The guardsmen wore battle helmets, gas masks, fatigues, and combat boots. The two sides looked, to each other, like the inhabitants of different worlds.

In thirteen seconds Blanket Hill was transformed into a national monument of death and tragedy. Campus Day was canceled. Blood shimmered on the grass. Bullet holes marked the trees. A generation of college students said they had lost all hope for the System and the future.

When the shooting stopped on May 4, the sound of wailing sirens could be heard miles away. The telephone system broke down; merchants instinctively closed their shops. The American Legion held an emergency meeting. Near Blanket Hill a boy with shoulder-length hair, bell-bottoms, and red-hazed eyes dipped a black anarchist flag into a pool of blood, did a bizarre dance, and screamed. Not far away, in downtown Kent, another boy took an American flag off a front porch, tore it up, and spat on it. Three policemen arrested him as he tried to light the flag with a Zippo lighter.

The volley of gunfire came on the fourth day of intense demonstrations against President Richard M. Nixon's decision to send U.S. forces into Cambodia. The demonstrations began the day after the Presidential commitment with the mock burial of the Constitution on the grassy area known as the Commons.

For most alumni the burial of the Constitution on this campus was hard to fathom. As far as they were concerned, Kent State was not a demonstrating school. Kent State was very much like its sister state schools, Ohio State University in Columbus and Ohio University in Athens. There was always a small, spring-is-here bash each year to the dismay of administrators and the delight of students. It usually took no more than a day to repair the damage and buckle down to study. At Kent State the annual bash was a mudfight, carried out with vigor on the first warm, rainy night of spring. Men would trip and twirl the coeds into the thick mud sloping off the hills. The coeds would protest and wear old clothing. The merriment would continue until everyone was caked with mud and worn out, when the participants would depart for the town's bars to cool their oats with beer. The annual ritual was still held at Kent State in 1970, exactly one week before the shooting.

Kent State, located thirty-three miles south of Cleveland, eleven miles east of Akron, near the steel cities of Youngstown and Lorain, was Ohio's second largest campus and ranked twenty-fourth in enrollment among the nation's public universities. The student population had quadrupled from five thousand in the early fifties to twenty thousand in 1969. Under state law the university is obliged to accept a graduate of any accredited high school in Ohio. Only 20 percent of its students can come from out of state.

The university was actively growing. Its physical plant on the carefully groomed eight-hundred-acre campus had mushroomed. New buildings went up each year. The design was the result of an administrator's decision. He said the emphasis would be placed on learning and he would have no hand in creating any fancy architectural monuments. The town grew, too, and prospered. By 1969 it had almost thirty thousand residents—its population in 1950 was 4,343—and 88 percent owned their own homes.

By the mid-sixties the university's physical plant was valued at $45 million. During the sixties an emergency construction program added twenty-three new dormitories to the campus, many of them high-rise structures like modern apartment complexes, visible for miles around. Kent State was planning for a campus enrollment of 24,000 students by 1974. To keep pace with the press of enrollment, it put on its drawing boards a nine-year $106-million campus development program calling for the construction of sixteen academic buildings, ten more residence halls, a new library, a new administration building, a new student union. University planners figured that twelve hundred new beds each year would have to be provided for the next twelve years.

To handle this exploding growth, in 1963, the board of trustees appointed a new university president, a fifty-five-year-old Illinois-born Phi Beta Kappa, Dr. Robert I. White, Jr. Dr. White was a quiet, soft-spoken man with a belief in hard work, a "Jeepers, gee whillikers" style, and an everpresent pipe. He came to Kent State in 1946 after teaching at the University of Chicago. In his inaugural address the new president quoted Dante: "'Consider what origins you had, you were not created to live like beasts, but to seek virtue and knowledge.'" He viewed his campus as the academic center of a megalopolis stretching from Cleveland to Pittsburgh. "Kent State," he said, "is now entering into a period of adulthood. Maturation has been forced upon us by location, youth, and a changing world." He said a state university must be marked by quality, must possess institutional freedom, and must avoid standardization and harassment from the outside.

By 1966 White was warning businessmen that the university's stunning growth and the increase of students on campus had produced strains on students which intensified the weighty, alienating impacts of industrialization and technology-

Campus sociologists were pointing to changes in the make-up of the student body. They, too, talked about alienation, noting that by the early sixties over a thousand students were committing suicide each year on the nation's campuses. Kent State University, each year, would have its student suicides. "We must become aware of those who are struggling on our campuses," Dr. White said.

Most campus psychologists and sociologists pointed to the continuing Vietnam War as the primary source of alienation. Others said students were rejecting the rat-race lives of their parents and, due to disillusioning parental example, were straying from the dollar-oriented suburban values of success. Kent State sociologist Dr. Paul Sites thought the university had outlived its purpose. "The only way to bring back alienated students into the university is to make the educational process more meaningful. The student is forced to work on the university's terms. By definition, alienation occurs when a student and a university's devices don't meet. Classrooms aren't flexible. They're prestructured and there's no way twenty thousand students can fit into one mold." Society, the experts said, was changing. So was the Kent State campus.

The university, like many other universities in the late sixties, was beginning to exhibit a split personality. The short-haired, button-down members of the fraternities and their independent counterparts were still in the majority. But another group of students began the exploration of personal life styles. Hair grew longer—from early Beatle length to shoulder-length Rolling Stones style. Dirty blue jeans, for some, were replaced by faded denim bell bottoms. The split nature of the student population was best exemplified by the *Kent Stater*'s coverage of SDS Columbia takeover leader and later Weatherman chieftain Mark Rudd's visit in 1968. There was a picture of Rudd on page three of the paper looking sullen and menacing and talking about "racism" and "repression." Most of the rest of the paper was devoted to pictures of floats in the homecoming parade and candidates for homecoming queen.

The factions grew apart. The Greeks found they could not backslap and share the racy jokes with those who disdained mugs of beer for a joint of grass. Black students formed a black power group, the Black United Students, and decried "institutional Tomism." White students formed a chapter of Students for a Democratic Society and began attracting membership.

Within the campus spotlight, focus shifted from Big Men on Campus to long-haired, Pancho Villa-mustached kids like Rick Erickson, the local SDS head. The *Kent Stater* covered Erickson each time he said three words. He was, with his long hair, his flowered shirts, his low-key manner, a different kind of hero for an Ohio campus.

Rick Erickson, back at Buchtel High School in Akron, had been president of the debating team and had been honored for his high-school achievement by the Kiwanis Club. He had renounced all of that "crap" and had become a personal symbol of the new life style. At one time he had wanted to become a politician. His father had set the example. Rick Erickson was the son of Ed Erickson, one of the best Democratic mayors the city of Akron had ever seen. Soon, though, Rick Erickson was arrested for smoking marijuana and leading countless protests and sit-ins. Defending him much of the time was his father, the ex-mayor.

"At Kent State," Rick Erickson said, "they turn out the middle-management drones. This is where they make teachers and all the other types that help maintain the system. The kids are more hip at Kent. A lot of them are from urban areas. They've seen things. They know some of the problems. That's what we're building on, the problems."

By 1968 a new mood was seen on the nation's campuses and at Kent State. A student poll showed that only 22 percent of the student population supported the Vietnam War. (When the *Kent Stater* published the poll, the local American Legion chapter asked: "Did the editors realize what effect the poll would have on our fighting men in Vietnam?") At Kent a group calling itself the Mobobrious Pit formed a kind of radical theater and vowed to fight "institutional apathy." On April Fool's Day in 1968 its members turned a residence hall into what they called a coeducated "Vietnam paradise." Members covered the hall corridor with brambles, leaves, and vines. Each room was turned into a grass hut. Eerie green lights filled the halls. Visitors to the hall that night were warned by a rigged-up public-address system of enemy attacks and advised to "get under cover."

There were signs, too, in 1968 that drug traffic of some quantity existed on campus. A detective said anyone could go to downtown Kent on any night of the week and buy any kind of drug he wanted. Three students were arrested in dormitories for possession of LSD. A score of marijuana arrests followed. The Portage County Grand Jury expressed shock over the extent of the drug traffic. Said university vice president Robert Matson, "This is typical of youth protest, the use of drugs. These kids are rebelling against what they consider the decadent values of their parents. They choose to show it in anti-social activity."

By mid-1968 university president White said his campus was "in a state of flux." Concerted radical activity began at Kent State on November 13, 1968, when student council vice president Bob Pickett, some eighty members of the Black United Students, and seventy-five SDS members participated in a sit-in at the Student Activities Center. The sit-in was to protest the presence of Oakland, California, police recruiters on campus.

"The university," said Pickett, an outspoken and brilliant black man from New Jersey, "is making no attempt to increase the enrollment of black students. The City of Oakland's police department has perpetrated a system of racism upon the black people of Oakland and they have made repeated attempts to kill Black Panther chairman Huey C. Newton."

President White, facing the first serious demonstration of his tenure, called it "intolerable" and said there was no need for such action. "Channels of communication have always been open."

Pickett replied that the university was "playing a game" and resigned from the student council. "You can have your student government," he said, "here it is." The Black United Students walked off campus for two days to Akron. Tempers cooled, however, and the university decided it would take no disciplinary action against the students. The lack of disciplinary action and the protest itself led an SDS spokesman to say, "The Oakland confrontation shows the possibility of mounting a move for further change at Kent State University."

On April 8, 1969, a group of twenty-five SDS members attacked the university administration building. They demanded the abolition of the Reserve Officers Training Corps program.

On April 16 a student suspension hearing was held against two SDS members who had participated in the demonstrations. A rally called by SDS against the hearings drew fifteen hundred students to the Student Union. Trouble began at four o'clock when a hundred shouting students attacked the speech building. An angry confrontation between radicals and fraternity men took place. One fraternity man reached over a policeman's shoulder and punched an SDSer. A cadenced shout began: "Kill the SDSers! Kill the SDSers!" Another fraternity man shouted: "The club, the club, use the club." A heavily muscled student in a mustard-colored jacket tried to take a swing at one of the protesters over three people. A short, pudgy professor who had just arrived on the scene said, "My God, what are we doing to ourselves?"

Fistfights broke out. The radicals yelled, "Open it up or shut it down!" The fraternity men sang "America the Beautiful." The crowd began to break up when thirty SDS members crowded up a stairway toward locked doors on the third floor. They batted down the doors to the hearing-room area, occupied the building, and hung a Viet Cong flag from the ceiling. Then they wheeled a color television set into the hall to watch themselves on the tube. At eight-thirty that night a platoon of highway patrolmen and one hundred riot-trained deputies from neighboring counties arrested fifty-eight demonstrators and cleared the building.

The demonstrators were taken to the Portage County jail in Ravenna, some five miles away. In the middle of the night a rumor spread that two hundred other students were heading toward the jail to free those arrested. Deputies loaded shotguns, donned their riot helmets, and surrounded the jail. Nothing happened.

The demonstration shook the university. "The very survival of this university is at issue," White said, "in both a philosophical and practical sense. Perhaps, too, this could become a question of whether or not we will finish the quarter." White banned SDS from the campus and suspended from the university the fifty-eight students who had been arrested.

"Parts of this campus," said Frank Frisina, the student government president-elect, "are a thousand miles away from each other." Feelings were high-pitched; the campus was polarized.

In an effort to unify the badly split campus, student government leaders agreed on a referendum asking students what the university should do about the April 16 demonstration. Of 18,900 eligible faculty and student voters, fewer than 9,000 cast a vote. Yet it was the largest turn-out for any election or referendum in university history. The issues were resolved this way:

On dropping the suspensions of the students involved in the incident, 3,100 approved, 5,151 disapproved.

On the administration utilizing its influence to have criminal charges placed against the students involved, 3,100 approved, 5,577 disapproved.

On reinstating the charter of SDS, 3,232 approved, 5,210 disapproved.

Frank Frisina pointed not only to the polarization evident in the vote, but also to the fact that more than ten thousand students didn't care either way. "I guess this is still Ohio," he said.

"But this is a different place than it was even two years ago," Frisina went on. "There is no interaction among students, among students and administrators, among students and townspeople, between the university and the town. There is no dialogue. Something is happening that I can't completely understand."

Weeks after the April 1969 disturbances, the president's wife,

Mrs. Robert White, sat in the Whites' restored farmhouse on the campus listening to the whine of sirens. "It's just an ambulance, not the police," she said. "This is how our life has changed." Outside, campus policemen guarded the home. "We didn't ask the police to come," she said, "but having them here makes me feel safer. Our lives have twisted. Extra phones were put in and the phone rings all hours of the day and night. One night Bob asked me to leave the house because there had been some threats and the Highway Patrol set up guards outside. I hated to think we had come to that. The officer came in the house armed, ready for anything."

From the fall of 1969 to April 30, 1970, the mood at Kent State was, as Frank Frisina said, one of "observing the cool." The confrontations of the previous year ended. So did the threat of imminent violence. Frisina thought he was making progress in his campaign to initiate campus dialogue. Vietnam, the Draft, and the System were still crucial issues, but bigger than ever Thank God It's Friday parties were being thrown at student hangouts along Water Street in Kent.

On Moratorium Day, October 16,1969, three thousand students marched and five thousand boycotted classes. At the same time there was tumultuous applause in Johnson Hall as one of the New York Mets hit a home run in the World Series.

A couple asleep on a couch didn't even look up. Another student walked past the education building and told a friend, "I'm going to bed. What else is there to do?" Some students prayed at the Newman Chapel. The ROTC drill practice was in session on the Commons. "Did you wash your ears today?" the drill sergeant shouted. A man in the front row yelled back, "Yes, sir!" Couples on Blanket Hill were oblivious to everything, as usual. The three thousand marchers sang "Give Peace a Chance." It was a mixed crowd of V-neck sweaters, dress slacks, cordovan shoes, work shoes, army shirts, and bush hats. An old woman flashed the marchers the peace sign. Hundreds of hands returned it. The march broke up peacefully. At 4:35 p.m. there was a big cheer on the Commons. The Mets had won!

In October the founding father of the Young Americans for Freedom, a rural, side-burned Ohio congressman, Buzz Lukens, was the featured speaker for Greek Week. A junior was arrested for wearing a T-shirt inscribed: "Kent cops are dirty pigs!" Campus police chief Donald Schwartzmiller presented his dispatcher's office with a color portrait of two pigs cheek to cheek. For the first time in years the Kent State football team was causing some excitement—the junior halfback was leading the nation in yards carried. Long lines formed each night in front of the new Roy Rogers King of the Cowboys carry-out beef restaurant where two roast beef sandwiches sold for seventy-nine cents. A student poll found that of 269 students, 195 favored gradual withdrawal from Vietnam. For its front page homecoming-weekend picture, the *Kent Stater* superimposed a map of Vietnam over the picture of a student sitting on Blanket Hill thinking. Musselman Hall built a ten-foot-high beer can for its homecoming-day float. A fraternity strip-in was canceled, members said, for aesthetic reasons. Workmen erected a six-foot-high chain-link fence the entire length of the Commons below Taylor Hall. Students protested, saying, "The Commons is not a classroom." Some said the fence was an administration ploy to trap potential demonstrators against the ROTC building.

In November poet Gary Snyder of the bygone Beat Generation visited and gave thirty-seven letters to the university. In one of them he said, "The whole Anglo-Saxon Protestant mentality in America is being replaced by a new consciousness which is uninhibited, relaxed, open, and self-aware." The *Stater* suggested marijuana be legalized. Dick Gregory, the lecturing comic, visited and said, "America has found a new nigger now—you, the youth of the country. Adults love you one at a time, but hate you as a group." Seventy-five marchers observed the November moratorium.

In January a student organized "No Bra Day," the first of its kind anywhere in the nation. Members of Alpha Epsilon Pi, a social fraternity, announced a forty-eight-hour dribble-thon. Five brothers dribbled two basketballs for two sleepless days. A voodoo session was held. Beer flowed by administration consent in the Student Union. Three dormitories bought pinball machines. Protesting cafeteria food, four students made signs saying, "A penny saved is a stomach turned." A group of four hundred students stood by and cheered on the Commons as the chain link fence was taken down by administration direction. Construction and subsequent leveling, a dean announced, cost $1,678.

In February a second winter homecoming was held as members of the 1951 Kent State football team—girthed and balding—were honored. A concerted ecology movement began. Main target: the Cuyahoga River flowing through Kent which, the year before in Cleveland, had burst into flames. Three basketball players were suspended from the team for drinking beer during practice sessions. Frank Frisina listed his achievements. Among them, he now sat in on Board of Trustees meetings. "I keep an eye on those guys," he said.

In March coed Sue Sanderson won a place on *Glamour* magazine's list of the nation's ten best-dressed coeds. In an essay she said, "If the morals are to be universally raised, it will be the feminine influence that will do it." In successive editions the *Kent Stater* suggested an end to the draft, the withdrawal of U.S. forces from Laos, and an end to pollution. A group of coeds protested cafeteria food, chanting "We want meat!" and "Alka Seltzer!" A pet hamster was publicly buried outside Tri Towers and a candle placed on its grave. A rat was beaten to death outside Moulton Hall to demonstrate the brutality of the War in Vietnam.

In April only a hundred students attended the anti-war march. An ecology Think Week was held and was determined to have had little success—beer cans and trash littered the campus. An ecology Earth Day was announced for May 6, the week of Campus Day activities. Stater editor Bill Armstrong urged that Ohio, like Massachusetts, sign into law legislation challenging the President's authority to conduct an undeclared war. Two students announced campaigns for the student government presidency. One called for better lighting on campus. The other called for a "hot line" to President White's office. A rowboat regatta was announced for May 23. Three students camped-in on the Commons in an "Eco-sphere," a large white tent built to show that "campus architecture is stagnant."

University president White was studying ways to carry out recommendations made to him in a report on campus unrest by Dr. Barclay McMillen, a political science lecturer. Dr. McMillen's basic finding was that the student unrest of the previous spring was partly caused by "disaffection" of the individual student among the thousands on large campuses. He recommended that the university be split physically into smaller units. He said the university should be personalized, urging that campus police officers wear blazers and slacks rather than military type uniforms. Teachers, he said, should live with their families in student dormitories. University administrators, including Dr. White, should teach one course a year, preferably on the freshman or sophomore level. Teachers and administration members should eat in cafeterias and be seen at student hangouts. Alienated students, McMillen said, were in the majority. "High quality disruptive leadership is able," he wrote, "to excite, ignite, and guide the alienated student."

The report was written as a result of the disturbances of April 1969. From September 1969 to April 30, 1970, both Frank Frisina and student government vice president Kathy Berry felt, radical campus organizations showed little if any strength. In September 1969 the Weatherman called a rally by the victory bell to protest the presence of ROTC on campus. Only twenty-five listeners showed up and some of them heckled the speakers. When a sophomore history major called a rally and announced that he would napalm his dog in protest of American use of napalm in Vietnam, four hundred students showed up chanting: "Save the pooch!" A girl grabbed the dog from its owner and the rally ended.

The radical happening of the year took place on the Commons on April 14, 1970, as a kind of anniversary of the disturbances the year before. Yippie leader Abbie Hoffman couldn't make it, so Yippie leader Jerry Rubin and his wife, Nancy, visited the campus. Pressed by some of his trustees to stop the Rubin speech, President White refused, saying, "Kent State will continue to be a citadel of free speech." Almost a thousand students turned out to hear Rubin on one of the year's first pleasant spring days. Nervous campus policemen stood by. "The kids enjoyed Rubin and laughed," said Bill Armstrong, the editor of the *Stater*. "They viewed it as good entertainment. Rubin was a kind of mad, holy wild-man."

Wearing an Apache headband, Rubin said, "We have to invent new laws to break. I have no respect for the court system in this country. Being young in America is illegal. We are a generation of obscenities."

"Speak for yourself, Jerry," someone yelled.

"The most oppressed people in this country are not the blacks," Rubin said, "but the white middle class. America is a sick society because it is a bunch of people just doing their jobs and unhappy. We are retired when we are born. American people don't do anything they enjoy, they do things for money."

As the days passed and the end of the school year came closer, Frank Frisina felt that most of the damage done in the previous year's demonstrations was healed. In early April anti-war demonstrations broke out at Miami University in Oxford, in southern Ohio. While the state's editorial writers condemned lawmen there for indiscriminate use of police dogs and tear gas, there was no show of sympathy at Kent and no demonstrations were in sight. Anti-war demonstrations broke out at Ohio State in late April and editorial writers once again condemned lawmen for over-reaction, but the mood at Kent was unshaken.

On April 27 Kent State held its annual campus mudfight. More than three hundred participated. Plastic buckets filled with water were thrown from dormitory windows. A car driving by was about to be doused by wastebaskets full of water when the car's attackers were surprised by a fire extinguisher the car's occupants had armed themselves with.

Until 10 p.m. on April 30, a Thursday, when the nation's television networks showed the grim expression of the President from the White House, it seemed that May 1970 at Kent State would be a tranquil month ending a year of recovery.

When Dr. Robert White heard the President's speech, he thought, "Well, here we go again." When Frank Frisina heard it, he felt everything he had worked for all year was collapsing—there, before his eyes, around the television set. "All the kids were around TV sets in the dorms. They had horrified stares on their faces."

3

Friday, May 1

"This is not an invasion of Cambodia," Richard Nixon told the nation on April 30. The camera zoomed in for a close-up of the Presidential palm covering the operational area on a wall map, a close-up the anti-war movement would later make into a poster that would be distributed by the millions. "Once enemy forces are driven out of these sanctuaries and their military supplies destroyed, we will withdraw."

But to those with deep feelings about the morality or wisdom of the war in Vietnam, the move into Cambodia was just that—an invasion, a widening of the conflict, a cataclysmic move that turned the War in Vietnam into the War in Indochina.

As some students saw it, the move was an invasion by a government that had become repressive, led by a President who seemed enamored of his role as commander in chief. They saw the mentality that sent the United States into Cambodia as the same mentality that practiced repression in Chicago, in the ghettoes, and on the campuses.

The next day, on Friday morning, the President, in an informal chat with Pentagon employees (which happened to be tape-recorded), contrasted "fighting men in Vietnam" with "those bums who are burning college campuses." Many students felt Nixon had shown his true colors.

Frank Frisina remembered that one of the reasons Nixon the Presidential candidate had appealed to him was what he had said about protest during the campaign. He looked the passage up:

We must listen to the voices of dissent because the protester may have something to say worth listening to. If we dismiss dissent as coming from rebels without a cause, we will soon find ourselves becoming leaders without an effect. By its neglect, by its insensitivity, by its arrogance, our present leadership has caused an unprecedented chasm to develop within our society.

At Kent State the reaction to the Nixon Cambodia announcement was almost immediate. Thursday night, hours after the speech ended, a group of students went into town and spray-painted anti-war slogans on some of the businesses in the downtown Main Street—Water Street area. The slogans read: "OFF THE PIGS!" "POWER TO THE PEOPLE!" "GET OUT OF CAMBODIA!" The small band moved to the heart of the town's entertainment area, known as the Strip.

The Strip is a short block almost at the center of town, lined with bars that cater to students. The bartenders skillfully look the other way when it is obvious a young customer has had a few drinks too many. It is a sleazy, down-beat block surrounded by alleys and parking lots, and so heavily patrolled that one of the town's four police cruisers is usually there.

When the group of spray-painters got to one of the bars on the Strip and tried to spray "Off the pigs!" on its red brick wall, the bar owner came out with two student bartenders, told the bartenders to hold the painters, and said he was calling the police. The police got there within minutes, but by that time the student bartenders had let the spray-painters go. The bar owner was furious and the next day some of the spray-painters would tell stories on campus about the repression they had personally encountered on North Water Street.

Friday, May 1, was Law Day. Small Ohio towns observe this day with great seriousness. Many businesses close at noon and the *Record Courier* editorialized about paying thanks to the lawmen who risk life and limb to defend residents' safety. The day gained added significance in showing that May 1 was no longer a Communist feast but a day dedicated to the security of America.

The year before, an SDS circular had said:

Today is Law Day, the day on which the ruling class pats the heads of its protectors: the pigs, the courts, and the lawmakers, for the fine way they keep all the people in control, the great way they keep the blacks in the ghettos, and the magnificent way they are trying to smash revolutionary groups like the Black Panthers. The pigs are to be congratulated today for their role as physical protectors of the ruling class. They are the ones who catch the "criminals" and throw them in jail. And keep them in jail.

At seven o'clock in the morning on Law Day, Zapata-mustached Steve Sharoff, the son of the retired police chief of Monticello, New York, a Kent State history student, was at work with some of his friends organizing a noon rally on the Commons to protest the move into Cambodia. He and a friend, Chris Plant, came up with a pop name for a new protest organization—WHORE—and decided that their protest would employ the techniques of guerrilla theater. The World Historians Opposed to Racism and Exploitation would dig a six-inch hole on the Commons and bury a copy of the Constitution in it. They couldn't immediately find a copy, but finally came up with a seventh-grade history book and ripped the Constitution from it. By nine o'clock that morning he and his friends were handing out leaflets announcing the formation of WHORE and the noon rally.

The rally was to be held two blocks from the heart of town, in the center of the campus, on the Commons, a flat, bowl-like expanse of green in a valley between several knolls. The victory bell is located at the eastern edge of the Commons near Taylor Hall and, due to past tradition, this rally would form at the bell. The bell's concrete backing would serve as Sharoff's platform. The ROTC building is located at the western edge of the Commons, about 150 yards from the victory bell. Blanket Hill stands immediately southeast of Taylor Hall, which is directly behind the bell. In the flat area immediately east of Blanket Hill is the practice football field.

Frank Frisina watched at noon on the Commons as the bell began to ring and as Sharoff, Plant, and others prepared to speak. Three to four hundred students were there and, Frisina knew, it was the largest protest rally of the year. His antennae told him that some of the vibrations he was picking up from the crowd were angry ones. As the bell rang, he remembered that the day before the Nixon speech he had been present at a meeting with President White and law-enforcement heads where the university's riot-control plans were routinely reviewed. During the course of that meeting, he remembered, several participants said that this year there was no forecast of trouble, that the meeting was just a routine part of the schedule made out early in the year because, after all, it was spring. Frisina's own thoughts had been that the only possibility of trouble, the slightest possibility, came from the Black United Students, who claimed the university was "Uncle Tomming" blacks on campus.

At most, Frank Frisina knew, as Steve Sharoff mounted the bell's backing and began to speak, trouble plans called for the summoning of the Ohio State Patrol and Frisina respected the Patrol's discipline, training, and "sense of cool."

Steve Sharoff, who would blanch at the very thought, began the meeting in the manner of a Jaycee toastmaster, with a few announcements. He reminded his audience of an upcoming underground film festival and of Project Earth, the week-long ecology symposium planned for next week. He announced a 3 p.m. rally, also on the Commons, to be held by the Black United Students in support of "all things happening in Ohio," specifically the anti-war demonstrations that had begun Tuesday at Ohio State University in Columbus. Sharoff paused.

"Brothers and sisters," he began . . .

Then he announced the formation of WHORE, and the new group's title was met with a few appreciative titters. "As president of WHORE," Steve Sharoff said, "I charge the Nixon administration with lawlessness in regard to Cambodia. I will now perform the deeply sorrowful task of burying the Constitution, which is being used to persecute true friends of liberty like the Black Panthers and the Chicago Eight. Nixon acted without the approval of Congress or the people. The executive is an all-powerful fascist organization. We now declare the Constitution dead."

Sharoff stepped off the bell's concrete backing and moved toward the six-inch hole dug into the Commons where the burial was to take place.

Before he got there a student leaped from the crowd onto the platform and yelled, "No, no, no, you can't do that." The crowd was surprised. Sharoff got down on his hands and knees to stuff the Constitution into the hole and stopped, Constitution in mid-air, to listen.

The student on the platform, wearing a pair of blue slacks and a blue button-down shirt, continued, "Khrushchev said he will bury us and look, we're doing the job for him. You're burying the Constitution for him which gives you your very right to be here."

"All right," someone yelled from the crowd, "if it gives us the right to be here, then let's get on with the funeral."

The button-down student was hissed and shoved off the platform. Sharoff stuffed the Constitution into the hole and covered it with dirt and the crowd cheered.

Another history graduate student, Jim Geary, who won the Silver Star in Vietnam with the 101st Airborne, leaped onto the bell backing, his discharge papers in one hand, Zippo lighter in the other. "I earned the right to burn these papers," Geary said, "and goddamn it, I'm going to do it." The papers burned.

"RIGHT ON!" the crowd yelled. "BURN, BABY, BURN!" Ralph Bevilacqua, an English instructor and former faculty advisor to SDS, took the platform and said, "Revolution must take the form of resistance. We're not going to class! We're not taking exams! We're not accepting grades! We're not going to take bullshit lectures from bullshit profs!"

As he spoke, a student spray-painted the word "STRIKE" in big white letters on the bell's backing.

The crowd was restless. It was time for a little fun. Bushy-haired, black-mustached Robert (Bobby) Franklin leaped onto the bell's backing. He was a non-student who, until the beginning of the school year, had been a research assistant in the university's chemistry department. He admired Jerry Rubin and, a month before, on a Cleveland television program, demonstrated his admiration by peeling his shirt off on camera to show that he, too, in Rubin style, was wearing a sweat-stained American flag. Among campus radicals he was the "Wild Man," eliciting more laughs than respect.

Franklin began to speak. "Right now I am a Communist," he said. "I don't deny it. We have to organize the people. What should we do at Kent State? There has to be a revolution in the heart and the mind. Go into your classes and ask why America goes into Cambodia, Cleveland, and New Haven."

He interrupted his rambling with the kind of stunt he is known for at Kent State. Jumping backward in mock alarm, he said, "Look, there he is, over there, Mr. Pig!"

Among his listeners was chief campus police detective Thomas Kelley—in his mid-fifties, pot-bellied, crewcut, redfaced, and thoroughly out of place. Kelley was a joke among the students. He attended every suspected radical meeting and took laborious notes. He always looked casual and nondescript and, students noted, every time he did undercover work, he always wore a blue windbreaker, brown slacks, and brown shoes.

"I want to welcome J. Edgar Pig to the meeting," Franklin said. "As you all know, J. Edgar Pig is the root hog wearing the blue windbreaker, the brown slacks, and the brown shoes."

As Franklin pointed, the crowd laughed and hissed. The laughter increased when they noticed Kelley was dutifully writing down every word Franklin had to say about him.

By the time Ken Hammond, author of a radical left column in the *Kent Stater*, began to speak, the crowd had dwindled to about a hundred. "The movement at Kent has fragmented itself too much," Hammond said. "If today can symbolize the start of a new revolutionary movement, that's real good." As he ended his remarks, Hammond told the crowd there would be another rally at noon on the Commons on Monday, May 4.

Meanwhile, university president White was having lunch in the student union near the Commons with Bill Resch, president of the Graduate Student Council, and other student leaders. It was a routine luncheon held for the purpose of dialogue and the group was seated at a window overlooking the Commons. They could see the rally but couldn't hear what was being said.

The sight of the rally reminded White of one of the problems facing the university and he mentioned it to the group. Kent was still receiving the usual number of state students, he said, but out-of-state enrollment was down. The drop, White said, could possibly have been a result of the press coverage of the SDS demonstrations on campus in April 1969. White said the publicity had given the university a "bad image" and asked the group how word could be spread to parents that Kent was a "safe" campus.

As the luncheon broke up, White and Bill Resch talked about trips they both planned later that day. White was going, as chairman, to the American College Testing Program convention in Mason City, Iowa. Resch would attend a meeting of Graduate Student Council presidents at Ohio State University. Resch figured the chief topic of conversation at his meeting would be the rioting on the Ohio State campus. There is no way anything like that could happen here, he thought.

President White, fearful of the repercussions of the Nixon speech, decided to wait for the three o'clock Black United Students rally before he committed himself to go to his convention. He wanted to be sure there wasn't going to be any trouble and BUS, of late, had used some strong language. On March 30 *Black Watch*, the BUS newspaper, demanded: "End all forms of mental mistreatment of black minds. This calls for the firing or, if need be, killing of all racist deans, professors, coaches, or university presidents."

White waited for the meeting anxiously, and when only forty-seven black students showed up, along with about twenty white radicals, he felt reassured. There wouldn't be any trouble. At 5:30 p.m. he caught a flight for Mason City.

As the hours went by on Friday, Kent police chief Roy Thompson, a white-haired man looking older than his fifty-nine years, a Kent resident since 1945, was more and more worried. "We had them painting up the stores the night before and my people kept telling me we'd have more trouble," he said.

In August of 1969 he had threatened to retire on January 1, 1970. "All these rocking-chair critics criticize you all the time," he said. "People who don't know anything about police work keep talking about civil liberties." He felt many Supreme Court decisions "cause us to babysit the criminals."

But he changed his mind about retiring. Seven hundred people in town signed a petition begging him to stay on. All the police chiefs in the surrounding towns issued statements like the one issued by Dickie Robison, in nearby Stow, who said, "It will take a mighty big man to fill his shoes." And then, in March, the university gave him a distinguished service award.

The people in Kent liked Chief Thompson. When he became chief in 1962, he replaced a town legend. Old chief Firmin Grubb had even been written up in Ripley's "Believe It or Not." A burglar fired point blank at him in 1936 and Firm's service buckle deflected the bullet. The buckle jammed into his stomach.

In 1964 a staff memo from the city editor of the Kent *Record Courier* to his new reporters said:

> Red Greer, the mayor, has done a great deal for the city. One of the biggest was the appointment of Roy Thompson after a two year drive to force Firm Grubb out. Thompson is one of the nicest people you will meet on your beat. The police department has two cruisers and one unmarked car. It uses a new radar unit for speed checks. You will find this department, in general, most cooperative.

Roy Thompson grew up in West Virginia and joined the Kent force after he got out of the service in 1943. He was the man who organized Kent's Civil Defense force and set up neighborhood fallout shelters well stocked with food and water. In 1958 he chased a bunch of panty-raiding students through a dormitory. In 1960, when eleven Negro students staged a sit-in at a bar, he told the waitress to go ahead and serve them.

Roy Thompson is militantly anti-Communist. "The minute the Communists destroy your first line of defense, the police department, you're lost," he told civic groups. He feels Communist elements have made great inroads on the campuses. "They got a lot of these people over on that campus who I don't suppose are plain Communists, but an awful lot of them are pinkos." As the years went by he found his job in the little college town, where he still liked to walk down the street checking parking meters, was growing more and more complex.

"I don't understand how they could let that Jerry Rubin speak on campus when everybody knows he's a Communist," he said.

Four SDS organizers of the previous spring's disturbances were released from the Portage County Jail on Wednesday. "I knew we were going to have a lot of trouble," Thompson said.

On Friday morning one of his men told him that Rick Erickson and Howie Emmer, two of those released from jail, were seen at 130 College Street, a rickety old house near campus, in the company of Robert Franklin. The house's backyard was filled with discarded pop bottles. "I was worried," the chief said. "I know pop bottles can be used for molotov cocktails. But I couldn't understand why they'd have those pop bottles out there for everybody to see. I figured they were being real cute and thought they'd trick us."

All in all, it wasn't a very good Law Day!

It was warm Friday night, very warm. Temperatures were in the high seventies. It was the second really warm day of spring. On the first warm night, that Monday, there had been a mudfight. Tonight, the bars on North Water Street were full. On a weekend night in Kent the bars on the Strip are usually full—not only with students but with visitors from Cleveland, Akron, and the neighboring towns; boys looking for pickups; girls waiting to be picked up. There are always groups of kids lining the sidewalks in front of the bars. It is just as easy to meet someone standing around outside and, if you're broke, more profitable. This night, observers said, there were more people lining Water Street than usual.

"The night had a political air," one student said. "Kids just wanted to rap with each other about what the hell Nixon the Madman was up to." Another said, "Some kids had heard about the bar owner calling the cops on the painters Thursday night."

The mood inside the bars and on the Strip was festive. Many inside the bars watched the New York Knickerbockers and the Los Angeles Lakers battle in the NBA playoffs. A group pitched pennies outside a bar. A few began dancing in a circle on the sidewalk and overspilled onto the street. A police car came by, was pelted with a beer can, and left. It was 11:27 p.m.

"It was hot as hell inside," said Craig Madonio, a bass player in a rock group. "The kids went out for fresh air and there were a lot of kids out there, too."

Outside what was known as the "freak" bar, a place where townies, heads, blacks, and motorcycle gang members congregate, stood a larger group partly composed of members of the Chosen Few motorcycle gang whose members periodically terrorized the neighboring small farm towns. Four or five Harley Hog motorcycles were parked in the street.

As the dancing spilled into the street, a cry of "Street Festival!" went up. Two of the Chosen Few stood in the middle of the street and, as the crowd applauded, urinated on each other. A traffic jam developed. A few of the kids went up to a young driver caught in the jam and asked if he would mind getting out of his car so it could be used as a speaker's platform. The driver smiled, said he wouldn't mind at all, and got out of the car, leaving it in the middle of the street. A young man with very long hair got on top of the car and said, "Have a good time, brothers and sisters, the streets belong to the people, we're going to have a festival."

An athlete from the university got on top of the car and said, "This is illegal. We can't do this." He was hissed and got down. Those who had parked their cars in front of the bars were asked to move them so the street could be clear for the festival. Others appointed themselves traffic coordinators and blocked off incoming traffic, detouring motorists to other routes.

Some of the Chosen Few collected trash in the middle of Water Street and built a bonfire. Gang members took turns urinating into the fire and doing stunts around it with their cycles. Others rolled large barrels, used as parking-lot blocks, into the street and further sealed off the area. A crowd of about four hundred sang and danced in the street. Another thousand watched from the sidewalks. The atmosphere was still festive. The street had been "liberated" and everyone was cheering.

"The blacks have taken over the administration building!" someone yelled. "Let's go to campus."

"No, no," someone answered, "the blacks are here among us. Keep the festival going!"

Sometime before midnight, as the festival continued without violence, a middle-aged man driving a new Oldsmobile refused to take the detour, rolled the car's windows up, and tried to drive through the crowd.

"Get the pig!" someone yelled.

The car was surrounded, its windows smashed, its body kicked in. The man backed up and fled. He was not hurt.

"That changed the mood of the whole thing," a student said. "Here was this guy driving his new flashy chrome car through these Commie-faggot-long-haired-pimp-freaks and if any got in the way, it was too bad. It was a grim reminder of actualities."

Chanting began:

ONE, TWO, THREE, FOUR, WE DON'T WANT YOUR FUCK-ING WAR!

FUCK THE PIGS!
BRING THE GIs HOME NOW!
FUCK AGNEW!
FUCK NIXON!

The group in the street surged south on Water Street toward Main Street. About twenty students began throwing rocks and bottles at windows. Most of the crowd stood on the sidewalk and watched.

Steve Sharoff, who had organized the noon rally, was sitting in one of the bars. "I heard a crash and a guy came in and said, 'Guys are throwing bottles out there!' Wow, I thought, that's pretty far out."

Someone took a manure spreader from the window of the Getz Hardware Store and threw it through the window of the Portage County National Bank. Someone yelled, "Get the bank!" No one followed.

Inside the bank two security guards, hearing the window smash, took cover behind pillars and trained guns on the window, ready to pull the trigger if anyone tried to come in.

"I thought in the beginning," said the editor of Kent's underground newspaper, "the purpose was to trash the banks and utilities. Someone, legend has it that it was an athlete, broke into a shoestore and took a pair of shoes. That took everything out of the realm of trashing and made it old-fashioned window breaking." The banks and utilities, he explained, were to be "trashed" as symbols of the System, "like you'd spank a child."

All the store windows along North Water Street, except one, were broken. The Smoke Shop's windows were left intact, though the owners, defending themselves against the town's wrath, later claimed that stones had struck the windows but had bounced off. "The Smoke Shop was left," said one participant, "because, you know, they sell pipes there and tobacco and it's kind of a symbol for dope."

From eleven twenty-seven, when the first police car had been pelted and left the scene, until nearly midnight there were no police in the festival area. Chief Roy Thompson said he wanted to see if the students would "simmer down" on their own. When it was obvious they would not, Thompson alerted his full twenty-two-man staff, dressed them in riot gear, and asked for the assistance of the Portage County sheriff's department as well as the help of dozens of tiny communities surrounding Kent.

He also called the Kent State campus police department for assistance, and was turned down. "I told them," said campus police chief Donald Schwartzmiller, "that we had the campus to protect and it was their responsibility to protect the town. My men were needed to guard the buildings on campus and I was afraid to be drawn away from the campus."

Mayor LeRoy Satrom had been out of town during the day, but Chief Thompson reached him at a friend's house. The mayor was playing poker and had won five straight hands when he got the call. He explained to his skeptical friends that he really wasn't trying to bolt with the winnings, and then left for town.

"When I took the oath, I thought my biggest problem would be planning budgets, not riots," Satrom said. The mayor who had preceded him, Johnny Carson, a drugstore owner, had never had this kind of a riot to contend with. Neither had Red Greer, who served in a time when the mayor worried about college students trying to get beer while they were still underage. Red Greer was always lucky. One time he won an election when the Board of Elections flipped a quarter after a tie vote. "The problems those guys had were the problems of a different world," Satrom said.

Led by Chief Roy Thompson the full police force in riot gear marched down South Water Street toward North Water and met the surging crowd. Kent City patrolman Tony Filomena, a good-natured Italian, had been reached at home by the police dispatcher and told there was a riot in town, "all hell was breaking loose."

"We formed just outside the police station," Filomena said, "and we got our helmets, gas masks, batons, and tear gas. People were coming into the station reporting damage to their cars and saying the students had gone mad uptown. Just about anybody who came into the station was deputized.

"We trotted down to the square. We saw a big fire burning in the middle of North Water Street—broken store windows, broken bottles, glass everywhere, chunks of concrete and pieces of wood all over the place and roving bands of students smashing everything in sight.

"It looked like the war was on and this was the first battle. We shouted 'Disperse, disperse' and made a sweep of the area. We arrested several students who didn't want to disband but who got wise, or argued, or tried to take a swing at us.

"I arrested a kid and didn't know what the hell to do with him. I couldn't take him to jail, and all the other guys were sure as hell busy. I saw the mayor and I asked him to take the kid in.

"The mayor got in the car and asked me how to turn the siren on. I showed him how and he pulled off. I yelled after him and he stopped. I told him to turn his red light on. I showed him how to turn the light on and the mayor thanked me and took the kid away."

After he'd taken the student to the city jail, Mayor Satrom came back, and, driving a police cruiser up North Water Street, read a civil emergency proclamation over a loudspeaker. He read the proclamation twice with no effect. His car was stoned. Police began sweeping down the sidewalks in phalanx. It was 1:07 a.m.

Police chief Thompson, on the scene, leading his men, seeing the damage, was convinced that before him lay the result of the conspiracy he feared. He made an on-the-spot decision. He would, now, at the height of the action, close all the bars and clear everyone out of the entire area. It was a decision he would later characterize as "probably a mistake." Policemen charged into the bars, routing everyone inside onto the street. At the height of the disturbance an additional fifteen hundred people flooded onto the street.

Thompson recognized the difficulty of the decision. He was concerned that if he let the students stay inside the bars, they would "get all boozed up." He was also concerned that the bars would serve as a sanctuary for the troublemakers. His initial thought was to lock all the bar doors, trapping the students inside, while a speaker went in to calm them. He decided against this because he remembered the discarded pop bottles at 130 College Street and feared the bars would be firebombed with the students trapped inside.

"Students scattered in all directions," Tony Filomena said, "into parking lots, up alleys, into buildings. Bricks and chunks of concrete and bottles were being thrown at us. I looked beside me and a deputy who had been hit on the right side of his face had blood streaming down his cheek. Several officers, hearing obscene language and pop bottles breaking, ran into the bank parking lot, chasing students."

The crowd surged east on Main Street, away from the downtown area, back toward campus. A line of fraternity houses stands on the block between the town and the campus. Fraternity men came out of the houses to see what was happening, and many were clubbed back inside by the police. "Some of the Greeks got radicalized that night," a student said.

"At Lincoln and Main," Filomena said, "the students formed on campus at the arch, by the campus gate, on the sidewalk and the grassy area. We stood pat opposite the students with periodic showers of bottles and rocks coming at us. We waited for the university police department to come since students were now on campus property. The students began to shout 'Sieg heil! Sieg heil!' at us and other obscenities from across the street. For half an hour or longer, there were still no university police and the student crowd was getting bigger and bigger with more students coming."

Facing a heavy barrage of rocks and bottles, the Kent police began using tear gas, shooting it onto campus property from town property. Students ran onto campus, then came back to regroup.

"I didn't know they needed help over there," said university police chief Schwartzmiller. "We weren't aware they were having a problem. We were protecting our buildings. We had the ROTC building surrounded. We arrested a boy for trying to break some of the windows of the building."

Half a block from the tear-gas area, at 2:27 a.m., as the demonstrating crowd grew, two Tree City Electric Company workers were fixing a traffic signal. It was a routine time for them to do their work. The traffic signal had been out for more than a week, and early morning, when there was no traffic, was the best time for them to work.

Glen Kruger and Blaine Baldasare, fifteen feet above their truck on an uplifted scaffold, with the traffic signal in hand, watched the action between students and police the way some people watch a football game from the upper grandstand.

"We had a good seat from up there," Baldasare said. "The whole thing didn't bother us too much. We figured the hell with them. Let's get it done and go home."

Suddenly, as they worked on the signal, a drunk driver from a nearby farm town hit their truck head-on at fifty miles an hour. Kruger was knocked off the scaffold and onto the ground. The impact caused Baldasare to somersault off the scaffold and catch the traffic light, cradling it with his feet, hanging on. The scaffold collapsed.

"I thought somebody blew the truck up," Baldasare said. "Suddenly I'm up in the air and holding onto the light. Then I look down and I see this guy stagger out of his car, look up, and laugh to beat hell. And then I see this huge crowd running right toward me."

When the crowd got to the intersection, accompanied by policemen, Kruger was on the ground in pain, Baldasare, with hands flailing the air, was yelling, "Get me off this thing!"

"It was eerie," Filomena said, "but not one student made a peep when they got there and saw Kruger on the ground and the other guy on the light. They'd been yelling about the pigs and all, but when they got there, it was quiet."

Students ran to help Kruger, putting jackets under his head. When the ambulance came to take Kruger away, the crowd cheered. Kruger waved. When a fire truck came to take Baldasare off the traffic signal, they cheered again. "I gave them the peace sign," Baldasare said. "I wouldn't do it now but I was pretty mixed up then." When the drunk was put into a police cruiser, the crowd cheered again and yelled, "Yea pigs!"

"Then Mrs. Kruger arrived in her car," Filomena said. "She came to a sudden stop and ran to the truck. She was crying and hysterical. Her little boy, about ten years old, was with her and some of the students started talking to him. He told his mother that daddy was okay and just had his leg hurt and was at the hospital. Looking around at the policemen and students under the lights, we were all very touched. Mrs. Kruger and her boy went to the hospital. The students went back to their dorms and we went back to the station."

The long night was over. Fifty thousand dollars' worth of damage had been done to businesses in the town. Seven policemen suffered minor injuries. Fourteen students were arrested. It began at eleven twenty-seven with a street festival and ended three hours later, with Blaine Baldasare clutching a traffic signal.

Sometime around midnight Mayor Satrom spoke with Roy Thompson. The chief told him about the discarded pop bottles and the release of the four revolutionaries. He added it all up for the mayor and pointed to the result: It was the worst downtown disturbance in the history of Kent. In his twenty-seven years as a police officer Roy Thompson had never seen anything like it.

It was his feeling, the chief said, that his department couldn't defend the town against something of this scope and the National Guard had to be called in immediately. The Guard was on duty in Akron and Cleveland. They wouldn't have far to come.

Mayor Satrom thought it over and called the adjutant general's office in Columbus. He wanted the Guard put on alert, he said, and if there was any more trouble, he wanted the guardsmen to defend his town. He was told that a National Guard liaison officer, Lieutenant C. Joseph Barnette, of the 145th Infantry Regiment, would be in Kent on Saturday morning.

4

The Movement

"We estimate that the pigs probably will not fire into
crowds, although they have done it once in Berkeley.
But they won't fire into white crowds."

—Mark Rudd, Weatherman, May 1969, Pittsburgh

That National Guardsmen were called into the City of Kent was due
in large part to the Weatherman. Police chief Roy Thompson's men
told him there were positively identified Weathermen on campus.
He relayed the information to the mayor, who relayed it to the adjutant general's office.

Weathermen on campus! The Weatherman, with dynamite,
raised fists, a New Red Army, "Eeh-ya-ya-ya-ya!" war whoops, and
flaming rhetoric: "The only direction is insurrection, the only solution is revolution!" And a goal, taken from a Bob Dylan song: "The
pump don't work cause the vandals took the handles."

As far as the city administration of Kent, Ohio, was concerned,
the Weatherman—children of the media, known coast to coast for
guerrilla warfare, bombings, and "Four Days of Rage" in Chicago—
did exactly what Mark Rudd, their Mao, and Bernardine Dohrn,
their La Pasionaria, intended for them to do. They scared hell out of
Middle America and small towns like Kent, Ohio. The Weatherman
told people like Roy Thompson and LeRoy Satrom that Armageddon and revolution were imminent. So, moving in self-defense, they
asked for the National Guard.

Yet the paradox is that there were no visible Weathermen at Kent State University. ("They saw something we didn't see," campus police chief Schwartzmiller said later.) During four days of disturbances no Weathermen were arrested. In the 1969-70 academic year SDS was nonexistent at Kent State. It was an overwhelming irony: the intelligence reports the town acted on were wrong.

But to small-town authorities adrift in a sea of long hair and bell bottoms, unverified rumors brought back staggering media flashbacks: March 1970, the house on Eleventh Street in New York's Greenwich Village, three die when a Weatherman bomb factory explodes. (One of the dead was subsequently identified by Bernardine Dohrn as Terry Robbins, a former Kent State SDS organizer.) October 1969, in Chicago, cadres of motorcycle-helmeted Weathermen, Kent State SDS organizers Robbins and Howie Emmer among them, carry rocks and sticks, attack policemen, and go on a three-day rampage to celebrate Che Guevara's birthday.

Authorities in small towns like Kent, Ohio, don't split hairs. Long-haired people, to frightened minds, easily turn into Weathermen; Weathermen easily turn into the Communist conspiracy; Jerry Rubin easily turns into Mark Rudd; and what difference is there, really, between throwing a manure spreader through the Portage County National Bank's window and burning down the town.

It was not surprising that the intelligence reports chief Thompson got had Weathermen at Kent State. After all, both Mark Rudd and Bernardine Dohrn had been there before.

The first and last Weatherman meeting at Kent State took place at the beginning of the school year, in September 1969. It was nothing but a rehash of SDS meetings of the previous year, the same demands were read. Mark Real, a Kent State junior, clean-cut, a former seminarian who had participated in SDS activities the previous spring, announced he was now a Weatherman. Someone nearby held the same Viet Cong flag used in the SDS demonstrations the previous year. "We must attack the ruling class," Real said. And he led a new cheer:

Hey, piggy wiggy
You gotta go now,
Oink oink

Bang bang
Off the pig!

But cheer and all, the meeting fell on its face. Somebody asked Real if his crew wanted to become the new military establishment once the old one was abolished. And somebody called Real a "pig." All told, eight members were present and twenty-five observers.

Mark Rudd and Bernardine Dohrn did, indeed, visit Kent State, but their visit came before their Revolutionary Youth Movement overthrew the old SDS Guard and reshaped SDS goals; before Mark Rudd announced a plan to recruit high schoolers by going into the schools and picking fights with students to prove how "tough" Weathermen were; before Bernardine Dohrn placed as much emphasis on not wearing a bra (Women's Lib) as on not continuing the war in Vietnam. They both came to Kent State before they purged SDS of non-Weathermen, before Students for a Democratic Society, founded on words like "love" and "creativity" in Port Huron, Michigan, was beaten to death by the raised fists of the Weathermen, participatory democracy be damned, yea Che! yea Mao! Off the pigs!

Mark Rudd appeared at Kent State in October 1968, during homecoming week. He appeared as Columbia's SDS chairman and wore a button-down shirt, rumpled, it is true, but button-down. He spoke at the university auditorium before eight hundred persons and brought with him a film of the Columbia takeover starring Mark Rudd as Mark Rudd.

But it was not a good night for the revolution. The projector kept stopping and the atmosphere in the auditorium was like the atmosphere at Kent's Nickelodeon Theater, with people cheering the demonstrators, hissing the police, and vice versa. Everybody had a good time until the New York police moved into the occupied buildings and bloodied heads. "I haven't seen a bloodier sight since Custer's last stand," said *Kent Stater* columnist M. J. Kukla in prophetic description since, later, Rudd would be criticized by his fellow radicals for engaging in just that: Custerism.

After the movie Rudd sat on stage and gave a little talk and, Kukla noted, "It's a good thing Rudd didn't try to hold Columbia with the people in the Kent auditorium that night because he wouldn't have lasted an hour." By the time Rudd finished his pep talk only about twenty people were there and they were hard-core and broke, so when the hat was passed for revolution, it went empty. The way Kukla saw it, the entire scene was vintage Mack Sennett, and the serio-comedy continued that night when two campus reporters tried to interview the famed student leader. One of them, Maggie Murvay, the sloe-eyed, plumpish director of the campus radio station, would say later, and in detail, to the House Committee on Internal Security: "As the interview started out, the way it was, Mark was sitting in a chair and Richard, the other reporter, was sitting on the floor with a tape recorder. All in all, we had to start the interview five times because the words that Mark used would not be fit for broadcast use. As the interview started the fifth time, after a few questions the interview became a debate between Richard, representing more or less the Establishment or administration side, and Mark, representing SDS and their ideas. It came to a point, instead of Richard asking Mark the questions, Mark would ask Richard the questions, which was a complete opposite of the way an interview should go. Each time Richard would come out of the question using logic, and Mark Rudd got more or less tangled up in his ideas. All of a sudden, the other SDS members, Rick Erickson and Howie Emmer, jumped up and said: 'The tape is no good, give us the tape, give us the tape.'

"We said: 'The tape is not ours, it belongs to the radio station.'

"They said: 'Well, we will buy the tape.'

"Since there were more of them and only two of us, we decided we would sell them the tape.

"That night, another reporter from the station, Marty Girard, went up to Howie Emmer. He more or less discussed what had happened with the tapes. Marty made the offer to Howie that Mark Rudd come up to the station or phone in a statement suitable for air use for a newscast and we would forget the incident. Otherwise, the story would be aired that the tapes were confiscated by the members. Eleven o'clock, no phone call, no visit. So we ran the story on the air that the tapes were confiscated by SDS members. Bob Carpenter, who had a talk show, made the statement that there is a cancer on campus and the malignancy is SDS."

Bernardine Dohrn, a brown-haired, poised, twenty-six-year-old University of Chicago law school graduate, appeared as the national SDS inter-organizational secretary when she spoke at Kent State on April 28, 1969. She told a meeting of a hundred people that "the inadequacies of society require an organized revolution to destroy the power structure which suppresses American society and subjects the many to the will of the few." She compared the struggle of whites to the plight of Negroes and said an American racist society was slowly suppressing the white majority as it had the Negro. "There is a need for radical change through revolutionary action," she said, and noted "the ultimate need of carrying weapons for self-defense." She cited, as example, a group of blacks in New York who were accused of fire bombing several businesses, one of them Macy's department store. Miss Dohrn said she thought Macy's a "stupid target" and said another target "made much more sense": the New York Police Department.

"No whites have been killed on campus yet," she said, "but that will come too and we'll have to carry guns in self-defense just like the blacks at Cornell."

Later, during a discussion of means with which to achieve radical change, when a student said love and not violence was the answer, Miss Dohrn took the platform and said: "I could murder in self-defense and murder in revenge."

That there were only a hundred students at the meeting to hear a national SDS spokesman was not unusual. Only 250 had showed up at the first SDS meeting at Kent State in September 1968, and SDS membership never surpassed more than one percent of the student body.

Before SDS there was no real Movement at Kent. Only three students, for example, participated in the freedom rides and sit-ins of the South, actions which symbolized the beginning of a movement from the "bottom up," a movement that would reject, rather than rely on, the vagaries of liberal politicians to achieve change.

When SDS was founded in 1962 in Port Huron, Michigan (its future president would be Kent State University dropout Carl Oglesby), the organization's principal emphasis was on decentralized decision-making. Based mainly on a draft written by Tom Hayden, who had been the editor of the *Michigan Daily* and would become one of the Chicago Eight, the opening sentence of the group's constitution, the Port Huron Statement, said: "We are people of this generation, bred in at least modest comfort, housed now in universities, looking uncomfortably at the world we inherit." The language was humanist rather than socialist, with words like "love," "creativity," and "participatory democracy."

"As a sound system," the statement said, "we seek the establishment of a democracy of individual participation, governed by two central aims: that the individual share in those social decisions determining the quality and direction of his life; that society be organized to encourage independence in men and provide the media for their common participation." SDS, in retrospect, in those days was hardly revolutionary. It held long, rambling "participatory democracy" discussions and the civil rights struggle was the focus of its attention.

Then, as American involvement in the Vietnam War deepened, the battleground shifted from civil rights and equality to the antiwar fervor of the campus. The first mass protest against the war was organized by SDS in April 1965 in Washington. Twenty thousand attended. A series of nationwide teach-ins, including one at Kent State, focused student attention on the morality of the conflict and, gradually, even the student in an institution like Kent State found himself questioning national values and, in consequence, his own values as well. This student had grown up with a reflex patriotism, a knee-jerk Americanism which took pride in "our country, the leader of the Western world." During the civil rights marches even the involved student had accepted his role: he viewed himself as a beneficiary of middle-class affluence and he was acting in behalf of those less fortunate.

Now he faced agonizing alternatives: Kill. Go into exile. Go to jail. He began questioning the system and his own place in it. He saw the university itself as better than the eight-hour-day, two-martinis-before-dinner existence of his parents. He began to reject middle-class values and experiment with new life styles. At the same time, he also saw the university as a bureaucratic maze of horrors, a carbon copy of the corporate way of life: dehumanized by large lecture halls, absentee professors, and standardized courses, exams, and programs. The ticky-tacky house in the suburbs was a mirror-image of the sanitized new room in the multi-story dormitory; the rat race for the buck was the rat race for the good grade. Soon this student realized that he was, at once, the beneficiary and victim of middle-class America. And, at the same time he realized that his cultural and political protests were synonymous. As he re-evaluated his own life, he saw the most gruesome reality on television each night: GIs killing an enemy that fought with captured weapons; Washington backing a government sick with corruption and moral decay.

SDS became the largest and most-influential anti-war group and took the new awareness from the classrooms into the streets for the first time when the Oakland Induction Center was shut down in 1967. "NOT WITH MY LIFE YOU DON'T," an SDS button said. ROTC programs came under attack. Programs like Kent State's Liquid Crystals Institute, operating under a Defense Department grant, became focal campaign issues.

When peace marches and protests contributed little to change, as Lyndon Johnson's credibility gap widened, as General Lewis B. Hershey continued his iron-fisted rule of the Selective Service System, the struggle became more desperate. Disruptive action to "stop the war machine" was used on more and more campuses.

SDS led an explosive take-over of buildings at Columbia University in June 1968 under Mark Rudd's leadership. The take-over disrupted the entire school, caused an estimated $300,000 in damage, and led to a general student strike and the arrest of 720 people. Columbia became a landmark and symbol of radical action.

The Black Liberation Movement, meanwhile, was hailed as the "soul brother" and sometimes the "big brother" of the white revolutionary movement. SDS continually supported the political viewpoints and actions of the most militant segments of the black community—Malcolm X, Stokely Carmichael, Rap Brown, the Black Panther Party.

With the use of the tactics of disruption, factionalization began and the Port Huron Statement began to look like a document from a gone world. The Progressive Labor Party faction attacked national SDS leadership, claiming SDS was losing touch with the working-man. SDS was preoccupied with ivory-tower issues like ROTC and the Dow Chemical Company, the Progressive Laborites said, and what did the workingman care about that? Trying to react to Progressive Laborite criticism, one of the issues of Mark Rudd's Columbia take-over became the university's role in a neighboring ghetto project, though Rudd took pains to point out that "we are not protesting any university policy, we are protesting the racism and repression of the System." When French workers went on strike in May 1968 in support of a student strike, some radicals envisioned an American worker-student alliance.

But one faction, which would become known as the Weatherman (after a line in a Bob Dylan song: "You don't need a weatherman to tell which way the wind blows"), concluded that it would be hopeless to try to turn clerks and construction workers into revolutionaries. The revolution, the Weathermen said, had begun elsewhere, in Cuba, in Vietnam, and especially among the blacks. When Mark Rudd declared himself SDS chairman in June 1969, he said, "You can look for pitched battles between the militants and the pigs on a scale that will make anything in the sixties look like a Sunday-school picnic."

Rudd's SDS leadership seemed to be based on right-wing tenets— SDS, Rudd seemed to say, my way, love it or leave it. The take-over cost SDS about half of its membership and SDS-Weatherman, under Rudd's guidance, issued a statement that was far, far away from the original Port Huron Statement of 1962. In fact, Rudd's SDS and Tom Hayden's SDS of 1962 were two totally different organizations. The Rudd statement said:

> We are within the heartland of a worldwide monster, a country so rich from its worldwide plunder that even the crumbs doled out to the enslaved masses within its borders provide for material existence very much above the conditions of the masses of the people of the world.
>
> . . . If necessary, black people could win self-determination, abolishing the whole imperialist system and seizing the state power to do it, without the white movement, although the cost among whites and blacks would be high. Whites must get on the right side of the impending black revolution immediately. There is no time left for leafleting at the factory gate. We must take action that will give material support to the black struggles, exemplary action that will show others the way to smash the state.

By the fall of 1968, when SDS was founded at Kent State, the organization had been greatly radicalized but was nowhere near the kind of fanaticism that Rudd would display in the future. Even so, the *Kent Stater* commented editorially about the new group and its action:

> One thing the Students for a Democratic Society have complained about has been students' rights on campus. Mainly, they want more of them. Therefore, it seems strange that some members of that group decided to show how well it can violate the rights of others with an inconsiderate and irresponsible act.
>
> Much has been heard about what SDS plans to do to disrupt elections today. No one will argue their right to their opinions. They do not like any presidential candidates. That's their problem. But when they march into Bowman Hall during an 11 a.m. political science 101 lecture conducted by Prof. Thomas D. Ung and completely disrupt the latter portion of the class just to show their beliefs, then it is time for some careful reconsideration about their worth on this campus.
>
> They marched into the hall, with four men carrying a large black coffin. The coffin bore such signs as "You can vote but you can't govern" and "Elections are crap." The group never uttered a word, but marched down one aisle, paraded in front of the stage and then exited up the other aisle. The fact that they were booed out of the auditorium made plain the class's response.
>
> As a university recognized group, SDS must realize that it must comply with certain regulations and rules of conduct. One such rule is conducting itself in a manner which will not disrupt any university function. SDS committed a serious faux pas Monday. It may live to regret it. The *Stater* does not object to the presence of SDS on campus. But it does insist that SDS exhibit the same courtesies as are afforded to it.

A week later, on November 12, 1968, SDS held a meeting in the education building. Attending were a large number of students from the Black United Students group. A film was shown depicting Black Panther Party chairman Huey Newton and the Oakland Police Department. "It was a very emotional film," campus radio director Maggie Murvay said, "geared to make police look bad. Following the film, someone started to speak and they said that the Oakland police were racist and they should not be here on the campus recruiting because they are a racist organization. They said that we have to take some kind of action tomorrow so that they won't be back tomorrow afternoon and they won't be back the following day."

"On November 9 I went to the meeting place of SDS," said university vice president Robert Matson. "I had asked their leadership to come in. They instead issued an invitation to come meet with them. I went and I asked them what kind of concerns they had. They referred to no specific concerns. Indeed, the final wrap-up statement of one individual in this meeting, one SDS member, was that 'If we had plans, do you think we would tell you?' Which makes communications, ongoing communications, very difficult."

On November 13 members of SDS and Black United Students congregated in front of the administration building demanding an end to Oakland police recruiting, the disarming of campus policemen, and a university guarantee not to infiltrate radical organizations. They marched over to the student activities center, where the recruiting was being done. About 150 SDS members and 200 Black United Students crowded into the building and staged a sit-in. It lasted five hours. The university gave in to none of the demands.

University president White told the House Internal Securities Committee:

"While the recruiting activity was temporarily disrupted and while campus tensions were on the fringe of large-scale disorder for several days, it should be noted that all students desiring to be interviewed did so, that there were no serious outbreaks of violence, that there was no destruction of university property.... There were no arrests made on that occasion. The reason why no arrests were made was because—and I refer to the fact that we uncovered some errors in our own procedures—university counsel advised us that the evidence we gathered would not stand up in court."

Maggie Murvay, who would herself later become an undercover agent for the campus police department, said: "The reason it wouldn't have stood up in court is because they forgot to mark the pictures. No one knew what time the pictures were taken and they had no witnesses when they were taken. Their whole security operation was unbelievable. One time they sent a student they recruited to do undercover work to live in a house where there was supposed to be narcotics activity. It took them about a month to notice that the kid had gone to the wrong house."

SDS was trying to work out a radical coalition with the Black United Students. But the visionary coalition was not to take place. BUS withdrew from SDS, to a kind of nationalism that had no room for white boys playing romantic games. "The trouble with all those guys . . . one BUS leader said, "is that they read too much. It was like they were trying to live their own fantasies out. They kept talking about 'revolution.' Shit, ain't gonna be no revolution in this white man's country. Those cats loved their headlines. They would read the papers to each other about themselves. They wanted to use us to get themselves some big headlines."

The Kent SDS chapter was going through a difficult period of adolescence, forming leadership, recruiting activists, and formulating a set of demands. Rick Erickson, the lanky son of Akron's former mayor, and Howie Emmer, the stubby son of parents who shared his beliefs, took the leadership. "Rick was Fidel and Howie was Che," a former member said. "Rick made a lot of pretty speeches and made converts, but when it came to organization and carrying out the plan, Howie was diabolic."

Rick Erickson had gone to Columbia at the height of the takeovers there. He met Mark Rudd and admired him. He claimed to have seen the System's hypocrisy and repression before then—"Mr. Charlie isn't a rich Northerner or some Southern white cat, he is The System"—but hadn't done much about it. "Until Columbia," Erickson said, "I figured—let the lemmings march into the sea." What caused him, a product of the middle class, to forsake the dreams of success he once aspired to? "War, greed, racism, hunger, ignorance, an economy based on war, the draft. Dig it? The System."

The System created Rick Erickson and now he wanted his chance to re-create the System. "It has to begin on the campus," he said, "but pretty soon we have to take it into the streets of the cities." Consciousness became the magic SDS word at Kent State. Get the apathetic Ohio kids thinking about the issues. Focus the issues. Act. Confront. "They just don't understand," Erickson said. "Let them arrest me. SDS is not Rick Erickson or Howie Emmer. It is an idea and you don't smash an idea by putting it in jail. You focus more attention on it. You bring it to more people."

In turn, when Erickson was arrested for possession of marijuana, the court's legal opinion was a good description of how the System saw Rick Erickson:

> The defendant's own statement to the probation officer reveals an obvious character weakness in that the defendant has associated with a number of social misfits and attempts to explain his use of marijuana by blaming it on the failure of college life to meet his expectations, his father's political friends and enemies, alleged false standards of conduct among people he knows. The defendant apparently believed and may still believe that because of this disillusionment in certain people and institutions, it was only natural and proper to smoke marijuana regardless of well-known laws against such conduct.
>
> Unfortunately, this attitude and line of reasoning is prevalent among growing numbers of young people in our society today, especially some of those college-aged. The defendant and his friends, and others of similar persuasion, substitute their lack of understanding for the true facts of the world about them. They substitute the unreality of marijuana dreams for the reality of being a man and facing the world as it is and meeting such problems as it may pose head-on.
>
> This court cannot help but wonder whether the public good does not require that this defendant be treated at this time in such a fashion that he and his friends of like inclination and attitudes, on the Kent State University campus and elsewhere, are snapped out of their dream world into the mainstream of life for the good of themselves and the general public.

Howie Emmer, meanwhile, Rick's Che, was not arrested for marijuana, got little attention, worked summers at an icecream company in Cleveland, and was known to his fellow members as "tough."

Gradually, SDS began attracting activist members. Many were bright, outspoken, driven young men like Mark Wagler, who was "raised to be a superpatriot" and "decided to be a political rebel."

When he gave the valedictory address at Lake High School in rural Stark County in 1961, he spoke on "Faith and Fortitude." At twenty-five a graduate student and teaching assistant, his concern was "America's racism and imperialism."

Wagler grew up on a Mennonite farm, and his metamorphosis began when he graduated from Kent State in 1964 with high honors. "I hoped Nixon would be elected in 1960," he said. "I had the whole American dream. I never realized there were people outside that dream." Following his graduation from Kent, he went to Switzerland for a year as an exchange student under a Swiss government grant and studied at the University of Berne. He returned to the United States and finished one year of a three-year National Defense Education grant at the University of Chicago, but left to work in a South Side ghetto. "One thing and another came down to the fact that white people were exploiting black people. My experience helped me to understand class structure and how the lives of those people were manipulated, dominated economically, politically, and socially. I was there as a white missionary. I began to realize that the power was in the white community. My efforts were like a Band-aid."

He came back to study at Kent, but his ghetto experience and his growing awareness of black powerlessness and white privilege began to convince him that his education had been irrelevant. "What I've got to say is basically this, there's a ruling class controlling the country and Kent State University, and it's the rich. I want the working class to take power from the rich. There is no right to exploit."

The SDS membership drive did not attract a large activist membership. University vice president Matson said: "We felt we had what we called the hard-core of SDS. This ranged from fifteen to twenty-five in membership. Now, depending on what the substance of a meeting might be or the particular issue might be, this would readily expand to roughly 150 students. Beyond that second circle it depended more and more on what the particular issue was. It appeared that 150 students could be called upon for most of the incidents and issues."

Later, Congressman Richard H. Ichord, of Missouri, chairman of the Committee on Internal Security, looking at pictures of Kent members, would say:

"Just looking at these photographs, I don't want to judge people by their appearance, but I think it is fair to permit one to judge that they are potential troublemakers. I don't know who they are trying to imitate, Che Guevara or someone else, but just looking at them and the television pictures leads one to believe they are potential troublemakers."

From Erickson, Emmer, Mark Real, and Terry Robbins, a Kenyon College dropout from Queens who worked as an Ohio SDS organizer, came a remarkable document in early April 1969 called "Time of the Furnace." It was a blueprint for revolutionary action on Ohio campuses and was sent to SDS leaders throughout the state. Another manual, called "The War Is on at Kent State," was issued applying the Ohio demands to the Kent campus. The demands were: 1. Abolish ROTC. 2. End the Project Themis grant to the Liquid Crystals Institute. 3. Abolish the Law Enforcement School. 4. Abolish the Northeast Ohio Crime Lab.

"The four demands," said Dr. White, "surfaced around April 6. As matters stood prior to that time, there was a whole grab-bag of possible issues, and we could not identify which were going to be the specific issues. When the four appeared, several of them surprised us. Ending ROTC, of course, was a normal, expected demand.

"Abolishing the Liquid Crystals Institute was a surprise. Liquid Crystals does hold a Project Themis Grant from the Department of Defense, but that would lead to presumptions which aren't necessarily correct. Its primary function is early detection of cancer. The development of weaponry is not involved with the institute. The assertion that liquid crystals were used to track Guevara down in Bolivia was terribly farfetched.

"They demanded that we abolish the Bureau of Criminal Investigation, known as the BCI, which is a state agency. It is not a university agency but they were allotted space on our campus. They worked in cooperation with the state BCI, which assists all law-enforcement agencies in the state with 'criminalistics,' the assessment of evidence and chemical tests.

"The demand that we abolish the Law Enforcement School, set up about six years ago, was equally silly. The school is a major curriculum within the department of political science, established by regular faculty-governed political procedures."

On April 8, 1969, SDS formally attempted to present its demands to the university, thereby beginning what was called the "spring offensive." The plan was to go to the administration building and there, Luther-like, pin the four demands to the door of the Board of Trustees' meeting room. The SDS rally began in front of the Student Union. Erickson and Emmer spoke and read the demands. Forty SDS members stomped through classrooms in three buildings yelling "Ho, Ho, Ho Chi Minh, the NLF is gonna win!" When they came to the back door of the administration building, they were 250 strong. University police blocked them from entering. About 700 anti-SDS students were also there to block the group. SDS members pushed and shoved at the door without success. They then went to the front door. Dean David Ambler, then vice president for student affairs, stopped Erickson. "I offered to allow three students into the building to present their demands. He said they all had to come in."

Fighting broke out between SDS members and the anti-SDS faction. Kent State University police sergeant Don Stiles testified that Erickson kicked him in the groin "five or six times." Sweating campus policemen held their arms out to block entry. The confrontation lasted about an hour. Then Howie Emmer yelled "We will quit now" and it ended.

The university moved fast. It suspended SDS's charter as a recognized campus organization. It suspended Erickson, Emmer, and five others. It pressed assault and battery charges against Erickson, Emmer, and three others. It sought, and received, a court injunction keeping Erickson, Emmer, and three others off campus property until May 1.

On April 9 SDS held a rally to protest the university's action. Three additional SDS members, sought on assault and battery charges, were arrested at the rally. A group of five hundred students watched and scuffling once again broke out among the factions. The anti-administration rhetoric heated up. "This rally wasn't as physical as the one on the eighth," said lieutenant Jack Crawford of the Kent State Police Department. "The three members came on campus and Joe Kuchta of the Kent Police Department arrested them. There were about five hundred students assembled to watch them being arrested. There were two brief scuffles. The crowd was heckling the SDS members so badly you couldn't hear what they were saying. When the three were arrested, the crowd had a mixed reaction. The SDS people were trying to take the people we arrested—their members—away from the officers by pulling at them, and the other students disliked this and were pulling the SDS people away."

The next day four hundred fraternity members marched in counter-protest in support of the administration. They surrounded about fifty SDS members and yelled "SDS Go Home" and "Greek Power." "We were running the risk of counter-violence," Dr. White said. "We were alarmed. We were afraid some students would take things into their own hands."

SDS responded to the university's ban and its actions, according to an SDS circular, "by violating the organizational ban as much as possible. We held several rallies and dorm raps in the next few days. We stressed the political nature of the administration's actions, reaffirmed our four demands and our determination to fight, and added a fifth demand: open and collective hearings for all those suspended."

The university ignored that demand, too, and set Wednesday, April 16, as the date for the first suspension hearing, of SDS member Colin Nieburger. "We resolve to open the meeting," SDS said.

On April 16 SDS held a rally on the Commons by the victory bell. Jim Mellen, a national SDS organizer from Chicago, was the main speaker. There were about two hundred SDS members and a crowd of eight hundred persons, many of them hostile. Mellen was heckled and responded to the heckling by saying, "I know that there are some pigs out there who still think we should occupy Vietnam. And there are some pigs out there who still think we should go into ghettos and push people around. Well, I'm telling you, you can't do it any more. We're no longer asking you to come and make a revolution. We're telling you that the revolution has begun, and the only choice you have to make is which side you're on. And we're also telling you that if you get in the way of that revolution, it's going to run right over you."

"OPEN IT UP OR SHUT IT DOWN!" the members chanted.

As Nieburger's suspension hearing began on the third floor of the Music and Speech Building, Father Robert T. Begin, a Cleveland Catholic priest who had poured blood over the Dow Chemical Company files in Washington, D.C., told the rally, "Property which houses repression is immoral. If it's immoral, it must be destroyed." The group of two hundred SDS members moved toward Kent Hall, where they thought the suspension hearings were being held. After about ten minutes they discovered they were beating on the wrong doors and moved to the Music and Speech Building.

They were met by about three hundred anti-SDS students who stood at the front door and chanted: "WE'RE NOT GOING TO LET YOU IN!" Fighting broke out. Campus undercover agent Maggie Murvay said, "One SDS member had a kid by the back of the shirt and she was pulling the shirt back like she was trying to choke him. I grabbed her by the neck and said 'Lay off!' and she did.

"All of a sudden," Maggie Murvay said, "I noticed the SDS members weren't around any more. I went around to the other side of the building because I figured they'd gotten inside. The glass was knocked out of the side door. I went in and started to go upstairs."

Lieutenant Jack Crawford was already on the third floor. So were Rick Erickson, Howie Emmer, and four other SDS members. The university had gone to court to modify the restraining orders against them so they could serve as character witnesses for Nieburger at his hearing. They were to be put in an adjoining room after they had been escorted there by campus policemen.

"We advised them," Crawford said, "as they came into the floor, this is the room they were to go in. They plainly told us they were not going. The only way we could have gotten them into this room, they said, was by force. They paraded up and down the hallway. A short time after they arrived on the floor, one of the members asked permission to go to the bathroom and we said yes. They all wound up in the restroom and they were at the outside windows. They had the windows open, shouting to the people who had started to gather outside the building. They were yelling for the crowd to come up and liberate them.

"We were able to get them out of the restroom and back down the north end of the hallway where the hearing was. There were outside windows in the corridor and Rick Erickson and Howie Emmer went up to those windows, too, and started yelling outside."

Erickson, Emmer, and the four others began chanting and beating on wastebaskets in the hallways. A large group of SDS members and sympathizers had gotten into the building and up to the third floor. They were separated from Erickson, Emmer, and the others only by a metal door. They began beating on the door. Policemen held the door from the inside.

Emmer walked up behind the policemen and, arms outstretched, yelled, "These are my people! Here we are! Come get us! Break the doors down!"

Lieutenant Crawford said, "Shortly after Emmer said that, the group outside started pounding on the door with metal objects. They had taken a metal clothes hanger apart outside. At one point a piece of metal pipe, approximately six feet in length, came through the bottom of the door and was pulled on into the hallway by one of my men. It looked like my men couldn't hold the door so I ordered them back down the hallway to surround the hearing room. Five minutes later they broke the door down and also broke a chain and padlock which had been on the outside.

"The first SDS member," Crawford said, "came through the door with a pipe approximately seven feet in length, and leveled the pipe, like a spear, and started running at full speed down the hall toward the line of police officers."

Rick Erickson screamed at him to stop. "He looked at Erickson for a minute," Crawford said, "and he dropped the piece of pipe which he had." SDS invaded the hearing room, the hearing broke up, and policemen lined the hallway at both ends, not permitting the SDS students who had broken into the building to leave.

At 5:42 p.m. university vice president Matson called the Ohio State Patrol. Inside the hearing room SDS members marked blackboards and walls with slogans: "REVOLUTION NOW!" "UP THE ASS OF THE RULING CLASS." One blackboard was scrawled with what was Rick Erickson's commentary on what had taken place. "An old bitch, gone in the teeth," Erickson wrote of the System. The State Patrol arrested fifty-eight people, Erickson and Emmer among them.

The following day SDS held a rally to protest the arrests. Terry Robbins said, "The first thing we got to talk about is how we are going to get some action. That may scare a lot of people, except a lot of us have been injured and feel better for it."

The action the group decided to take was mild. SDS members and sympathizers went into dormitories to convince students the arrests were unjust. Asked what chance SDS had to sway the student body, vice president Matson said, "Who was that World War II general who replied 'Nuts' when he was asked to surrender? Well, that's the way I feel about their chances of success." That same day, Erickson, Emmer, and two others were charged with inciting a riot.

Student government leaders like Frank Frisina did their best to campaign against SDS, even writing "scare circulars" that said outside agitators were coming into Kent to cause physical damage to the university.

("I would agree," Frisina said later, "that there was no factual backing, support, substantiation for what we did in print. I had no qualms about putting out false rumors because I thought it would avert more violence. Whether what we did was morally right or ethically right, that's another question. Violence to facts doesn't mean much. What's violence to facts?")

In a newsletter SDS assessed the success of its spring offensive at Kent State:

The situation at this point in the struggle is very mixed. On the one hand, the repression has clearly hurt us: over sixty of our people have been banned from the campus, at least eleven face heavy charges, with total bail exceeding $120,000 and the Administration has succeeded to some extent in scaring a lot of people and obfuscating our original demands, allowing civil liberties whiz-kids to spring up.

On the other hand, SDS has made several key advances. We have fought, and fought hard, making it clear that we are serious and tough.... And we have clearly raised the political consciousness of almost the entire campus, winning over many new people, and making it possible to win over many more in the future.

But most important of all, through struggle, we have made it clear that the war being waged in Vietnam, in the black colony of America, will be fought as well at Kent State University.

On May 22 SDS attempted to disrupt ROTC review day. It began with a rally where Rick Skirvin, SDS member, said, "We'll start blowing up buildings, we'll start buying guns, we'll do everything to bring this motherfucking school down. When I was locked up at the Portage County Jail, I had one obsession: I wanted to take a machine gun and kill every bastard there."

The ROTC review was held on the Commons. The field had been marked off by chalk. The cadets were standing at attention when six SDS members came into the area chanting "Off the pigs!" The cadets never broke formation.

SDS retreated to the Liquid Crystals Institute and put a chain on the door. Kent police brought a large clipper within minutes and Liquid Crystals was liberated. It was the final SDS action of the year and only six members took part. For all practical purposes, SDS at Kent State was dead.

Rick Erickson and Howie Emmer became two of the biggest desperadoes in Kent history. It was not a difficult achievement in a quiet little county where deputies have shot only one man in twenty years.

When they went to the Portage County Jail in March 1970 to serve forty-five days for inciting the previous spring's riot, almost as many cameramen were there as policemen.

The town was treated to a constant stream of jailhouse gossip. Rick and Howie, it was said, read nothing but Marx and Mao Tse Tung while they were behind bars. "Studying," Roy Thompson said.

When they were released from jail on Wednesday, April 29, cameramen once again crowded around them. Rick and Howie gave the handshake of brotherhood for the cameras and then got into a brand new Cadillac and peeled away.

The revolutionaries traveled in style.

5

Saturday, May 2

Early Saturday morning the merchants surveyed the damage and made out insurance claims. A glass-company salesman went from door to door on Water Street offering special cut-rate prices. "We need boards, not windows," a shopowner complained. Two service-department trucks were filled with broken glass. The town's prohibitionists looked at the damage and sneered "I told you so!" Policemen like Tony Filomena, bruised and worn out, were back on the job with only three hours' sleep. A quiet fear spread. There had been trouble before, but nothing like this.

Police chief Roy Thompson, who had advised Mayor Satrom Friday night to call in the Guard, sent his "intelligence agents" into the field.

"I'm not going to say who the agents are," he said, "because then they couldn't be agents any more. I trust them, though. Oh, sure, sometimes they tell me things that don't happen, but then I figure the other side has either planted that information or the other side has found out our people know about it and they were forced to cancel the plans."

The townspeople were enraged at the damage the longhairs had wreaked on their town. Many others, having heard about the riot on the radio, came in from the county roads and little farms on Saturday morning, shopping day, to sightsee. By midmorning traffic in downtown Kent was so heavy that Roy Thompson had to assign one of his men to keep it moving. One sightseer, involved in shaking his fist at a long-haired student, plowed his pickup truck into the car in front of him.

A truckload of young self-proclaimed Hindu monks stopped on the Strip for a little drumbeating and chanting of "Hare Krishna." This stopped traffic just about completely. Bald-headed and wearing flowing saffron robes, they moved among the townspeople and handed out "Spiritual Awakening" leaflets. Even the merchants, used to eccentric student behavior, stood agape near their broken windows. When the chanting had gone on for several minutes, one of Roy Thompson's patrolmen went up to the monks and said, "Get on, we don't want you here." The young monks, amazed at this violation of their religious liberties, put their bald heads together in a huddle and conferred. Surveying the situation—merchants, sightseers, rubble, police—they got on the truck and, still chanting, left.

Mayor Satrom announced a state of emergency early in the morning and placed a dusk-to-dawn curfew on the town, effective at 8 p.m. "In the interest of public safety and welfare," he ordered the closing of all retail liquor stores, taverns, and private clubs; the discontinuance of the sale of beer, wine, or liquor; the discontinuance of the selling, distributing, or giving away of gasoline or other liquid flammable or combustible products in any container other than a gasoline tank properly affixed to a motor vehicle; the discontinuance of the selling, distributing, dispensing, or giving away of any firearms or ammunition of any character whatsoever.

That afternoon's *Record Courier* announced that the National Guard had been placed on alert. "If there's any trouble tonight," a policeman said, "it's going to be on campus." A town theater director whose production of *Long Day's Journey into Night* was to be held that night on town property called police and told them of his plans. "I don't care if it's the Chamber of Commerce putting it on," a policeman told him, "if it's held tonight, we'll be there." The director canceled the show.

By noon Roy Thompson was getting anxious phone calls from town merchants. Many of them had received anonymous calls saying that unless they put "Get Out of Cambodia" signs in their windows, their places would be burned. One merchant said a young, bearded man wearing Ben Franklin glasses came into his store and said, "Take this as friendly advice. Put up an anti-war sign tonight or you won't have a store tomorrow morning." Merchants responded by putting up the largest anti-war signs they could fit in their windows. One merchant stopped a reporter and proudly displayed his sign, asking if he'd spelled Vietnam right. "Veetnam?" The reporter corrected him and the merchant got busy painting a new sign. "I don't want them getting mad because I didn't spell it right," he said.

Lieutenant Barnette, the Ohio National Guard liaison officer from the 145th Infantry Regiment, arrived at eight o'clock in the morning. At eleven, he called on university vice president Robert Matson. Matson, a young, soft-spoken man who worked his way through Ohio University as a construction worker and dishwasher, was concerned. He was not happy to see Barnette.

Barnette told Matson his unit had been put on alert to come to Kent if needed. Matson was visibly surprised. The university hadn't been consulted, he said. It was the first he had heard about it. He explained that the university had its own riot contingency plan. First, Matson said, the university police would be called in. Second, the Portage County sheriff's department would be called in. And then, only if absolutely necessary, the Ohio State Patrol would be called in.

A man in his mid-thirties, dressed casually in chino slacks and a sport shirt, Barnette listened to Matson's contingency plans carefully. Unfortunately, Barnette said, if the Guard came in, the contingency plan was just a scrap piece of paper. If the Guard came in, he said, it would take "complete control" not only of the town but of the campus. He pointed out, though, that at the moment the Guard was only on alert. Chances are, Barnette said, the Guard wouldn't be needed.

The words "complete control" stuck in Robert Matson's mind. He didn't like the sound of them, and he relayed his conversation with Barnette by telephone to President White in Mason City. White also disliked the sound of the words and ordered Matson to send the university's twin-engine Piper Aztec for him. In case of trouble he didn't want to be stranded on an Ozark Airlines flight in some place like Chicago.

In mid-afternoon, after he'd been briefed by his agents, police chief Roy Thompson met with Mayor Satrom. The chief reminded the mayor that he had recommended calling up the Guard the night before. Now, the chief said, all his new intelligence confirmed his previous judgment. The Guard was needed as soon as possible to defend the town. Weathermen had been observed on campus and positively identified. There was evidence of guns on campus. ("Guys with red headbands on we never saw before," the chief said later, "call 'em Weathermen or whatever you want to call 'em.") His agents, the chief said, had also learned of plans to burn down the town. Special targets would be the banks, the town post office, the campus ROTC building. LSD would be placed in the water supply. The chief pointed to the threats the downtown merchants were receiving.

LeRoy Satrom thought about what the chief told him. At 5 p.m. he decided there was nothing else to do. That kind of intelligence could not be ignored. With the town's safety at stake it was his responsibility to do something about it. He called the adjutant general's office in Columbus and told them of the Weathermen and guns on campus. He asked for help and the request was quickly granted.

The National Guard after-action report noted:

> The first battalion, 145th Infantry was ordered to move from Akron to the City of Kent to assist civil authorities in the City of Kent. The Adjutant General (Del Corso) and the Assistant Adjutant General (Canterbury) for Army departed Columbus for Kent to observe the situation and to determine specific missions and requirements.

University vice president Robert Matson, at 5:30 p.m. that afternoon, did not know the National Guard had been called. It was another beautiful spring day. It was quiet. There was no trouble. No one from the city had been in touch with him. Late in the afternoon he was beginning to feel a bit relieved. There were rumors of a rally that night but he had been told it was not garnering much support. He had seen no more of Lieutenant Barnette and that was fine with him. He had organized several student activities in a hurry so the kids would have a place to go that night. One of them was a big dance to be held at Tri Towers dormitory complex. He had even gone to the trouble of lining up a rock band. He had ordered that a green circular be issued. The circular told students it would be unwise to go to the rally. On the back was a list of all the university activities scheduled that night. He was keeping a close watch on things.

He talked to campus police chief Donald Schwartzmiller, who told him his intelligence indicated there would be no trouble that night. As LeRoy Satrom was asking the National Guard for protection, Robert Matson was again on the phone with President White in Mason City telling him he might as well stay there. It looked as if it would be a routine night. The university plane had arrived in Mason City, but, Matson told White, there was no reason to come back.

In mid-afternoon ROTC Captain Don Peters, a Vietnam combat veteran, went to the ROTC building to do some paper work. As he left, long-haired youths in denim bell bottoms told him, "Be sure you come back tonight so you'll be in the building when we burn it." Peters knew that for many students the building was a convenient symbol of the military complex. It was there, on campus, and they could lash out at it. The rickety old building had been threatened periodically ever since SDS, the previous spring, made the abolition of ROTC one of its main demands.

The building had some of Captain Peters' war mementos in it. His typewriter was there, his tape-recorder, his correspondence. He decided to go back inside to get these things. When he got inside, he thought, the hell with it. He'd heard that song before. He took only a pair of old Levis and a rumpled shirt. He was going fishing that night. As he drove away, he thought to himself that somehow the kids who'd talked to him about burning the building seemed different. He couldn't figure out why they struck him that way. Then, after a while, he came up with the answer. They seemed so confident! By that time, though, he had gone too far to turn back and, besides, he looked forward to fishing and wanted to get going as fast as he could.

Bill Resch, president of the Graduate Student Council, was on his way back from Columbus that afternoon. He heard the details of Friday night's disturbances over the car radio and tried to put things into perspective. What caused it? Cambodia? Sure, but . . . When Rubin spoke, his speech did nothing to the kids. Either Rubin was getting bad-rapped as the Great Inciter or the kids at Kent were just politically apathetic. With all his rhetoric Rubin couldn't even get the kids to stay away from classes that day. And a lot of them had laughed. He stuck by his original feeling. Cambodia, yes, but mostly cold beer and hot weather. That, Bill Resch thought, equaled Friday night. Friday night was a fluke. It was over. No one was hurt and nothing else would happen. His car radio told him that the mayor had slapped a curfew on the town. He got into Kent a little before eight o'clock and noticed many students hurrying away from town to the only part of Kent they were allowed to roam that night, the campus.

By mid-afternoon on the campus everybody seemed to know about the rally that night, though no one knew who was sponsoring it. Word had spread by mouth. Everyone seemed to know, too, that the National Guard had been placed on alert.

At 6 p.m. there were only about fifty students on the Commons. At 8 p.m. the victory bell began to toll. Within twenty minutes a group of eight hundred students had gathered on the Commons. The bars were closed, it was illegal to be in town, and it was warm. Most of the students wore the usual uniform: beads, bell bottoms, Levis. Some wore red headbands. Some had marked their faces with warpaint. A reporter in the crowd saw a student with a hunting knife on his belt. The sheath was tied to his thigh. Three protesters made their way around the crowd, talking to newsmen, telling them they would "get it" if they took pictures of the demonstrations. "We don't want to go to jail again," one of the three said. He threatened to kill three Kent *Record Courier* newsmen who were also Kent State journalism students.

The victory bell stopped ringing, and a young man with long, flowing blond hair and denim jacket and pants jumped up on the bell's concrete backing. Everyone expected a speech. The young man had university vice president Matson's circular in his hand.

"The university is holding activities today so no one will come here," the young man said. "We need more people. There's a dance at Tri Towers! Let's liberate the dance!"

Led by a small group screaming war-whoops and yippie-yells, the crowd surged around Taylor Hall, across the parking lot facing Blanket Hill, up a plowed field, and through a wooded area to Tri Towers. They jammed up a stairway to the second floor to "liberate the dance." The only problem was that there was no dance—there were three students and the rock band. For a few minutes the crowd was disoriented and didn't seem to know what to do. Then they swarmed back outside. Anti-war slogans were spray-painted on buildings, trees, and sidewalks. Someone turned in a false fire alarm. Watching the group from nearby was campus police detective Thomas Kelley, wearing his blue windbreaker, brown slacks, and brown shoes. "Good old Kelley!" someone yelled. Also nearby were tow trucks driven by incognito campus policemen. Some of the demonstrators spotted the tow trucks and waved.

Continuing on through Eastway Center, a four-dormitory area for freshmen, the crowd picked up additional demonstrators. It now numbered about twelve hundred people. "Join us!" they yelled. Some picked up rocks at a construction area. "As we got back to the top of the hill toward the Commons," one participant said, "the people in the front of the group started running down the Commons toward the ROTC building. When they got to the building, they stopped. There were no cops there. How could you have a confrontation without any cops?"

A chant of "DOWN WITH ROTC!" began. A reporter felt a rock whiz by his chin and turned to look in the direction it had come from. "I looked quickly to my right and I saw the guy who threw it. There was hatred all over his face. The crowd was fifteen feet away from the building. A second or two later a barrage of rocks filled the air. The group was turning into an angry mob. After the initial barrage the group retreated back toward the victory bell, apparently to await any reaction. There wasn't any."

The crowd milled around.

A demonstrator to the side of the main group unfurled an American flag, ripped it, and set it afire. Holding the burning flag aloft, he walked toward the cheering mob. "Right on!" the crowd yelled.

A student with a camera kneeled down to take a picture. Ten or fifteen members of the crowd charged, tackling him with an audible thunk, and knocked him to the ground. The student was kicked in the face. "Pig!" they yelled. He cried for help. His camera was taken from him and the film pulled out. As he lay on the ground, the camera was thrown back at him. Another group of demonstrators picked him up and carried him to his dormitory. "I thought they were going to kill him," said a witness twenty feet away who was afraid to help.

The flag burning touched off another attack on the ROTC building. A demonstrator raced to the building with a stick and battered in the windows that had not been broken by rocks. This time, in addition to rocks, demonstrators also threw railroad flares. One flare bounced off the roof, others landed nearby. One landed inside the building, but the glow slowly went out. A few campus policemen stood on the western edge of the ROTC building, near the Student Union, away from the Commons, watching. One of them was campus police chief Donald Schwartzmiller.

"I was there with three of my plainclothes men. We had mobilized our entire force. They were getting ready, putting on their riot gear. The Portage County sheriff's office had also been notified. I wasn't about to stop that mob with just a few of my men."

A young man and woman ran to the eastern side of the building near the Commons and threw burning rags inside. "BURN, BABY, BURN!" the crowd chanted.

"It was an emotional thing now," a participant said, "you couldn't talk to anybody rationally. Everybody was strung up."

Schwartzmiller went inside the Student Union, leaving some of his plainclothes men on the other side of the building. He told university vice president Matson to call in the State Patrol. Things were out of hand, he feared, and it was time to take the final step of the university contingency plan. Matson asked the Patrol for help. He was told two busloads of highway patrolmen would be sent from the Warren Barracks, forty miles away.

Schwartzmiller called the City of Kent police department and asked for immediate help. "They returned the favor of the night before," he said. "They told me they couldn't help. They said they were all tied up protecting the town. They said the town was their responsibility and the campus was mine."

Outside, the crowd cheered and waited for the fire to start. But the glow went out again. A young man ran up to the building, pulled himself up to a window, and looked inside. He announced that the fire had died out. The crowd groaned.

A long-haired youth ran to the eastern side of the building and touched a burning rag to one of the curtains. Flames shot up and the crowd cheered wildly.

Minutes later a City of Kent fire truck with six firemen arrived at the scene. They had no police escort. "My men were still getting ready, putting on their riot gear," Schwartzmiller said. The firemen unrolled their hose and began pumping water into the building. They pumped enough water in to kill the fire. The crowd began stoning them. Several persons ran up and took the hose from the firemen. Some fifty demonstrators pulled at the hose, trying to yank it away while other demonstrators stoned the firemen from close range. Others jabbed the hose with pocket knives. Water finally began spurting from the hose and a part of it was ripped away. When another rock barrage began, the firemen got back on their truck and fled.

One of the demonstrators put a piece of hose over his head and snake-danced back to the crowd on the Commons. The mob cheered him. "It was a very emotional thing," a participant said, "people were thrilled. They wanted the building burned to the ground."

As the fire truck roared away in retreat, another demonstrator went up to the ROTC building and held a burning rag to a curtain until flames shot out of the window. The building finally blazed.

Campus policemen accompanied by Portage County sheriff's deputies arrived in full riot gear armed with sidearms, shotguns, and carbines. The firemen were back with a new hose minutes later and, defended by a line of rifle-toting officers, fought the fire. A demonstrator started for a fireman, and the fireman turned the hose on him and knocked him to the ground. "If anybody gets near that fire truck," a sheriff's deputy told a reporter, "I have orders to put a little round hole in him." The sheriff's deputies laid down a barrage of tear gas.

The demonstrators broke into two groups. One group of about four hundred headed off campus toward the downtown area. The other swarmed around the Commons toward the tennis courts as policemen formed a skirmish line.

In the university's communications center in the administration building, vice president Robert Matson sat listening to a police radio, waiting for the State Patrol to arrive. It was 9:14 p.m. He heard what the police radio said and he couldn't believe he had heard right. It said: "THE GUARD IS MOVING INTO KENT!" The Guard? But what where they doing here? He had called the State Patrol. The ROTC building was still in flames, the fire had started only minutes ago. How could the Guard get here so fast after the fire broke out? The police radio went on to say that three hundred students were moving toward the downtown area.

The group of demonstrators marching down Main Street toward the downtown area destroyed signs, telephone booths, anything breakable. Demonstrators turned cars away as they approached. As they marched they picked up stones and pop bottles. They met and stoned the National Guardsmen, marching up Main Street toward campus. The National Guard after-action report said, "The crowd was ordered to disperse and to return to their abodes. The dispersal order was given a total of three or four times. People in the crowd made no move to comply with the dispersal order and Guard troops finally fired tear gas and moved against the mob to break them up. The effort was successful."

The demonstrators scattered across campus. An information booth near the university library was showered with kerosene and lighted. So was a tree. Parking meters in the lots were damaged. Demonstrators filled their pockets with change that rolled onto the sidewalk. University lights were broken as the group weaved back toward the Commons.

Meanwhile, the confrontation with the group on the Commons continued. The Commons is separated from the tennis courts by a six-foot-high cyclone fence. When sheriff's deputies began moving demonstrators toward the fence, someone yelled, "Get the fence! It's a trap!" A group of about twenty students flattened the fence in less than a minute. An archery shed containing bows and arrows was doused with kerosene and set afire. One demonstrator grabbed a bow and arrow and war-whooped.

As the shed burned, the demonstrators found themselves in a confrontation with their fellow students. A group of students swarmed from a nearby dormitory when the shed was torched, carrying fire extinguishers, wastebaskets, and water buckets.

The ROTC building was now burning so fiercely that the fire could be seen five miles away. A fireman called for everyone to back off because of a gas canister inside. A thick yellowish curtain of smoke could be seen inside the building. Firemen were also hindered by target ammunition inside that began to explode and by a car nearby that began to steam. They feared its gas tank would explode. They finally lost control and flames began shooting through the roof. Colonel Arthur W. Dotson, a twenty-nine-year career man who had been appointed Kent's ROTC commander in October 1969, stood by the burning building and said, "Vietnam would be a pleasure after this."

In the president's house, overlooking the Commons on campus, the housekeeper looked out the living-room window and saw the fire. Panicked, fearing the president's house would be next, she called Dr. White in Mason City. He had not yet been notified that the building was on fire. He called Matson and learned that the National Guard was on campus. White called his pilot at the airport and asked if he could take off immediately for Kent. The pilot told him the airport tower would not let him take off until dawn due to a heavy fog. White's worst fear was realized. His campus faced its gravest crisis and he was a thousand miles away, trapped and isolated.

A contingent of National Guardsmen, personally led by Adjutant General Sylvester T. Del Corso in a blue business suit, reached campus and formed flanks near the burning building. They immediately laid down a tear-gas barrage. A gusty wind swept the tear gas away and back at guardsmen and sheriff's deputies, many of whom hadn't had a chance to don gas masks.

A Portage County sheriff's deputy, using a bullhorn, asked the crowd very politely to disperse. The crowd, now down to about five hundred demonstrators, was strung out on the rise overlooking the Commons near Taylor Hall and Blanket Hill.

The deputy said: "Ladies and gentlemen, please go back to your dormitories. If you remain outside, you will be arrested. We do not want to arrest you."

He was answered with a chorus of "OFF THE PIGS!," "OFF THE GUARD!," and obscenities.

Del Corso ordered his junior officers to form the troops into a skirmish line. Bayonets were fixed. The troops broke into platoon-sized units and, rifles ready, advanced on the students, who broke into smaller groups.

Del Corso led his men across the Commons and up the knoll toward a group of students standing near Blanket Hill. Rocks began pelting down. Del Corso called for an M-79 man to launch tear gas into the crowd. Once again the wind took the gas away. Guardsmen herded groups of students into Johnson Hall. Other groups ran between the dorms and onto the parking lot behind Taylor Hall.

"It was really chaotic," one witness said. "You could see individual guardsmen chasing kids with their bayonets."

A twenty-one-year-old senior suffered an eight-inch bayonet cut on his right cheek and a deep stab wound in the leg when two guardsmen chased him up against the Johnson Hall wall.

"I was trying to run away and I got panicked. These guys were chasing us. I didn't know which way to go. I started running for Johnson and I saw these two guardsmen coming at me from two directions. I crumpled up against the wall and one guy, the guy who got me in the leg, ran up against me, tackled me kind of, and fell over me. The other guy was running too, and I think he wanted to hit me with the butt, but as he pulled the rifle down, he slashed me in the face. They picked me up and pushed me into the dorm."

Del Corso's platoon, after pursuing a group into Johnson Hall, started in pursuit of a group retreating toward the Tri Towers complex, along the same route taken by demonstrators earlier that night to break up the dance. Students ran into the woods near Tri Towers. As the troops came toward the woods, the students, now into the tree line, turned and let loose a hail of rocks. One rock landed at Del Corso's feet.

Del Corso, sweating and angry, bent down, picked up the rock, and threw it high over the heads of troops in front of him. Cleveland *Plain Dealer* reporter Carl Kovac heard him say, "Throw 'em back at those bastards," as he threw the rock. Kent State student Martin Kurta, a former member of the student government, heard him say, "If these goddamn kids can throw rocks, I can, too." The students escaped into the woods. Del Corso's platoon wheeled and marched back toward Johnson and Taylor Halls.

As they marched, a group of girls from a women's dormitory leaned out of their windows and yelled, "YEA ARMY! GO GUARD!"

A number of platoons lined up in an area known as the Quadrangle. A number of dormitories line the Quad, a flat area. Tri Towers is nearby. Del Corso stood in front of the platoons. Groups of students stood outside the dorms, watching. No rocks were being thrown. There was no chanting.

A group of students against a dormitory wall said they wanted to talk to a Guard commander. "Dialogue!" they yelled.

A group of guardsmen near them told them to get back inside

their dormitories. When the students didn't move and yelled "Dialogue!" again, Del Corso said, "All right, get 'em inside, I don't care how. Through the doors! Through the glass! Through the walls! Any way!"

The troops, bayonets fixed on their M-1s, began advancing on the students, still backed against the dormitory wall.

"No! Oh, no!" a sheriff's deputy screamed and ran in front of the guardsmen's bayonets, putting himself between bayonets and students. The deputy grabbed the platoon leader by the fatigues and screamed at him to stop. When the guardsmen's bayonets were less than five feet from the students, the platoon leader ordered his men to halt. The deputy turned to the students and begged them to go inside the dormitories. They did. The guardsmen about-faced and marched away.

A reporter asked a guardsman if he could stand near their formation. "If you're scared, get the hell out," the guardsman said. The reporter asked the guardsman if he was scared. "You're damned right I am," the guardsman said.

Cleveland *Plain Dealer* reporter Carl Kovac, an ex-Marine, and Kent *Record Courier* columnist Robert Hoiles, who had been near Del Corso and got separated from him, walked together toward a group of guardsmen. A guardsman ordered them to halt. They stopped and told the guardsman they were newsmen. The guardsman ordered them to get back to their dormitories. When Kovac told the guardsman once again he was a newsman and reached for the press credentials in his breast pocket, the guardsman told him to "Freeze!"

"For the first time I noticed his hand," Kovac said. "He was holding a .45 held at hip level toward my head. He was no more than three feet away. The safety was off and the hammer cocked. I asked him if he would reach in and get the press pass and he refused. Another trooper stopped beside him and leveled a grease gun at Hoiles and me. We saw Del Corso and waved. When they saw Del Corso, the two guardsmen forgot about us."

By midnight the situation was under control. Del Corso went to the dormitories and made arrangements for students who were trapped there to be escorted back to their dormitories by armed guardsmen. Some of the men who had taken refuge in the women's dorms objected. At Tri Towers a large group of students gathered in a little television room hoping to see films of the burning ROTC building.

Early Sunday morning, tired National Guardsmen stood ready with bayonets around town and campus buildings. A large armored personnel carrier was parked by the campus gate. A National Guard helicopter and two State Patrol helicopters, armed with searchlights, hovered overhead. The squelch of police radios could be heard all over town and campus. The ROTC building, burned to the ground, still smoldered. Target-practice ammunition popped in the night. It sounded like gunfire.

6

General Del Corso

It seemed as if much of the bitterness and rage over the shooting on Blanket Hill came to settle on one man, a man who was not even there, the commander of the Ohio National Guard, Major General Sylvester T. Del Corso. In the days following that awful afternoon at Kent, reason became mired in heated accusations. U.S. Senator Stephen M. Young, Democrat from Ohio, spoke to his colleagues on the Senate floor and assured them with sadness that the Ohio Guard was "trigger happy."

"He's a senile old liar," stormed General Del Corso about the eighty-year-old senator's comments.

"Del Corso is a two-by-four politician," retorted the senator. "My father told me never to get into a spraying contest with a skunk."

Nearly every liberal voice in Ohio and many across the nation condemned Del Corso. "It is not those kids on the skirmish line that I blame," many would say. "It is that damn Del Corso." On the other hand, the general received several thousand letters commending him for doing his duty. Veterans' organizations passed resolutions attacking a critical press and praising the Guard. The polarization that divided the country wound tight on one end and was anchored by the stubby general.

In times past the commander of the Ohio National Guard lived out his term in relative obscurity and passed from the scene with stiff little newspaper notices that mentioned old campaigns, worn decorations, and dim memories. Sylvester T. Del Corso should not have been any exception to this.

In appearance Del Corso is not an overly impressive man. He stands five feet seven inches and has a paunch. His mouth is a narrow line that seems to be fortified against humor and he speaks in a soft voice that sometimes makes listeners lean forward to hear.

The general works and directs the Ohio National Guard from Fort Hayes, a military compound covering the space of a couple of city blocks on the north side of Columbus, the state capital. He is in his office, in a rambling old building that has housed the Guard headquarters for years, by seven-thirty each morning.

The general is neither a complicated nor boastful man. In fact, it took him a few moments to remember where he won his first Silver Star, and he related the action in an almost bored manner. He usually wears a conservative business suit, but his dress uniform carries five rows of ribbons topped by the Combat Infantryman's Badge. His decorations include five for efforts under enemy fire. One writer close to Del Corso described him as a "man of simple tastes and Spartan habits."

When he took the job as head of the Ohio Guard in 1968, the general considered himself as something of a homebody. He plays tennis on his home court, golfs in the high eighties, and after work will take a shot of bourbon and perhaps work in the yard after dinner. "My typical schedule has been disrupted of late by civil disturbances," he said offhand. "Those things turn my day into a twenty-four-hour ordeal."

The son of an Italian stonecutter and sculptor, Del Corso was quiet and almost shy in his manner as a student at Berea High School in Berea, Ohio, a suburb of Cleveland where he and his seven brothers and sisters were raised. There were two things that people in Berea remember about him in those days: he was very disciplined and very tough and both of these qualities made him an excellent fullback.

"I remember him as a boy," said one woman. "He never seemed to be interested in social things. I don't think he dated much. He was the kind of boy that you would see walking down the street like he had someplace to go. He was never aimless that I recall. You know, he loved that National Guard, too."

Tony Del Corso was fifteen years old when he lied about his age and joined the Ohio National Guard as a high-school student. He enlisted in 1928 as a buck private in the 145th Infantry Regiment, a unit he was destined to serve in virtually every capacity.

After graduating from high school he enrolled at Baldwin-Wallace College, a small Methodist school located in Berea where his conversion to guard on the football team took place. Behind the school's chapel stands a large stone fountain made by his father, T. A. Del Corso. The general fondly remembers that the fountain was once in the backyard of his boyhood home.

On Front Street in Berea there are still a few who remember Tony Del Corso and the 1935 and 1936 B-W football teams. They led the nation in scoring for those two years and in 1936 went undefeated after beating Syracuse University. Del Corso was considered one of the best guards in Ohio college football then. Some say he was the absolute best.

In 1939 the Ohio National Guard did two things for Sylvester T. Del Corso. It straightened out his age on the records and made him a second lieutenant. Later that year Company D, Berea's contribution to the Ohio National Guard, then being formed into the 37th Division, was called to active duty and before it left for Camp Shelby, Mississippi, Lieutenant Del Corso was given command of the unit.

In the spring of 1942, now a captain with his nation at war, Tony Del Corso began what would be a distinguished combat record with the 145th Regiment. There followed Guadalcanal, Bougainville, and a promotion to major with an appointment as executive officer of a battalion. At New Georgia in the Solomons he was hit with a grenade fragment but refused evacuation in order to direct the withdrawal of two infantry companies that had been trapped by enemy fire. For this act he was awarded a Silver Star. He already wore a Bronze Star for leading an assault on a hill on Bougainville.

The youngsters and old-timers who shot pool at Schuerlein's Recreation in Berea could see a Japanese flag that the major had sent home and talk of the far-off war as the balls were racked.

In a letter to a friend Del Corso wrote of his wound and the fighting:

We are in action and have killed plenty of Japs. The Berea boys have accounted for plenty of Japs with machine guns and mortars. I received a small grenade fragment in my leg but it

wasn't enough to stop me and I am on the front line all the time. I
have a few souvenirs among which is a Jap flag. The general congratulated me for a fine job, but everyone is doing a fine job here.
    Don't let Berea forget the boys out here. You have no idea what
they are going through and how well they are doing it.

The Pacific campaign was to be a holding action until the war in
Europe was concluded and the 37th Division bore much of the brunt
of the gnawing day-to-day fighting. The Marines might make the
big beach assaults, hitting quick and grabbing island after island,
but it was the 37th that followed, slogging through the tropical rain,
hacking the jungle, and weeding out the remnants of the Japanese
force. In three and a half years overseas Sylvester T. Del Corso saw
over seven hundred days of combat.

"There were some bad days," the general recalled. "The time at
Munda airport. We fought the Imperial Japanese Marines. They
were the best they had. That's where I was wounded. I still carry
those fragments."

Del Corso was elevated to lieutenant colonel and given command
of the third battalion of the 145th. Of the three battalion commanders in the regiment at that time, Del Corso was the only one to live. It
was the third battalion that took Manila City Hall in a fierce engage-
ment in which Del Corso personally led an assault into the building
after five of his company commanders were killed.

"The city hall was a modern structure, several stories tall, and
commanded the entrance to the walled city where the Japs had a
stronghold," Del Corso said. "It was a casketshaped building with
a courtyard and a tower on one end. The men attacked and were
driven out four times. One platoon was caught in a hallway and
almost wiped out by a machine-gun. I took the entire battalion into
that building. We started at one end and went through it room by
room, floor by floor. We finally took control of the roof and courtyard."

After sustaining casualties that included thirty dead, Del Corso's
battalion had taken the entire building with the exception of a single
room on the ground floor next to the walled city. The troops had
tried everything: grenades, flame throwers, and more grenades. The
Japs would answer every assault with the clatter of machine-guns

that would send rounds slapping around the tile corridors of the building.

"We couldn't figure it out," Del Corso said. "We tried everything on that room and we couldn't crack it. Then I got hold of our demolition expert and asked him if we could blow a hole in the ceiling above the Japs. We used TNT and blew it. You know, those Japs had a dugout in there and could seal it off from our fire. We caught them by surprise from above. There were forty-one dead Japs in that room." The body count for the Japanese force in the city hall was 340.

For that action Del Corso was awarded another Silver Star.

Years later, during a prison riot in Ohio State Penitentiary, Del Corso, now commanding the Ohio National Guard, would recall the battle for the city hall in Manila and order a charge of explosives placed against a prison roof. It would enable nine guards held hostage to escape with their lives. Five prisoners died in the fighting.

"We needed shock and speed," Del Corso said. "We needed them in Manila and we needed them here [at the penitentiary]."

As the war drew to a close, Sylvester T. Del Corso was promoted to full colonel and given the command of the 145th Infantry Regiment. His rise in the regiment had begun in 1929 when he was promoted to corporal. There was probably no one who knew as much about the operation of the regiment as Del Corso. The unit motto was "Excel" and it seemed as if the new colonel had adopted it as his own.

In the South Pacific there was one more major event that would conclude World War II for Colonel Del Corso. That was the surrender of the Japanese forces in northeastern Luzon. The "One-Four-Five" was spread out over a 120-mile line as the war drew to a close. General Yamashata, supreme commander of the composite Japanese forces in the area, was officially notified of the surrender of his nation to the Allied Forces. The surrender of his troops was to be made to Colonel Del Corso, who made ready to receive the Japanese delegation with full military courtesy.

It was a sunny, cloudless day as Colonel Ryzuki Sakamaki stepped forward, exchanged salutes with the American colonel, and presented his sword, which Del Corso still possesses, a memento of long, difficult days. The Japanese officer bowed and there were tears in his eyes as he signed the surrender document that officially ended hostilities in the area.

"Sakamaki hated to lose," Del Corso said many years later. "The man told me he had not seen his wife in twelve years. He was a professional soldier and had begun his war in Nanking and ended it here in Luzon. We were a hundred miles from Manila, but the Filipinos heard we had Sakamaki. They wanted to do away with him, he was a mean customer, but we protected him. He later stood trial. I never heard what happened to him."

Del Corso felt no compassion for the vanquished Japanese. "The feeling that came over me during the surrender ceremonies was a sense of loss, the loss of so many human beings. I thought of the men we lost over the years. It flashed through my mind what a tragic loss of young men. No, there was no love. We extended a few military courtesies between professional soldiers, that's all."

V-J Day came. The war was over and the troops returned home. Del Corso returned to Berea and took a job with the Veterans' Administration's testing and guidance program. He was assigned to help with the program at his alma mater, Baldwin-Wallace. At first, the postwar years seemed destined to pitch him into obscurity.

In June 1946 he married in Baltimore. Emma Louise Engle was a former nurse with the Army Nurse Corps and she and the colonel had met in the Fiji Islands while both served with the 37th Division. By November there was more good news for the colonel. The "One-Four-Five" was reactivated and he was designated its commander once more. The cold war was beginning its freeze. That same year Baldwin-Wallace College honored him as its outstanding alumnus of 1946.

Three years later the army honored Del Corso for his World War II service with the presentation of the Legion of Merit Award, but as far as the public was concerned the big news about him appeared on the front page of the Cleveland *Plain Dealer* later in the year. "Col. S. T. Del Corso, a young man with an amazing military record and a headful of ideas for rehabilitation of Warrensville Workhouse inmates, was appointed superintendent of the workhouse late yesterday by Mayor Thomas A. Burke."

The job was a prickly one in Cleveland politics. The former superintendent had resigned after a police investigation revealed he had offered special privileges to certain inmates at the city's chief penal institution. There had been a rash of escapes in the previous months and the hard-nosed combat veteran quietly stated the new policy:

"I shall let all inmates know when they attempt to get away they can expect to be shot at and expect to be hit."

He spoke of better rehabilitation of inmates and emphasized a continuous training program for guards in "handling personnel, leadership, discipline, and marksmanship."

Not long after he took over the Workhouse, the Cleveland *Press* sent a reporter with a City Council inspection team and found that Del Corso had made some remarkable changes, beginning with the prisoners' diet. He had restructured the menu on sixteen cents a meal to give the inmates decent fare. Under Del Corso a night school was begun and other improvements made.

When war broke out in Korea, and after two years as chief of the Workhouse, Del Corso was recalled to active duty by the army and later assigned to command the U.S. Disciplinary Barracks at Camp Gordon, Georgia. His accomplishments at the prison were favorably reported and many of his directives were regarded as innovations as he allowed a great deal of freedom to prisoners.

There was an honor farm run by unguarded inmates, a program of temporary home paroles, a visiting area far from the camp where prisoners could have picnics with their families. It was all quite liberal for those days, and the cigar-smoking commandant reported he had no trouble with prisoners, no attempts at escape, no real problems that he could not handle. When his tour at the barracks was completed, the army sent him to Command and General Staff College and then dispatched him to Germany, where he assumed command of the Augsburg Sub Area.

When the citizens of a small German town called Gablingen complained that American military vehicles were ruining the roads, Del Corso put his troops to work. The German newspaper *Augsburger Landbote* wrote: "The military authorities showed understanding of the situation in Gablingen community and assigned several trucks for the transport of gravel to the roads most affected. The gravel was provided without cost. . . . Col. Del Corso personally assured the Gablingen burgomaster that the vehicles would be at his disposal as long as the community needed them."

The action was typical of Del Corso's decisiveness. His whole method consisted of a direct and immediate answer to the problem at hand, whether it was blowing a hole in the roof of a city hall or a jail or paving a road. He identified the problem and solved it. Complexities neither existed nor were allowed to take form.

Governor James A. Rhodes named Del Corso the adjutant general of the Ohio National Guard in the spring of 1968. Newspaper accounts said he was the seventy-first to hold that office since 1803. It is doubtful if any had been more controversial.

"I felt very flattered that the governor elected me," Del Corso said shortly after he received the two stars that made him a major general. The job was appointive but Republicans really could not count Tony Del Corso as a staunch GOP member. He may have voted their way, but he did not participate in any of their political functions. "He may have bought a ticket or two at some point for a fund-raising dinner but that was the extent of it," said one county chairman. "The governor just wanted someone who could handle the Guard and Del Corso was a good man." Much later, Del Corso admitted that the right-wing American Independent Party had asked him to run for office. He refused.

As things turned out, General Del Corso did not get through his first summer as Guard commander without trouble. He was in the news and embroiled with controversy stemming from a bloody racial disturbance that erupted between white policemen and black militants in Cleveland's Glenville area. Ten persons, including three policemen, were killed and nineteen others wounded after an angered band of blacks opened fire on police. Cleveland's mayor, Carl B. Stokes, the first black to be elected mayor of a major U.S. city, called for the Guard to help quell the violence after forty-seven stores had been burned and looted. The situation exploded with such force that Governor Rhodes alerted sixteen thousand guardsmen and ordered twenty-six hundred to Glenville.

Stokes, who was riding the crest of his political popularity, ordered all white police and guardsmen out of the area on the second night of disturbances in order to give patrolling black citizens a chance to cool their own people. The mayor faced a bitter verbal attack from his police force as more violence broke out after the Guard and white police withdrew.

Del Corso advised the mayor to forget the experiment with the black patrols and use the Guard. "I just made the recommendation," he told reporters. "I respect the mayor and what he was trying to do, but I felt that he had had his chance and we should have ours to do the job we are here for." Finally, the Guard was ordered back into the riot-torn streets and the general issued orders not to shoot looters unless they resisted efforts to keep peace.

Earlier in the year Del Corso had praised Stokes for his personal action of taking to the ghetto streets and talking down trouble following the stunning news of the assassination of Martin Luther King. But when the Ohio Crime Commission convened hearings on the Glenville incident, Del Corso testified and rebuked Stokes for his handling of this disturbance. He told the Associated Press that the mayor had "surrendered to black revolutionaries."

The AP reported that "Stokes had acted against his advice when he ordered guardsmen and white policemen from the troubled area."

"Widespread looting and burning became prevalent," the general said.

Cleveland city offiicals were amazed at Del Corso's remarks to the commission. The *Plain Dealer* reported that several of the mayor's aides complained that Del Corso's comments to the commission did not square with those he made to Stokes while the Guard was on duty in Cleveland. This dispute passed and yellowed in newspaper files, but it was not long before Del Corso again found himself quoted in public. This time he launched a verbal blast at the student demonstrators who had begun to draw his professional attention.

Speaking to an organization called the Progressive Adults of Ohio at a meeting in Cleveland, the general called the New Mobilization Committee to End the War in Vietnam and the Students for a Democratic Society "part of the international Communist conspiracy." He told the conference that persons connected with the New Mobe were closely associated with the Communist Party. The general roundly criticized elected officials who joined peace demonstrations and said the SDS had been stopped in Ohio because of vigorous law enforcement.

"These groups have been infiltrated and we know them," he said. "We can move against them fast when laws are violated."

The Cleveland *Press* quickly took him to task in an editorial entitled "Del Corso Pops Off." It said:

"Going beyond the fatuousness of the statement, Del Corso has no business airing his political views publicly. Traditionally the military stays out of the political area.

"Del Corso ought to have plenty to do running the Ohio National Guard without giving gratuitous political advice."

Two months later he addressed the Rotarians in Columbus in a speech entitled "Civil Disobedience" that attacked both Communist militants and public officials who scorned the use of the National Guard in riot situations.

"We have listened too much . . . and too long to those who handle dissidents with permissiveness and tolerance," he said. He spoke against those who placed restrictions on the police and military. "Just see how the military has been prevented from going all out in Vietnam and Laos and Cambodia now . . . sitting there in a defensive position, when to surrender our freedom there is to surrender it here, and if we have to fight for it, let's do it away from our shores, that's what I say, because I'd rather die fighting than live the life of a coward."

Again he challenged the New Mobe and the SDS, calling them Communist-inspired organizations, and pledged:

"I for one have no intention of standing back and letting them get away with it. I will fight psychological warfare with psychological warfare—by publicly exposing them for what they are."

His speech was met by applause. When it was concluded a reporter from a Columbus newspaper asked him why he did not speak of Ghandi, Thoreau, or Martin Luther King while discussing civil disobedience? "I just didn't have time to get around to all that stuff," he replied.

As commander of the Ohio National Guard, Del Corso urged his troops to write letters of support to President Nixon for his war decisions. He came under fire for what he termed simply "a response from the silent majority." One state legislator called for his ouster, charging that the Guard commander had become active in politics. The American Civil Liberties Union threatened suit.

"We issued a sample draft letter in support of the President's policy and suggested that guardsmen, if they so desired, could sign it, reproduce it, rewrite it, write in the opposite vein, or totally ignore it," the general said.

In a letter responding to charges of political involvement, the general said he would "fulfill the responsibilities of my office with determination and vigor and react with positive action against any activity which adversely impacts on our national security or the civic safety of all Ohioans."

A month and a half after the Kent State shooting the general sat behind his desk in the Adjutant General's Building at Fort Hayes and spoke of dissent. He was afraid, he began, that dissent would continue on campus. He talked with his characteristic softness, his small eyes betraying no emotion, his voice steady, never varying in decibel.

"I don't see an end to this," he said. "Not until the students clean it up themselves. The individual student is going to have to step in and get rid of the troublemakers.

"I think college administrators have lost control. They've lost their sense of responsibility. They have turned the colleges over to faculty committees who are unable to act, unable to solve the problems that we have on campus. They talk about academic freedom and confuse its meaning. Academic freedom has nothing to do with breaking laws. When laws are broken the courts are to decide right and wrong. I say when academic sanctions are violated suspension should follow.

"Where we are getting in trouble is where we have the student who is not well adjusted and he's utilized by individuals, groups, or organizations. They do this to gain an objective. I don't think there is any question about it. Some of these organizations like the SDS, not the member on campus necessarily, but the steering committee of SDS, would like to have control of our colleges and universities.

"Some kids are sincere in that they want peace, but how they are being utilized by the steering committee we can see at every turn. They have demonstrations and desecrate the American flag in front of photographers and fly the Viet Cong flag. These pictures are shown around the world, which certainly gives aid and comfort to Hanoi. The people participating in these demonstrations don't know this is going on—some may—but it is not coincidence that they have demonstrations in the U.S., England, Germany, or in France and in other places at the same time. They are all coordinated very carefully."

On May 4, 1970, at 12:22 p.m., Sylvester T. Del Corso was in Columbus. He was concerned that students demonstrating at Ohio State University would reach a fever pitch. Several thousand of his Guard were mounted to preserve peace on that campus and it was there he thought his presence was required. In his mind, the situation at Kent State, a hundred and some miles away, was well in hand.

7

Sunday, May 3

The telephone rang somewhere between quarter and half past five Sunday morning. It was the third time that morning the phone had roused him and Ronald J. Kane, the thirty-four-year-old prosecuting attorney of Portage County, answered it with the apprehension that comes from accepting too many early morning calls requiring immediate and sometimes difficult decisions. His uncertainty quickly sprouted into anger.

"Hey, this is the third time you people have called about this case," Kane said with a voice gritty from sleep. "Damn it, how many times do I have to go over this with you."

The lawman on the other end of the telephone patiently absorbed Kane's anger. After all, Kane was known to be quick and masterful with expletives, but he had good common sense, solid common sense. Eventually he would again explain the legal complications of the rape and sodomy case that had added to the sheriff's department's early morning misfortunes. Rape and sodomy, on a morning like this. The voice seemed to lament its duty.

"We're all tired as hell down here, Ron," the voice explained, hoping to distract the prosecutor's wrath and draw some quiet word of sympathy. "The little bastards kept us up all night over at the university."

"What the hell happened down there?" Kane's voice assumed a tone of cross-examination as his anger reached a new apogee. He personally had informed county officials before his bridge game last night that he was to be notified the moment any more trouble broke out on the Kent State campus.

Kane had little regard for the ability of the school's administration to handle any real trouble. The year before he had endured a campus SDS problem and won convictions after the university had quietly asked him to drop charges.

"I told them to go to hell," he said later. "They gave the SDS a legal status on campus and then refused to negotiate with them. Then there is all this trouble with the SDS ripping up doors and causing a riot and then they don't want to prosecute. That was a lot of crap.

"They tried to pressure me but I got the convictions. Those people have to learn that Kent State University is part of Portage County and Portage County is not part of Kent State University."

It did not matter to Kane that he had to bump heads with academic minds residing in the lofty reaches of an ivory tower. Once, meeting with a faculty commission, Kane brought his dog, a German shepherd. He walked into the room and immediately proclaimed that this animal had more common sense than half the people around him. Perhaps there is a special bitterness in Kane when it comes to Kent State, although he denies it. A Kent State dean once asked him to leave the university when he was a student because his grades were substandard.

Asked about this, Kane said, "Hey people. I lost both my parents, had a bad kidney, and was living by myself earning my way through school when that happened. I was so tired I couldn't keep it up. I went to Fenn College and then Baldwin-Wallace College and finally graduated from Cleveland-Marshall Law School. I had some bad times but I pulled myself through."

It was always Ron Kane's opinion that the people at Kent State would do well to learn from the common people around them.

Because of the way the trouble in the spring of 1969 had been handled, university president White and his staff were applauded by various organizations, including a Congressional subcommittee investigating SDS activities. White had even given a dinner to law-enforcement people who had been involved in the case. Kane felt that the school was lucky. He knew that what had taken place was hardly the test the others considered it.

After demonstrators had thrashed their way through downtown

Kent on Friday night, Kane immediately considered closing the university if the violence could not be contained. "You've got twenty thousand students on that campus and if they decide to go we don't have a thing to stop them."

All this had contributed to his mood this morning of disgust and alarm.

"Now don't tell anybody I told you," the voice begged as Kane sat up in bed. "They burned the ROTC building last night!"

"Why in the hell didn't anybody tell me?" No one had called with news of either the burning or the arrival of the Guard.

The sun had been up for more than an hour when Kane and an assistant, Thomas J. Sicuro, drove past the remains of the ROTC building. It was still smoldering and the spiral of smoke rising from its charred innards wafted over the dewy Commons. The wet grass sparkled in the morning light and only the stench of smoke ruined the beginning of a beautiful spring day.

Kane and Sicuro were surprised to see the bulky, olive-drab shapes of National Guardsmen stationed on campus. Everything about the Guard looked old: their helmets, their fatigues, their rifles, their pistol belts and canteens. Everything but the tired faces beneath the helmets.

There is a certain crispness, a certain efficiency, about a good military unit. It is almost a smell that is a mixture of polish, gun oil, and a faint tincture of sweat. Belts ride on hips and roll in a uniform manner, shoe laces are taut, webbing is straight, fatigues are tailored and the shoulders square out in a government-issue stance. The Guard did not have that look this morning. The Teamster strike had taken energies from them and their minds were at home.

At the request of Cleveland Mayor Carl Stokes, Governor Rhodes had called up the National Guard to watch interstate highways after dissident Teamster truck drivers walked off their jobs and the strike exploded into shooting and rock throwing around the Cleveland area. The men had stood guard for long hours over the freeways, standing on overpasses with rifles drawn. Many cruised up and down in jeeps and were afraid—they had heard about the shootings, and the Teamsters weren't playing games. They had to be continually alert and the tension had worn them down.

Kane looked over the campus and chatted briefly with some

guardsmen and then an odd thought struck him. The college was using the Portage County Airport, and among the never-ending flow of rumors that he dealt with there had been one that threatened sabotage to the airstrip. Kane told Sicuro to drive on to the airport. It was a nagging hunch. An itch somewhere that demanded attention.

Kane arrived at the airport to find six private planes had been wrecked and a mobile office ransacked and burned. The planes had been rammed with a three-ton truck stolen from a nearby construction site. The mobile office had been doused with kerosene. A note found on the seat of the stolen truck said: "If air and water pollution continue in Portage County, all the airports will be burned."

A sheriff's car pulled up to the airport and a deputy told the two prosecutors that Governor Rhodes was flying in for a meeting and a press conference. The meeting was scheduled for 10 a.m. at the fire station in Kent.

"I'm going to try and close that school down," said Kane. "I'm afraid we're in for trouble if we don't do it."

A police radio call reported that a truck had been stolen from the airport. Kane shook his head. How could this be happening in Portage County?

On campus the first students awoke and wandered from their dormitories to inspect the havoc of the night before. Some dressed for church and made their way past guardsmen who stood with heavy M-1 rifles near the remains of the ROTC building. Only a skeletal section of the entrance was still standing. A few metal filing cabinets leaned stubbornly in the middle of the wreckage, occasionally blocked from view by billows of blue smoke that danced with every shift of a soft wind. Where the archery shed had stood only a scorched circle remained. The five-hundred-foot section of cyclone fence lay on its side, sprawled on the Commons like a metal serpent.

The university yawned and awoke to the sight of jeeps and tracked armored personnel carriers. Students knowledgeable in such things pointed out that the APC's were the same as those used in Vietnam and Cambodia. They were good vehicles but vulnerable to a rocket the Viet Cong used that could make the inside a flaming hell for the occupants.

At ten o'clock Governor Rhodes arrived at the fire station in

Kent red-faced and visibly upset at what had taken place. In recent days there had been disturbances at other state universities. At the moment Ohio State University appeared to be the scene of greater trouble. James A. Rhodes was tired and angry. He considered higher education, the kind of education that he did not personally possess, a privilege and a necessity. There was no room for this kind of disturbance. It would not be tolerated. He would not tolerate it. For personal and public reasons, both hinging on an election, he would stand tall and tough against long-haired rabble and complicated conspiracies. In other words, the governor would match and square the violence if need be.

He pounded the table as he addressed the press:

"The scene here at the city of Kent is probably the most vicious form of campus-oriented violence yet perpetrated by dissident groups and their allies in the State of Ohio. . . .

"We've asked the complete cooperation of the county prosecutor for a comprehensive investigation and there's some people now out on probation that there has been a strong word to the fact that they had participated in this. Now we're going to put a stop to this for this reason. The same group that we're dealing with here today, and there's three or four of them, they only have one thing in mind, that is to destroy higher education in Ohio.

"And if they continue this, continue what they're doing, they're going to reach their goal, for the simple reason that you cannot get replacement from the Ohio general assembly for these buildings. And last night I think that we have seen all forms of violence, the worst. And when they start taking over communities this is when we're going to use every part of the law enforcement we have in Ohio to drive them out of Kent. . . .

"We are going to eradicate the problem. We are not going to treat the symptoms. And as long as this continues, higher education in Ohio is in jeopardy. And if there continues to be permissive consent, it will destroy higher education in this state.

"We were fortunate last night. We had seven hundred National Guardsmen in this area on the trucker strike. Had they not been there, there would have been fourteen or fifteen other burnouts. And I'm talking about buildings. . . .

"These people just move from one campus to the other and terrorize the community. They are worse than the brown shirt and the Communist element and also the night riders and the vigilantes. They're the worst type of people that we harbor in America. Now I want to say this, they are not going to take over a campus. And the campus now is part of the country and the state of Ohio. There's no sanctuary for these people."

Rhodes was followed by General Del Corso, whose face radiated intense seriousness. In a soft, even voice, bereft of the emotion that Rhodes had shown, Del Corso said: "We have sufficient force in the area, we will apply whatever degree of force is necessary to provide protection for the lives of our citizens and his property."

A few moments later a reporter asked Kent police chief Roy Thompson how many arrests had been made. The chief answered: "As far as that goes our reports aren't complete yet. There are about forty to fifty that I can recall. We can't tolerate this burning and threatening of our merchants and our citizens."

"Yes," interjected General Del Corso. "And I'll be right behind them. The Ohio National Guard, we'll give him our full support, anything that's necessary. As the Ohio law says, use any force that's necessary even to the point of shooting.

We don't want to get into that but the law says that we can if necessary."

Governor Rhodes added, "Let me say this—that if they can intimidate and threaten the merchants of this community and other people, no one is safe in Portage County. It is just that simple. No one is safe and I, I do not believe that people understand the seriousness of these individuals who are organized in a revolutionary frame of mind."

Ron Kane followed: "I think in the face of responsibility it is the students who have a privilege to go to school and not a constitutional right. And as a prosecutor of this county my responsibility is to the citizens of this county and anyone violating a state or local law is going to be prosecuted to the fullest extent."

As the governor and Kane stepped into the men's room at the end of the press conference, the lanky, pipe-smoking Kane offered his conclusion.

"Governor, I think we ought to close the goddamn place down. I'm telling you now. There's going to be trouble."

"I like the way this man uses the language," Rhodes said to an aide. "But we can't close the university," Rhodes continued. "No, because we would be playing into the hands of the SDS and Weathermen and the others who want to see this university closed. I say no."

"It seemed to me," Mayor LeRoy Satrom later said, "that the governor was going to keep that school open if he had to put guardsmen on every yard of that campus."

"I told the governor," Kane later told newsmen, "that as far as I was concerned, we were sitting on a keg of dynamite that could blow any minute. I wanted those kids out of town.

"I was afraid of what might happen. All you had to do was look around to know that those kids were doing a hell of a lot more than protesting war and calling for peace. They had burned down a building on campus and then smashed half the windows in downtown Kent. We had real trouble on our hands."

As Governor Rhodes was walking to his plane at the airport, he encountered Kent State president White, who had just flown in from Iowa.

"I remember him breaking from his group and walking toward me," White said of the governor. "Even before we shook hands he was talking about my problem. I don't recall exactly but he was saying that we had every bit of riff-raff in the state of Ohio on that campus and under no circumstances should we think about closing down because that is what they are after." There was not much White could say or do at this point. The Guard was on campus, a curfew had been established in the city of Kent, and a state of emergency had been declared.

The afternoon passed peacefully enough on campus. A number of parents visiting that weekend walked with their sons and daughters, stopping to pose for snapshots before the Guard's armored vehicles. Outwardly, the trouble appeared calmed and defused. Curiously, the students examined the guardsmen, their equipment, and the mood of the day. The stories of Saturday and Friday night were becoming stale after having been repeated so many times.

"It seemed as if it was all over," said a bearded student who would find himself peering into the face of a dead friend the next day. "If we would've only known that they would go that far."

"I went out and talked with some of the guardsmen," Dr. White said. "It was my impression that they were exasperated with the whole thing. They just wanted to get home. I didn't feel that they were frightened."

A group from Black United Students cheered Dr. White as he stepped from his office, a gesture that made him smile for he had no reason to be the recipient of any applause that afternoon. At least that was the way he felt.

The students idled in the sun and contemplated a special message they had found in their mailboxes that afternoon. It was signed by vice president Matson and Frank Frisina.

The message said:

During the last two days, the disruptive and destructive activities of a dissident group comprising students and non-students and numbering 500 to 600, escalated from a peaceful rally through illegal threat to life plus property damage leading eventually to the Governor's imposition of a state of emergency encompassing both the city of Kent and the university. As currently defined the state of emergency has established the following:

1. Prohibited all forms of outdoor demonstrations and rallies—peaceful or otherwise.

2. Empowered the National Guard to make arrests.

3. A curfew is in effect for the city from 8 p.m. to 6 a.m. and an on campus curfew of 1 a.m. has been ordered by the National Guard.

The above will remain in effect until altered or removed by order of the Governor.

At present the campus is calm. Several hundred National Guard and state police are presently on campus to maintain order. They are under the direction of Governor James A. Rhodes and will remain on alert on and around the campus until normal conditions return.

We are most thankful that thus far there has been no loss of life. However, five students and several law enforcement officers did report injuries that were apparently not serious.

We plan to resume our normal class schedule on Monday with the exception of classes scheduled for the floor of Memorial

Gymnasium. Currently the gym floor is being used to provide barrack facilities for the National Guard troops.

More than 40 persons were arrested Saturday night by law enforcement officers for violation of the city curfew. All face court action.

Consequently, there is gravest concern in all quarters of the University community over the campus violence and the destruction of property.

We urgently request anyone with information concerning the identification of participants in the violent and disruptive actions of this weekend to come forward. Any information you have may be reported to either the Student Activities Center or the University Police by phone, letter, or in person.

We congratulate the many students who continue to volunteer their time and efforts to return the campus to normal.

Naturally we will make every effort to keep you fully informed as the situation may change.

There was fearful prophecy in the language of the message.

Cheerful banter was exchanged between guardsmen and students that afternoon. Many of the troops, as young as the students themselves, engaged in brief conversations with onlookers.

One guardsman talking to two students suddenly looked right and then left before turning the lapel of his fatigue shirt back to reveal a button that read: "DOWN WITH REPRESSION." The students laughed, flashed the peace sign, and moved off somewhat relaxed, knowing they had some reinforcements in the ranks of the Guard.

"You have live ammunition in there?" asked a quizzical student who would later learn firsthand the sound of a cracking .30-caliber round whizzing by his head.

"Yup," the guardsman grunted.

"You going to shoot?"

"I'm not going to shoot anyone. They can tell me all day and I'm not going to do it. All I want to do is go home. You kids going to cause trouble?"

"Are you kidding. This is little Kent State. The trouble is over."

Allison Krause, a nineteen-year-old freshman from Pittsburgh, and her constant companion, Barry Levine, another freshman from

Valley Stream, New York, wandered about the campus observing the Guard and talking to the troops. Suddenly, Allison saw a guardsman with a flower stuck in the muzzle of his M-1. She smiled and together with Barry, who wore his hair shoulder length, spoke with the soldier.

"Where did you get the flower?" Allison asked.

"A girl gave it to me," answered the trooper, a young fellow who attended Akron University.

A Guard officer stepped over and interrupted the conversation.

"Where did you get the flower?" The officer's manner was brusque and impatient.

"It was a gift, sir."

"Do you accept all gifts?"

"No, sir." The soldier was braced.

"Do you intend to leave that flower in your weapon when we fire at camp?"

"No, sir."

"Well then, get it out of there!"

The soldier gave the flower to Allison Krause, and as the officer walked away, she called after him, "Why can't he keep the flower?"

The officer ignored her.

"Flowers are better than bullets," she called in frustration. In the days that followed those words would be quoted across the globe.

The officer continued to ignore her.

"Pig," she screamed. "Pig."

Elsewhere, Erwind Blount, the sophomore president of Black United Students, did not share the easy feeling that some thought existed on the campus. "The black man and the cops in this town are no different than any other place. If the cops get a chance to kick a black man's ass you can bet they will."

After seeing the mood of the town Saturday morning, Blount established a Black Protection Patrol that would look after black students and keep them from being sucked into the stream of violence that might be expected. Blount and his field marshal, Ruddy Perry, did not want to give police an excuse to brutalize any of the brothers.

Blount and Perry stopped before a young guardsman near a construction site on campus and asked what buildings and grounds might be considered restricted.

The guardsman lowered his rifle.

"Shit, I put my hands in the air as fast as I could," said Blount.

"You get moving, boy," the guardsman said as he fumbled with his bayonet. "Get moving!"

"Man, those dudes were so up tight I couldn't believe it," Blount said.

It was still light when a guardsman found two bottles and a rope in the bushes near the university police headquarters. They were identified and reported as the makings of a fire bomb. Less than fifteen minutes later five gallons of kerosene were found nearby.

The sun began to decline and with it came the stutter of helicopter rotors biting into the evening air with loud "wop-wops." For anyone who had spent time in Vietnam the sound was familiar. One Marine combat veteran, now a student, felt his mouth go dry. He remembered the heliborne assaults along Route 9 in South Vietnam's I Corps. He remembered the "Street without Joy" area along the coast. The "wop-wop" was a rotating reminder of a hot landing zone in the middle of a bomb-pitted jungle with craters filled with multi-colored water from rain and the chemicals of explosives.

An uneasiness descended with dusk, and the intelligence reports, more rumors of undetermined origin than "hot intel," renewed their emphasis on the possibility of snipers perched in shadowy redoubts.

At 8 p.m. Guard officers noticed students gathering on the Commons and asked that more troops be moved into the city to support the 1st Battalion of the 145th Infantry. Immediately, the 2nd Squadron of the 107th Armored Cavalry Regiment was relieved from truck-strike duty and ordered to Kent. Commanders talked with Brigadier General Robert Canterbury, who authorized roving patrols of troops to be used on the campus.

A Guard report noted what was taking place on campus at this time:

The movement of students on campus after 1800 hours [6 p.m.] appeared to be increasing as time went on. During the late afternoon of this day, several students were observed in the vicinity of the Administration Building and burned out ROTC building in an obvious state of stupor, floating along, eyes glazed and appearing under the influence of something. They did not appear intoxicated. At 2000 hours [8 p.m.], numerous groups were observed numbering 20 to 30 people each. The campus police were concerned and remarked that this was not a very good indication. An additional company was brought in to protect the wooden structure buildings near the power plant [ROTC buildings].

At eight-thirty the victory bell began to toll on the Commons. In fifteen minutes a State Patrol officer reported concern and suggested that the curfew be immediately put into effect on the campus.

One student, Joseph B. Cullum, described the scene on the Commons at the time:

"I arrived at the Commons at about 8 p.m. to see only a few onlookers present. In a few minutes a crowd of students arrived on the Commons. After asking a few questions I learned that these students intended to purposely break curfew in order to demonstrate that the curfew was an unnecessary infringement on the students' rights.

"It was the intention of these students to march off campus and peacefully march downtown with the express purpose of not causing a disruption, but demonstrating that the curfew was unnecessary.

"The students, myself included, began to leave the Commons and march down Main Street toward the business district."

The Kent State campus slopes down and flanks Main Street on one side and is separated from the city proper on another side by Lincoln Street. At the corner of Lincoln and Main there are a couple of restaurants and some shops that cater to the college crowd. A number of houses look up at the campus and an archway called Prentice Gate marks the main entrance to the university. Trees dominate the rolling slope and a lush green lawn is tailored between winding drives to give the campus a classical and inviting look.

A coed related her impression of what took place:

"I thought there was a certain kind of mob psychology being used by some kids in the crowd there near the Commons. I can't explain it, but I couldn't understand what the purpose of our gathering and demonstrating was directed toward."

A helicopter flailed above, and a rasping, metallic voice from a bullhorn descended as the students were grouping on the Commons.

"Now hear this, now hear this," the voice from on high rattled. "You are in violation of . . ."

The rest of the message was drowned in a chorus of boos and a flood of obscene retorts. No one paid any attention to the helicopter or the warning.

The Guard report on Sunday's action continued:

At approximately 2055 [8:55 p.m.], the riot act was read to the crowd. The police furnished the amplifier [bullhorn] and the crowd was ordered to disperse and to return to their quarters within the next five minutes and that the curfew was in effect. At this time a ¼ ton truck was furnished campus police to ride around campus to announce the curfew was now in effect. The crowd appeared to be well organized; after they ignored the order, the troops were ordered to disperse the crowd. The crowd broke up in small groups and went in several directions. One group made a march for the President's house which was stopped by a platoon of guardsmen that was patrolling the area.

"The demonstrators arrived at Lincoln and Main and just sat there in the street," the coed said. "I didn't go near them and I watched for a few minutes before I decided to leave. A group of us began to walk back toward the dorms, away from the entrance of the university, when we saw ten National Guardsmen coming toward us. We were near the library at the time.

"I must be naive, or I was naive, but kids around me started to run. I didn't. It was like the beginning of moments of panic. They started to go through windows in the library to get out of the way. The Guard was coming, swinging their bayonets and rifle butts back and forth. I could see their eyes. You know, there was a look like hate in those eyes.

"Before I knew it I was surrounded by them and someone was pushing and pulling me into the library. Another girl was screaming. I went through the window and it took me a couple of seconds to realize that I had been bayoneted. Once in the lower abdomen and once in my right leg."

The contingent of guardsmen continued to charge the students, yelling, "Get back! Get back!" as they moved at a brisk pace toward anyone in their way. The scene at the library was filled with terror and confusion as students desperately tried to cram themselves through the windows to avoid the bayonets and rifle butts. A girl screamed. She had been butted in the small of the back. Withering in agony, she was helped through the window by a friend. A guardsman bent to lift her, too. There were cries for help all along the side of the building.

"Several of the people around me in the library had been hurt by the Guard," said one girl. "I'd say three or four that I knew of. There were others in other parts of the building. Honestly, there was no provocation. None whatsoever. I heard that other kids were bayoneted but never bothered to go to the hospital. They were afraid."

The Guard report stated:

The mob moved again down the street and through the edge of the campus toward the downtown area which already had been partially destroyed two nights previously. Another detachment of troops were dispatched to cut them off and seal off the downtown area. This was accomplished but the mob stayed on the edge of campus near the main gate, taunting the police and guardsmen and throwing articles at them. Finally, after repeated requests by loudspeaker to disperse, the guardsmen fired tear gas and moved in riot formation to disperse the crowd. Some of the crowd did not move and at least one bayonet injury occurred. The dispersion was successful, however, and the mob left the area, after some of them ran into the library, breaking windows and necessitating the early closing of the library. A search was conducted with university officials but no rioters could be identified. During all this time the guard was utilizing helicopters with searchlights affixed to keep the mob under observation.

Tear gas popped with regularity. Its acrid smell drifted over the students and many choked and gasped for fresh air. The crowd was finally subdued. About two hundred demonstrators retreated and sat down in the street at the corner of Lincoln and Main.

"This was it right here," said a Portage County sheriff's deputy. "I knew we would either win the whole thing here or lose it. The kids said they wanted to negotiate. They wanted to talk to the mayor and President White. Jesus, they were sitting there when we got the report of a sniper."

A State Patrol officer did not want to move on the students for fear of a sniper in the library. Fire from this direction could endanger the massed students. University police were sent into the building but they found nothing.

At the moment a student spokesman engaged the combined force of guardsmen, police, and highway patrolmen at the intersection, the lights in the Kent Post Office suddenly went out. Calls flashed back and forth. The shaky and spooked condition of the city heightened. Snipers, sabotage, fire bombs, that was all anyone could think about as the students sat there.

Sergeant Joseph Myers of the City of Kent Police Department was the recipient of the student demands. They wanted the National Guard to retire from the campus by 1:30 p.m. on Monday. They demanded amnesty for all students arrested Friday and Saturday. The ROTC had to go. So did the Liquid Crystals Institute. Black students reiterated a demand for a larger enrollment of blacks, more Negro faculty, and a cultural center.

The request for a meeting was relayed, and in less than a minute Dr. Matson vetoed it. Mayor Satrom was on his way to the intersection when a tear-gas round fired by the Guard landed in the midst of the students.

In his report a Guard officer wrote:

> The spokesman for the group was reading a list of demands they were going to take to President White. At this time the spokesman was told that the curfew was in effect and that he was to get off the street or to his quarters, or he and the crowd would be arrested. He told me that they had until 1 a.m. and that I should leave them alone or there would be trouble or words to that effect. I immediately took the microphone from this individual and informed the crowd the curfew was in effect and that they were to disperse immediately or be arrested. Without hesitation the crowd started throwing rocks, tear gas and broken bottles.

A searing hatred coursed through the crowd as the tear gas exploded. The students had offered to negotiate and they saw themselves betrayed. They rose with an unnerving wail of frustration, anger, and confusion. The air was filled with stones.

"It was the Guard's decision to move," said Sergeant Myers. It seemed as if police sergeants had run the city's attempts to quell the violence since Friday. Now they had no control.

One student tried to slip past the Guard on South Lincoln and was bayoneted in the back before he could get away. He ran screaming into the kitchen of a nearby house, blood dripping behind.

"You fucking lying pigs," students shouted. "You fucking pigs."

"I'd say that at this point we lost all hope of establishing a peace with the kids," said the sheriff's deputy. "I felt sick."

A student at the scene agreed:

"At this time it appeared to me that control of the situation was passed from the local police to the National Guard. A National Guard officer announced that we had five minutes to disperse. Within thirty seconds a line of National Guardsmen with billy clubs advanced into the ranks of students, most of whom were already dispersing. I was walking quickly away from the area when a National Guardsman actually ran after me to get into striking range and hit me in the back with a club."

The Guard report said:

The city police, campus police and National Guard troops started moving in making arrests and dispersing the crowds. Ten National Guardsmen were injured within the first ten minutes of this confrontation. Several rioters were apprehended and were arrested by the city police with the aid of sheriff's deputies and National Guard troops.

Several guardsmen were pelted with rocks and one young trooper later said:

"It was incredible. You could hear the rocks falling all around you. One brushed my sleeve. It was scary as hell. We were worrying about the snipers. They kept saying there were snipers out there."

Another guardsmen was hit by a wrench and required hospitalization. One fell to the ground and was curling in pain when a girl came up and kicked him twice, once in the stomach and again in the face.

"I'm not saying that all college students are like animals—I'm saying that the people attacking us that night were like animals," one guardsman told the *New York Times*.

Later, Kent police chief Roy Thompson said he possessed a photo taken that evening of a youth in a tree with a gun. Several other law enforcement agencies certified its existence, but refused to reveal it as it constituted important evidence.

A student covering events for the Cleveland *Plain Dealer* was subsequently arrested for failure to produce proper press credentials. He wrote: "After being housed in a cell overnight, a student who inquired about his rights was told through the bars not to 'worry about that crap' by a jailer who threw cups of water on the students in the overcrowded cell."

Days after the incident President White was asked why he never responded to the students' wishes at Lincoln and Main. "I didn't know about it," he said. The word had not been relayed to him. "I'm not sure I would have done it had I known," he said. "I don't know what could have been accomplished at that point."

Vice president Matson, who had been praised for his handling of student disorders the previous year, explained that he did not feel it was proper to talk with the demonstrators at Prentice Gate. "They were in violation of the curfew and any negotiations would have been under duress," he said.

Lloyd Agte, a student instructor, remembered the mood of the students as being furious at the "pigs." If an attitude of mistrust had existed before the incident, it had now escalated to a point where words no longer sufficed. Even students who were considered moderate found themselves as heated as campus radicals.

The Guard drove the remaining demonstrators back onto campus and into dormitories while a helicopter equipped with a spotlight hunted the rooftops and knolls for the elusive and mysterious snipers that had been reported during the day.

Erwind Blount, the black student leader, and several of his friends were heading toward their dormitories after conducting a sweep of the area with the Black Protection Patrol when they suddenly encountered a group of police. It was dark and Blount could not make out who the police were or whether they were sheriff's deputies or highway patrolmen.

"I saw them and figured we better approach them kind of easy," he said. "Black cats walking around on a night like this are bound to make the police edgy.

"They didn't say anything, at least I didn't hear them say anything.

We suddenly broke and moved out. They fired. Two shots. I heard two shots and I was eating dirt. Nobody was hurt or anything. We didn't report the incident because we're black and there is no policeman around here who is going to listen to us. I was happy that we were able to keep black people out of the mess that day."

There was no official record of such an incident and none of the other students seemed to know anything about it.

A flare burned red on the Commons. At the "Pit," a gathering place located in the center of the three dormitories that make up the complex known as Tri Towers, people vied with each other for a position near the television sets as the late news began with a video replay of the night's action. Some of the students from other dormitories decided to spend the night with friends. The helicopters continued their hectic vigil. The chop and swish of their engines coupled with the flash of their probing lights kept many students awake during the night.

The guardsmen on duty huddled in the shadows and kept a watch for snipers, Weathermen, or anyone else who, their superiors had warned, might be lurking nearby.

8

Governor Rhodes

If you were fleet enough and possessed a tolerance for that sort of thing, you could usually catch a glimpse of James Allen Rhodes at one of Ohio's county fairs. He would be there on the midway, his graying hair brilliantined to a shine, his face pudgy and squinty, his moves peripatetic and jerky, his intention all politick. Rhodes, the governor of the State of Ohio, was a man born to promote himself with fickle come-ons and grandiose schemes that often left voters confused and a little bit awed at the audacity of the man. Voters felt safe with Jim Rhodes because he never made an effort to conceal the fact he was an archetype politician. In this a large segment of the public took refuge, for he fit the classical mold of the hawking, bawling politico and, therefore, people did not have to think very hard about him. They could wave off his imperfections with an exasperated gasp, "Hell, he's just a politician." Jim Rhodes was a man a voter could look to and not have to trouble himself with the complications of new politics. New politics to Jim Rhodes was a lot of chromed-over bunk. He maintained there was nothing new about it.

But wait a minute, there he is now, down on the fairway, down near the basketball contest at the Cuyahoga County Fair. He is the tall fellow in shirt sleeves. See the younger man next to him, he holds the governor's coat and carries the pocket money. Watch.

"O.K., O.K., let's see a little action here," the governor says as he pounds on the counter of the basketball contest. His rapping stirs a sleepy-eyed attendant to a semblance of attention.

"Hey there, Governor, good to see you all again," the man says. "Here you go. Shoot away."

"Alright, we'll burn the nets right off for you, yes sir," the governor calls as he weighs a basketball in his hand.

A crowd is slowly circling him, their whispers pleasing background to the governor's ear. The cuff links on his shirt sleeves give off glints of light that make a youngster with a stick of cotton candy stare at them with a transfixed gaze.

"Going to put it right in, eh, Johnny," the governor says as he bounces the ball. Johnny is the man who runs the game for a traveling carnival and he has seen Jim Rhodes do this for so many seasons that he feels sure that one of these years he is going to run for public office himself. After all, if putting basketballs through the old hoop can get votes it shouldn't be that hard to win.

Jim Rhodes shoots old-fashioned. No one handers. No new politics. He tucks his elbows in and shoots with both hands like they used to do until they started the one-handed business on the West Coast just before World War II. The ball arcs up and through. The crowd cheers.

"Ain't bad for a governor," Johnny offers. By now he's part of the act and he has a hard time keeping enthusiasm in his voice. The governor has so much enthusiasm.

The ball rolls down the large net suspended beneath the basket and Johnny retrieves it, gently flipping it to the governor, who is bouncing around on his toes and clucking away to the crowd like some peppery infielder trying to stoke a phlegmatic pitcher.

"Alright, alright, we'll do it again," he chants. "We'll put the ball right through. Hey, this is a great fair. My name is Jim Rhodes, what's yours?"

He bends to shake hands with the boy who is mesmerized by the cuff links. The sticky cotton candy comes off on Jim Rhodes' hand and he pats the boy on the head.

"Hey, Johnny, get one of those teddy bears ready for this lad," the governor chirps. "We'll have it right down for you boy."

The ball is up, hanging in the air for an instant before it plops neatly through. Swish.

"Way to go, Governor," a teen-ager shouts. "Way to shoot, baby!"

"O.K., Johnny, O.K. Get the boy's prize ready because this is going to be three in a row, yeah!"

The rim yawns, the ball is nearly there, the crowd is gasping, hoping, secretly giving it all the body english it can muster. The shooter has made this basket the most important thing in the world. A hell of a lot seems to be riding on it.

It rolls on the rim. The crowd is magnetized by the ball, its collective spirit is tipping it. It goes in, the ball goes in! The crowd rejoices with a loud whoop. Johnny already is passing the teddy bear to the governor, who tries to look modest about the whole thing. He bends and hands the stuffed animal to the boy, who clutches it with one arm while he squeezes the remainder of his cotton candy with the other.

"Tell Governor Rhodes thank you," the boy's father says.

The youth turns his head shyly away and mumbles something.

"You've got a real fine son there," Jim Rhodes says. He shakes hands with the father and then signs an autograph or two. An elderly woman offers her veiny hand and the governor whispers something that makes her smile.

The governor signals the young man who has been standing aside so as not to get in the way of the basket. The man reaches into his pocket and slips Johnny some money as the governor and the crowd move on to the ring toss.

"I've never seen a man get so much out of one crummy basketball shot," says Johnny. "Hell, he had those people thinking they were watching the importantest shot ever made in the history of the game. Their old hearts were just pumping away when that ball was in the air, yeah, he does that all the time. He may not make three in a row like that, but I usually let him shoot until he does."

It was pretty good shooting for a fellow who once flunked physical education at Ohio State University.

Ever since James Allen Rhodes entered public office and was elected mayor of Columbus in 1943, his political campaign literature noted that he had attended college at Ohio State. It did not state that he had taken only thirteen hours for one quarter in 1932 before dropping out "for financial reasons."

The Cleveland *Plain Dealer*'s Columbus bureau once wrote:

Rhodes received "D's" in a five-hour course in English and a five-hour course in geography. He failed hygiene, physical education and military science, all required one-hour courses. The record also shows that Rhodes failed military science because of non-attendance.

Conversely, the governor's records at Ohio State also include a notation stating he was the recipient of an honorary doctor of law degree from the university. He was honored similarly by six other Ohio universities. During his two terms as governor Rhodes displayed a keen interest in education and saw to it that the state's universities grew. In recent years his attention had turned toward vocational education. He even took time to write a book on its virtues.

The governor was always a good promoter. He served two terms as president of the Amateur Athletic Union and founded the Pan-American Games. He skirted the globe—from Japan to Israel—on trade missions, extolling the goodness of tomato juice from his home state and pointing with pride to the industrial products of Ohio. He sought new industries for the state and clamored out the need for "jobs, jobs, and more jobs" for his people.

When Neil Armstrong, the first man to walk on the moon, returned to walk in his native Ohio, Jim Rhodes declared he would build a museum to house the space suit used in the adventure. He said it during his campaign for the Republican nomination, and comedian Bob Hope, another native Ohioan, helped him greet the astronaut.

"I think Governor Rhodes is the best governor Ohio ever had," said Hope.

The governor beamed and accepted the cheers of the assembled who came to see Neil Armstrong. Then he announced that the state would build a million-dollar museum that would house Armstrong's equipment from the Apollo 11 flight.

"We'll grab it before some other museum," he said.

One day the governor awoke to find campaign cards circulating the state booming him for baseball commissioner. Another day, a news story speculated that he would become president of the Cincinnati Bengals football team. The newspapers were always full of things Jim Rhodes said or did or might be expected to do. "People who do things are called controversial people," the governor said. "I do things."

When it became evident that he was going to run for the U.S. Senate, a newspaper columnist had this to say:

> After years of promoting tomato juice and ice fishing and fishing derbies, camping in state parks and poking around historical caves and burial grounds with reporters and cameramen in tow, what would happen to the real Jim Rhodes if he were to find himself sitting through committee hearings in Washington—hearings which would chafe, fret and bore him utterly?

Jim Rhodes was sixty years old, but he looked ten years younger and exuded energies that left those at his side exhausted. His brusque manner with newspapermen could switch to the unctuous when he talked with voters. He never ended "Ohio" with an "o" when he spoke, it was always "Ohia" this and "Ohia" that. He was part hayseed and more than a little carnival barker, and in many ways a good governor for Ohio. As a politician he was very good, until his timing went and then he was in trouble.

For seven years James A. Rhodes traveled the length and breadth of Ohio, cutting ribbons, tasting jelly, promising jobs, and talking about education. At times he was not wholly believable. For instance, he wanted to build a bridge across Lake Erie to Canada. But there were few who would not credit him with being a pretty good governor. Some people did not like him because he was a Republican. Others said he was loud and too much of a P. T. Barnum. His relationship with the working press grew worse as time passed. His relationship with publishers was better and this offset the losses he suffered in his dealings with reporters. Even when scandal splashed around him, there were important newspapers in the state that shied away from any attack upon him. Others, like the Cleveland Press, took after him as if they were predatory beasts attacking a wounded animal. But Jim Rhodes played his cards out to the end even though it was obvious that he was in serious political trouble.

Rhodes is not what you would call a complicated man; not that he would have anything against being one, it was just that he was built to come on strong and gushy, spilling over front pages and speaking his political conscience. When his political clock wound down, he slowly became an anachronism. A man who slowly sank into a bog of obscurity while assuring everyone that at any moment he would return, courtesy of deus ex machina.

He first failed to calculate Richard Nixon's great strength during the 1968 Republican Convention and chose to hold the Ohio delegation for a favorite son on the first vote. There was only one ballot and Jim Rhodes was left holding fifty-five meaningless votes. There is nothing that Nixon values more than loyalty during hard times. The President has great admiration for men who make the right decision at a risky time. Jim Rhodes was the antithesis of this and later the word in Washington was that he could expect a courteous but icy reception at the White House.

If his indecision cost him precious political points in Washington, what followed would cost him his political career. In the spring of 1969 *Life* magazine, scrambling for circulation and employing traditional forms of muckraking, ran a color photo of Jim Rhodes and an article entitled "The Governor and the Mobster."

The magazine named the mobster as Thomas (Yonnie) Licavoli, a convicted murderer and alleged Mafia don from Toledo who had been sentenced for first-degree murder thirty-five years before. The article said that despite his long prison term, Licavoli still had his thumb implanted in the Toledo numbers-game operation.

Early in 1969 Rhodes commuted Licavoli's sentence to second-degree murder, thereby making him eligible for parole. *Life* went on to say that ex-Governor Michael V. Disalle had once been offered a bribe to free Licavoli. It was a well-known story among law-enforcement agencies that a $250,000 "Free Yonnie Fund" existed and was available for distribution to those persons who would take the necessary action. Shortly before the *Life* article appeared the parole board turned down Licavoli's request for a parole. He still sits in the Ohio State Penitentiary.

Jim Rhodes could survive Yonnie Licavoli easily enough. There was no proof of any attempted bribe and the *Life* story would have been labeled a smear and the voters of Ohio would have forgotten about it. However, *Life* did not stop with Licavoli. Not many persons remembered or cared about the convicted mobster, but they did pay income taxes and when *Life* said Jim Rhodes had once had trouble with his tax return they began to entertain doubtful thoughts about their governor.

When word reached his office that *Life* was about to publish the article, Rhodes canceled a trip to Punderson State Park where he was about to dedicate a golf course. He sat in his office for three hours and waited for excerpts of the magazine article to be passed out to the state house reporters.

In essence, *Life* charged that the governor had to pay nearly $100,000 in taxes, interest, and penalties on unreported income, much of which came from campaign contributions that were used for personal purposes.

The article said the tax case extended over ten years to the time when Jim Rhodes was the state auditor, a position he held for a decade. The accusations left the governor reeling. He issued a simple statement through aides denying any bribe offer or extension of privileges to Licavoli.

The statement went on to say: "Contrary to the outright lie reported by *Life*, I have never been assessed or paid a penalty for either failure to report or failure to pay any federal income tax. I challenge and defy *Life* magazine, or anyone else, to prove that I was ever required to pay a penalty for failure to report or failure to pay any federal income tax."

At the Ohio State University Hospital, where Licavoli was undergoing a medical examination, he talked of the case, denying any connection with the Mafia or the existence of large amounts of money being collected to "spring" him. *Life* had run a picture of him looking from a hospital window after it had been reported that he was bedridden following a massive heart attack. Licavoli maintained he was ill and had only partial vision left in one eye.

"I've reached the age where I can't get around even if I wanted to, let alone trying to think of doing anything wrong," he said. "The story is a lie."

"I'm just as clean and I think Governor Rhodes is just as clean as any person could be in regards to these matters," Licavoli told a television reporter.

At first, the *Life* article was viewed with skepticism. One newspaper editorial said: "*Life* casts aspersions and raises questions but does not make its case." If the allegations were true, it was obvious that *Life* reporters had been given access to highly confidential material, material that could have come only from the Internal Revenue

Service, the Justice Department, or even the White House. There was the possibility, of course, that it could have come from someone close to the governor. Many awaited Jim Rhodes' next move. Some advised him to open his income tax records for the years in question. That alone would put a quick end to the allegations.

But Rhodes and his aides chose to attack the article with words, noting that his tax returns had been examined and audited by Internal Revenue Service agents over the years and every one of them had been cleared.

"I have nothing to fear morally or legally in the handling of my respected tax obligations to my country," he said. "I have paid all my taxes."

Not long after the *Life* article, Ray DeCrane, a knowledgeable tax writer for the Cleveland Press, reported that Rhodes had been told that "everything you say here might be held against you" during one session with IRS agents during their investigation.

Spring slipped into summer and the governor, intending to run for the Senate, shied from the press. When he did meet with reporters he refused to discuss the *Life* article. A buzzer-and-lock system protected his inner office and he often remained in this sanctuary while press conferences on industrial development and other favorite programs were held in his cabinet room by other officials.

There seemed to be a sense of anxiety about him when the press was near. Once in the office of Secretary of Commerce Maurice Stans in Washington, Rhodes hurried through a brief meeting with reporters, mostly journalists representing Ohio papers, and hardly gave them a chance to ask a question. The governor seemed to be visibly relieved when the ordeal was waved to an end by a Commerce Department official.

When Jim Rhodes decided to run for the U.S. Senate, it first appeared that he would not have to face any serious opposition. Then John Glenn, Ohio's first astronaut and the first American to orbit the earth, retired from the space program and announced that he was running for the Senate. Political observers looked ahead to a Rhodes-Glenn contest that would be a "barn burner" of a race.

Some Ohio GOP leaders, Rhodes no doubt included, sought to assure the party's continuing hold on the governor's chair by running Congressman Robert Taft, Jr., in the gubernatorial race. A Taft-

Rhodes ticket was considered a Republican's dream. If Bob Taft ran for governor there was no way that Rhodes could lose his senatorial primary. A victory in May would help erase the *Life* smear and a well-timed libel suit would show Ohioans that Jim Rhodes was hitting back at slick New York journalism. All this would have been possible had it not been for Bob Taft himself.

For all his drum beating and promoting, Jim Rhodes could not give his name the familiar and respected ring that went where a Taft did in Ohio. Robert Taft, Jr., could claim to be part of a political dynasty that stretched back to the likes of Alphonso Taft, who served at one time or another as Secretary of War and Attorney General under President Ulysses S. Grant. His grandfather was President William Howard Taft, later Chief Justice of the United States. His father, U.S. Senator Robert A. Taft, appeared destined for the Presidency before General Dwight D. Eisenhower decided to become a Republican and took the nomination from him in 1952.

Compared to Rhodes, Taft was quiet and unspectacular. A graduate of Yale and Harvard, at fifty-three he could campaign steadily but not with the flamboyant verve of the governor. Taft worked his way through the Ohio House before going on to Congress. In 1964 he decided to take a crack at Senator Stephen Young, Ohio's elderly and outspoken Democrat. He won the Republican primary and was the betting favorite to beat Young in the fall. But in the end, it was a cataclysmic year for the Republicans as Barry M. Goldwater fell mightily to Lyndon B. Johnson, dragging Bob Taft and the party with him.

As Bob Taft approached the 1970 campaign, his desire to be a U.S. Senator was undiminished, but his time was running short. It could very well be his last chance and Jim Rhodes looked vulnerable. The *Life* article loomed larger and offset the governor's ability to go for the throat during a close-in political fight. Even with this disadvantage the governor would be a formidable opponent since he could begin collecting interest on a fistful of political debts around the state.

As they squared off for battle, Jim Rhodes insisted that Bob Taft would have run for governor had it not been for *Life*. Taft's rebuttal was simply not to mention the article in public, while his forces implied that something was amiss by using an old Rhodes slogan against the governor, but with a new twist. Jim Rhodes was fond of saying, "Profit is not a dirty word in Ohio." Taft adjusted this to read, "Integrity is not a dirty word in Ohio." Because of his sensitivity to the *Life* issue, Rhodes at first refused to debate his opponent or meet with him in press panels. He would later have to accept the challenge when it began to appear that he was in trouble.

The governor waited almost a year to file his long-promised lawsuit against *Life*. He asked for a $10.3-million judgment against the magazine for causing him irreparable injury as governor. Well-known New York attorney Louis Nizer filed the suit that complained that all aspects of the magazine article were untrue.

The beginning strains of what would ultimately become a major campaign issue were voiced by Jim Rhodes in the fall of 1969 as he made a tour of Cleveland State University. In his usual anxious, direct manner, the governor made several things quite clear.

"These buildings were built by the taxpayers and I have a duty to see that they are not damaged or destroyed," he said with a firm set of his jaw. "I will use every force possible to maintain peace on the campus."

Rhodes explained that his office was set to deal with campus disturbances and had discussed the matter with representatives of each of the state's universities. Not only was the governor ready to move against any uproar, he promised he would do it with force whether or not campus administrators requested it.

John D. Millet, chancellor of the Ohio Board of Regents and a Rhodes appointee, was at the governor's side as they inspected the Cleveland State University campus which the governor had been instrumental in building. Millet echoed the governor's firmness.

"Public opinion in this state will not tolerate take-overs or any such thing," he said. "If students have been led to think disruption and violence will bring about change, they have been misinformed. It can only bring about the destruction of higher education."

The Cleveland *Plain Dealer* saw fit to comment editorially on the governor's remarks and after agreeing that violence and disruption have no place on campus, the newspaper went on to say:

> However, we are concerned about the governor's emphasis on the force he would use to quell campus disturbances. He indi-

cated that he would call out the Ohio Highway Patrol and, if necessary, the Ohio National Guard to restore order on a riot-torn campus.

Perhaps, there may develop circumstances under which such extreme measures would be necessary. In the meantime, though, it would be more productive for the governor, other public officials and school administrators to spend more time trying to rectify the causes of campus unrest than to go around talking tough.

In the next six months there would be plenty of tough talk. It would take Kent State to soften the language, and by then it would be too late. As the campaign progressed, Jim Rhodes must have begun to feel the darkness of defeat closing around him. Vice President Spiro T. Agnew's rhetoric stoked the so called "silent majority" and there was no constituency as silent as that in Ohio. Jim Rhodes seemed to take the cue and push his hard-line attack, but not before he stopped and supported President Nixon's handling of the Vietnam war.

In February 1970 a group of four hundred students at Ohio University staged a protest over a proposed ten-dollar quarterly increase in tuition fees. Stones were hurled through the windows of the administration building and the Ohio State Patrol was called. Forty-six students were arrested. A court injunction was issued prohibiting students from interfering with university operations.

Jim Rhodes sat behind his desk at the capitol in Columbus and told newsmen that Ohio taxpayers were fed up with students destroying other people's property. At the governor's side was Major General Sylvester T. Del Corso, commander of the Ohio National Guard, which had been alerted and was waiting in armories in the event the violence spread.

The governor alerted the Guard for possible action at Miami University in April 1970 and was criticized for an excessive display of force. Rhodes said the Guard was sent when it appeared the situation had become an aggravated case.

"You have to protect buildings and property which belong to the taxpayers of Ohio," he said. "And I assure you the people want their property protected. What we don't want in Ohio is a Harvard or MIT or Columbia."

Afterward, in a debate in Cincinnati between the senatorial aspirants, Rhodes was asked about the use of force at Miami. He explained, "What we do, we order the Ohio National Guard for precautionary measures. There's no little fires in a five-million-dollar building. . . .

"We cannot permit people to burn down, whether they are students or nonstudents, to burn down property belonging to the State of Ohio. And I have taken that position and we're going to retain that and we have, I think, less trouble in Ohio as far as net results of buildings and fires than any other state. . ."

Rhodes continued:

"Now, we're not going to have a Harvard or an MIT or Columbia in the State of Ohio. It may be well and good to have your philosophy that you're going to get a court injunction. Going to the courthouse and back may take half a day. By that time there can be twenty-five fires and three or four people killed on a campus.

"All we're trying to do is stop immediately by getting everybody on the campus in the face of law enforcement from the State of Ohio, especially the Highway Patrol. We do not use the National Guard. They are not on the campus. They're off of the campus.

"But we're not going to permit outside students that belong to some organization that may be a Communist front to destroy the very basis and foundation of higher education in the State of Ohio."

A month before the election, polls showed that Taft and Rhodes were even in the race, but there were indications that the governor's strength was waning. Another poll, published a week before the election, gave Taft a 7% lead. He seemed an easy victor. Rhodes was strong in his home county and led in the labor and black voting blocs. Taft out-polled the governor in virtually every other category.

With less than a week to go until election day, warm weather settled over Ohio's colleges, bringing students together to embrace spring, abandon the confines of study, drink beer, ogle girls, and enjoy themselves after an icy winter. Coeds ran barefoot and basked in the sun.

Then at Ohio State University in Columbus a series of peaceful demonstrations by small groups of students suddenly erupted into a two-day ordeal of violence resulting in ten shootings and more than three hundred arrests. Jim Rhodes ordered the National Guard to the campus.

While the students were threatening a massive strike and more violence seemed in the offing, a National Guard officer dramatically reversed the growing tension by talking with the demonstrators. First, he removed his pistol belt and gave the peace symbol "V."

"I'll keep my men back as far as possible," Captain Phillip Wright said. "I'll do that if we avoid violence here."

The captain received cheers and an ovation when he added that the students should "go right on—do your own things" and peacefully boycott classes but remain orderly and non-violent.

A long-haired Ohio State student wearing blue bells and a look of exasperation walked into Jim Rhodes' office and placed a used tear-gas canister on a receptionist's desk.

"Here, give this to your governor," he said. "I'm one of those students who wants to get an education, but you can't do that with things like this being thrown at you."

Late Friday night radio reports said that a mob of students was terrorizing the City of Kent in Portage County, breaking store windows and hurling stones at police. Saturday afternoon Rhodes and Taft had their final confrontation at the traditional Cleveland City Club debate. The governor said the Guard's presence in the trucker strike and on the Ohio State campus had relevance to the campaign he was waging.

"These decisions from the governor's office relate directly to some of the issues in this campaign," he said.

In discussing campus violence Rhodes said the disorders were following a pattern that was becoming increasingly evident across the country. He called it an obvious conspiracy to encourage campus disorder to destroy higher education in the United States.

"This is not the action of legitimate protest," he said, "this is anarchy.

"The way I have handled the situation at Ohio State points up the sharp difference of opinion and philosophy between my opponent and myself," Rhodes said. "He [Taft] said he would have gone much more slowly and obtained a court injunction against the rioters.

By the time an injunction is obtained campus buildings could be burned to the ground and people maimed or killed.

"My opponent's soft attitude on campus violence is not surprising since in 1968 he voted against an amendment to the higher education bill requiring colleges to deny federal funds to students who participate in serious campus disorders."

By nightfall the governor had ordered the Guard into the City of Kent. The next day, Sunday, two days before the elections, the governor pounded the table in the fire house at Kent and vowed that he would not tolerate this kind of disorder. True to his earlier word he had moved the Guard in without notifying university officials. He summarily rejected advice from Portage County prosecutor Ronald J. Kane to close the university, citing the need to keep the school open to counteract those who would like to close it.

Jim Rhodes lost the election to Bob Taft by about forty-five hundred votes. Political analysts differed on the effect of the shooting at Kent State. Some say it helped Jim Rhodes. They cite the polls a week earlier that showed a disastrous defeat in store for Rhodes as compared to Taft's slim victory margin of less than one percent of the vote.

"Between the poll that showed Taft far ahead and election day something had to happen," said one county chairman. "I think it was the governor's move to keep order on campus. I think his action in the truck strike helped. Remember, there are a hell of a lot of people who have had it with these kids."

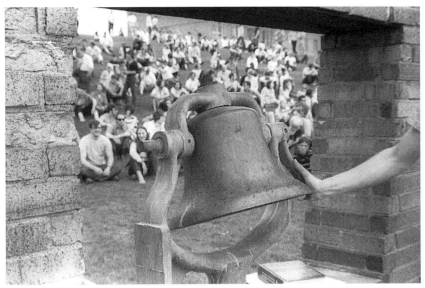

Friday, May 1, noon, the ringing of the Victory Bell calls a rally to protest President Nixon's expansion of the Vietnam War into Cambodia. © *1970 by Howard Ruffner*

At the noon rally on Friday, May 1, graduate student Steven Sharoff throws a shovelful of dirt on the buried U.S. Constitution.

© *1970 by Howard Ruffner*

The Kent State Reserve Officers Training Corps (ROTC) building fire burns out late Saturday night. © 1970 by Howard Ruffner

Early Sunday morning, a pain-faced Governor James A. Rhodes (left) visits the burned-down ROTC building. With him are Kent mayor LeRoy Satron (in dark glasses), university ROTC director Arthur Dotsen, and Ohio National Guard adjutant general Sylvester T. Del Corso. © 1970 by Howard Ruffner

Students pass a National Guard convoy parked in front of the school administration building on Sunday morning, May 3. © *1970 by Howard Ruffner*

At noon on Monday, May 4 guardsmen line across the Commons, opposite the victory bell, waiting to break up the rally. © *1970 by Howard Ruffner*

Students crowd the Commons and the knolls at noon Monday, watching the guardsmen lining up. Among them is Jeffrey Miller of Plainview, Long Island (wearing a western shirt and a headband). © *1970 by Howard Ruffner*

After the students refuse to heed their order to disperse, the guardsmen fire tear gas across the Commons. © *1970 by Howard Ruffner*

Some students race to the tear gas cannisters and fling them back at the guardsmen, who have begun to move in a skirmish line up the Commons toward the victory bell and Taylor Hall. © *1970 by Howard Ruffner*

Most students flee the tear gas and the oncoming guardsmen. These students, on a knoll near Taylor Hall, are running away from the guardsmen in the direction of Blanket Hill. © *1970 by Howard Ruffner*

Instead of stopping when the crowd has been dispersed, the guardsmen continue chasing students past Taylor Hall, past the crest of Blanket Hill. Allison Krause is the woman under the pagoda. © *1970 by Howard Ruffner*

The guardsmen station themselves in an isolated position at an old practice football field. Hemmed in against a cyclone fence, some guardsmen take a kneeling position and aim their rifles at the students. They do not fire. An officer in the field (not in photo) fires a pistol into the air. Minutes later, the guardsmen will retrace their steps back up Blanket Hill. © *1970 by Howard Ruffner*

A few steps past the crest of the hill, back down toward the Commons, the guardsmen turn and fire. The picture was taken an instant before the moment of fire. Note the concerted activity on the group's right flank while other men have their rifles aimlessly in the air. © 1970 by Howard Ruffner

Company C is led away from Jeffrey Miller's body as a crowd gathers.
© 1970 by Howard Ruffner

Numb and in shock, the students administer to the dead and wounded. Here, Jeffrey Miller is being taken away on a stretcher. *© 1970 by Howard Ruffner*

A student waves a flag and jumps in the blood of Jeffrey Miller in protest. *© 1970 by Howard Ruffner*

More of Howard Ruffner's photographs can be seen at www.hruffnerimages.com

9

Monday, May 4

Guardsmen stirred at their posts, their forms drab and bulky in the early morning mist. Dew stretched white on the Commons, awaiting the sun. On the practice football field, guardsmen sleeping under tents awoke to see the first students of the day: the dishwashers and board jobbers who worked in the university dining halls. They trudged by with hardly a glance at the young soldiers.

"Think we'll get out of here today?" a soldier asked his sergeant.

"Man," the sergeant said, "I hope so." The collar of his fatigue jacket was turned up against the chill.

By 8 a.m. the campus was alive and the wet grass on the Commons was criss-crossed with the trails of students hurrying to their first classes. Mrs. Charles Lavicka, a French teacher, was walking to her class, watching for a clue that might indicate the mood of the day. It was quiet and she felt the worst was over.

Joseph Carter, a graduate student, was sipping coffee in his off-campus apartment. The radio told him U.S. forces in Cambodia had captured a sixty-ton Viet Cong rice cache.

The weather for the Kent area would be mostly sunny and mild, with variable winds and temperatures in the seventies.

When the newscaster started talking about Kent State, Carter's attention was sharpened. He was told Governor Rhodes had banned all assemblies on campus. The announcement seemed odd to him in light of the fact that classes were to be held as usual.

The news that interested him, though, was the noon rally that was said to be scheduled that day. He made up his mind he would go. Carter thought the university administration had been strangely silent during the weekend disturbances. Maybe they would explain.

Major John Simons, chaplain of the 107th Armored Cavalry and an Episcopal minister from Cleveland, arrived on campus around 9 a.m. He was wearing the new black subdued insignia that the Guard had recently adopted. It annoyed him that he was not readily identified as a clergyman because of the blackened symbols on his helmet. He saw the tired troops standing at their posts. That bothered him, too. "The only thing I saw among the guys was fatigue and nerves," he said.

Donald Schwartzmiller, chief of campus police, was in and out of the Guard's command post on the second floor of the administration building above his headquarters. He was a mere observer with the Guard in control. He, too, thought the Guard was jumpy. "There were all sorts of reports of snipers that morning, totally unverified reports," he said. "There were rumors of caches of explosives."

On campus the word was out. "See you on the Commons at noon," students called to each other as they trekked to class. Chaplain Simons watched them, talked with some, and noticed an atmosphere of peaceful togetherness. Every now and then a student who passed him would flash the peace sign.

Lou Cusella, who lived off campus, climbed out of bed and heard about the rally on the radio. He decided to go. "I thought I was going to be smart for a change. I was going to dress for this rally. I wore a pair of dress slacks and a button-down shirt and a tie. I wanted to look as much like a Jaycee as I could." Sunday night, dressed in bell bottoms and a denim jacket, he had narrowly escaped arrest.

A friend told Michael Erwin about the rally the night before. He was going to go. There were two reasons for his decision. He wanted to protest the Cambodian invasion and the presence of the Guard on his campus. Erwin picked up his gas mask. "I did not intend to cause trouble." He knew about the ban on gathering and because of this the chances of being gassed were, he felt, "fairly high."

At the fire station a few blocks from campus, the authorities were gathering: Guard commander General Canterbury, a State Patrol representative, Mayor Satrom, Chief Thompson, and university president Robert White. They were there to discuss rumors and plans, specifically plans about the noon rally. It was a moody meeting.

President White felt intimidated. The general and the mayor insisted the Ohio National Guard was in complete command. "It was hammered at me from all sides that the Guard was in complete command," White said. "They told me the noon rally was illegal and they'd break it up."

It was Mayor Satrom's impression that Robert White was being very "cocky" during the meeting. "He sat there doodling on a pad and nodding his head," the mayor said. "I think he felt above the rest of us. He didn't say much."

Oddly, the Guard report pertaining to the meeting said, "The President of the University informed those present that a rally was scheduled for noon on the Commons. He said it would be dangerous and should not be permitted. It was agreed that the rally would not be permitted."

Dressed in what he considered an unobtrusive uniform, Lou Cusella made his way across the campus and watched two long-haired, denim-clad students spoofing with guardsmen perched on an armored personnel carrier. They were ducking behind trees and shouting to the soldiers. Cusella thought, Where do these idiots think they're playing their war games, in the jungle? Twenty minutes later he saw the same two longhairs handing out leaflets advertising the noon rally. "They gave each other the brotherhood handshake and with about fifty people they trooped out to the Commons. They seemed real happy."

When the Guard took over the campus it insisted that all newsmen arriving on campus carry a special Ohio National Guard press pass. Greg Sbaraglia, a reporter for the Canton *Repository*, was on his way to get one when he saw one of the sportswriters from his newspaper. The writer had been called up for duty with the Guard. "What the hell have you been doing here, loafing as usual?" Sbaraglia called. "Yeah, I'll bet," replied the part-time soldier. "We had some action last night and I really nailed some kid's head with a rifle butt. That'll teach those damn hippies to run faster." He showed Sbaraglia the rifle's steel butt plate and it had dried blood on it. Sbaraglia walked away.

Alan Canfora, a junior, made his way to the Commons with a

black flag on which the word "Kent" was spray-painted in red. "I did this to signify the sad turn of events in the city and on our campus. I was sad and angry."

Chaplain Simons was in the command post when General Canterbury returned from the meeting at the fire station. The general seemed in a hurry and announced there would be no rally on the Commons. Then he said he needed troops. The burned-out shell of the ROTC building was cordoned off by guardsmen, but there were no men in reserve. Reinforcements were due shortly, but there was no time to wait. Already students were gathering. Chaplain Simons made a suggestion. "Let's collect together a bunch of guys, some drivers, and wake some guys up at the gym and we could use them for the rally."

"That's a great idea, John," Canterbury said.

The troops had been on twelve-hour shifts since arriving from Akron. They were tired and anxious. Sergeant Russell Repp, a tile and floor installer, had not had a chance to go to the bathroom. He had not slept in two nights and he was hungry.

Lunch had been prepared for the Guard but tension and fatigue stunted appetites. There was chow mein and fruit salad for 250 men. About ten stopped to eat.

A number of photographers were getting ready to cover the rally and Jerry Stoklas, a photojournalism student, thought if he could get on the roof of Taylor Hall he would have a good vantage point and might be able to get some exclusive pictures. A journalism professor thought it was a fine idea and escorted him to the roof. "I figured I'd screw all those other *paparazzi*," Stoklas said.

After returning from his disappointing meeting with Mayor Satrom and General Canterbury, Robert White took his vice presidents, Ronald Roskens and Robert Matson, for a quick lunch at a restaurant a mile or so from campus. Before leaving he instructed his secretary to call if anything important happened. It was 11:15 a.m.

Groups of students continued to gather on the Commons near the victory bell. Someone started to ring it and the clang could be heard across the campus. There were no announcements that all of this was illegal, Joseph Carter noticed.

Meanwhile, Chaplain Simons had finished helping to gather a force of nearly a hundred men to be used in dispersing the crowd from the Commons. As General Canterbury was leaving the command post, Simons asked if he might go along. "He turned to me and said, 'Sure John, come on,' " Simons said. " 'Del Corso and I had a great time throwing rocks at those kids the other night.' "

Five or six students were huddled around the victory bell, ringing it with force. A professor emerged from Taylor Hall and scrambled down the hill. "Please stop ringing that bell," he called. The students gathered around him. One shouted, "Get away, old man."

By now the west side of Blanket Hill was filled with people and from across the Commons it looked like a gallery at a sporting event. "It had a surrealistic, an unreal-like quality," said Michael Stein, a graduate student. "It struck me as sort of distant. Even though I was there, it was sort of like watching it on a screen instead of being physically part of it."

By a few minutes before noon nearly fifteen hundred students had gathered around the bell. Another two thousand to three thousand students were assembled on the opposite side of the Commons behind the National Guard lines. Another two thousand were on the northern edge of the Commons near the tennis courts.

Not all of the students had come to participate in the rally. The noon hour at Kent caught many between classes and the central location of the Commons made it necessary for most to pass by on the way to lunch or their next class. "There were people who were just curious," said Yvonne Mitchell, one of the passers-by. "There weren't just kids messing with the National Guard, or radical kids or conservative kids. There was just an integration of everybody."

Bill Montgomery, a twenty-three-year-old Marine Corps veteran of Vietnam, watched and saw what he said were clean-cut fraternity types. "Really, I saw few you would call radicals there," he said. "There were a lot of kids there who had just come back from the weekend and didn't know what was coming off."

When he looked over the crowd, Michael Erwin felt the same way. "The crowd was made up of the Greeks, athletes, and the largest segment of the group were, like me, anti-war moderates." Student Buzz Terhune described the crowd this way: "You had super-straight Joe Fraternity and ultra-radical Joe Freak out there."

Guard sergeant Mike Delaney looked out at them from the other side of the Commons and said he felt sympathy with the students.

"I don't think I should change what I think because I'm wearing a uniform."

The crowd was growing and milling. The anti-war chants with obscene stanzas began to roll over the Commons and fall upon the ears of the authorities. Among the crowd, people began to call out a telephone number where students could get legal help if anything happened. Lou Cusella wrote it down. Jeffrey Miller, a sophomore, wrote it down. Hundreds of others did the same.

"Pigs go home," the crowd chanted.

"Guard off campus."

"Peace now. Peace now."

In the midst of the protestors Alan Canfora waved his black flag. He was angry at the stories of Guard harassment the night before.

Standing near the remaining ROTC buildings on the Commons was Captain Don Peters, an Army instructor assigned to the officers' training course. He was a combat veteran of Vietnam. Peters thought the beginning of the demonstration had the merry atmosphere of a mudfight.

A campus policeman armed with a bullhorn stood near the ROTC building and shouted out to the students to disperse. The wind and noise drowned his call. He yelled again. The other side of the Commons was too far away and no one heard his command. The noise swallowed it.

"Yell your head off," Chaplain Simons called. "Get a jeep and drive out there."

A guardsman pulled a jeep over and the policeman climbed awkwardly in the back. In the front seat was Major Harry Jones, a forty-three-year-old native of Tennessee who served full time in the Guard as the 145th Infantry's training officer. He wore a baseball fatigue cap and was unarmed except for a baton he carried.

The jeep drove slowly across the Commons, the bullhorn calling its message to the crowd that stood on the hillside.

"This assembly is unlawful. The crowd must disperse at this time. This is an order!" The jeers increased as the jeep neared the hill. It swung within a hundred feet of the crowd. Lou Cusella had the impression that the man with the bullhorn was not ordering, but begging. "There was all kinds of pathos in his voice. He looked like a high-school band director."

"We just shouted him down," said Steve Tarr, a freshman. The chants taunting the Guard continued to come over the green.

Then a rock arched out of the crowd, bounced on the ground, and hit the jeep. Several more followed. The chanting of the crowd increased in tempo:

"Off the pigs, off the pigs."

"One-two-three-four, we don't want your fucking war."

"Ho, Ho, Ho Chi Minh, the NLF is gonna win."

"Two-four-six-eight, we don't want your fascist state."

Paul Schlemmer, a university sports information publicist, looked at his watch and noted that the time was eleven fifty-eight.

The jeep was pelted by more rocks. Kathy Berry, student government vice president, saw two rocks "hit the jeep's hood with a ping." Al Thompson, a reporter from the Cleveland Press, saw a "rock bounce off the jeep."

Quickly the driver swerved from the crowd and raced across the Commons to General Canterbury and his composite force of cooks, drivers, messengers and sleep-hungry guardsmen. The general was dressed in a business suit.

Some of the guardsmen standing by recall the moment: "If I wouldn't have been in uniform, I would have been on the other side of the line, but I wouldn't have thrown rocks," said Sergeant Mike Delaney. "This guy would have been throwing rocks and wrenches," said Staff Sergeant Jim Thomas.

Earel Neikirk, a reporter from the Elyria *Chronicle and Telegram*, himself a Kent State graduate, was near Canterbury when Jones returned from the jeep ride across the Commons. The two officers huddled. Seconds later, guardsmen were ordered into a skirmish line, Neikirk said.

"I heard an officer say, 'Fix bayonets, gas masks, load,'" the reporter said. "I could not believe it. What were these guys going to do, mount a charge against a bunch of kids who weren't harming anything or anybody?"

The students were nearly a hundred yards away when the order went out to launch tear gas. Men armed with M-79 grenade launchers stepped forward and fired their gas rounds. The grenades fluttered through the air and the mass of students parted as the missiles, streaming trails of smoke, dropped near their front ranks.

The tear gas was necessary, a Guard report said, because "the size of the crowd was increasing rapidly by the minute and it became apparent that the order to disperse would not be heeded."

The wind, which had been shifting from time to time, was blowing toward the Guard when the gas rounds were launched. It carried the fumes away from the students. Several rushed forward, grabbed the smoking canisters, and hurled them back toward the Guard, far out of throwing range.

Donald Schwartzmiller watched the Guard skirmish line move toward the demonstrators. He "felt there would be trouble" when the students refused to disperse and such a small contingent of Guard went after them.

More tear gas was fired. As the canisters tumbled on the ground students made an attempt to throw them back. The Guard noted "members of the crowd quickly donned gas masks and put gloves on—these people picked up gas grenades and threw them back."

Applause and cheers broke out for those who pitched the steaming missiles back. "I saw one student throw back a tear-gas canister," said Michael Stein. "He was applauded by his fellow students as a kind of folk hero. Tear gas was very ineffective since the wind was blowing toward the National Guard."

Robert Roepke, a graduate student who was standing on one end of the Commons, said, "People thought it was a game, a circus." Sergeant Mike Delaney, on the other end, also described it as a game: "A serious game of Frisbee."

"I picked up a canister and threw it back, but I stuck my face in the damn stuff," said Ben Parsons, a twenty-two-year-old drama student. "It almost got to be a joke because the guardsmen were laughing. It was just a game."

Michael Erwin, who had put on his gas mask, threw "four or five canisters of gas" back at the advancing troops. "I was winded," he said. "I thought that I was out of range of the gas but the wind shifted and blew gas into my face as I took the mask off."

Captain Don Peters, the ROTC adviser, thought "a lot of guys were throwing those canisters back for heroics. The broads loved it."

Staff Sergeant Jim Thomas looked at the carnival atmosphere and wished he had a popcorn stand. "I could have made a thousand dollars."

All the while, the victory bell clanged its challenge.

Major Harry Jones advanced with the troops he commanded. "Some of these kooks had to be on dope," he said. "I bet they've got needle marks on their arms." The troops moved forward, firing gas and stepping with an even pace.

A ripple of panic passed through the crowd. Some students began to run. "People were yelling to walk, not run," said Alan Chesler, a teaching fellow.

Bayonets fixed and before them, the Guard stepped forward, scattering straggling students. "This is mad," thought Steve Smith, a freshman. "These guys are chasing kids all over this area. They don't have a chance to catch them. This could go on forever."

By now the entire Commons was covered with a shifting haze of gas. Students ripped up shirts and rags to protect their faces from the sting. Jim Nichols, a student, was in Taylor Hall at the top of the hill and saw teachers and staff members tearing up cloth, toweling, and pieces of girls' skirts. "They were dousing them in water fountains and in the restrooms and handing them to kids."

Outside, John P. Hayes, a journalism student, saw one student run toward a soldier and throw a tear-gas canister at him. "Three soldiers began chasing the student up Taylor Hill. One soldier caught the student and began hitting him with a billy club while others pointed their rifles at him." Dennis Taruben saw the same student being clubbed. "One of the guardsmen fired tear gas at him point blank." Screaming, the student ran off.

"I saw one student who was a little slow in leaving the hill behind Taylor Hall," said Michael Stein. "The National Guard advanced up the hill and they managed to reach him. He was beaten rather severely and fell to the ground and someone pulled him into Taylor Hall."

Private Paul Naujoks was coming up the hill with the Guard, breathing heavily because of the equipment he carried. "The rock throwing was just occasional," he said. "The guy beside me got hit in the shoulder. I never got hit. It seemed like we were trying to drive the bad guys out of there. I still remember this one guy with an Apache headband with a flag. I thought to myself, these guys are crazy. You never knew who was a spectator and who was a rioter."

As the Guard force began to climb the hill it broke into two elements, one going to the left side of the hill so Taylor Hall was flanked on both sides.

Joseph Carter, who had once served in the Guard, said, "I presumed the entire line of guardsmen would move up the hill and divide into two units, one driving the crowd away from the front of Taylor and the other dispersing kids around the side." Carter thought it strange that "only a platoon of men came over the crest of the hill and marched directly into the practice football field where there was no one to be dispersed."

Lieutenant Roy W. Drew, a guardsman, thought it odd that the right flank pushed onward. "When they got to the edge of the building, on top of the hill, they should have stopped. They didn't have enough men to go over the hill."

Bill Montgomery, the Marine Corps Vietnam veteran, was equally amazed. "They maneuvered themselves into a stupid position. They walked right down into the field against the fence and the kids surrounded them."

Chaplain John Simons thought, "That silly Canterbury; they're supposed to disperse the crowd, the crowd is dispersed, where in the hell is he leading those men?" The general was in the practice football field with the men.

"The students began to realize that the National Guard had maneuvered themselves into a partially enclosed area and were, in a sense, encircled," said Joseph Carter.

Harold Froehlich, a student, saw the Guard move onto the field. There was a fence in front of them with only a small gate. There were fences to the right of them and to the left. "They couldn't pursue and they couldn't contain," Froehlich said. "The students started gaining the upper hand for the first time. And they knew it."

Specialist Fourth Class Karry Werny, a twenty-three-year-old guardsman, was standing in the practice football field. He was scared stiff. "It's only a natural reaction, I guess," he said.

Joseph Carter said he saw about fifteen students throw rocks at the boxed-in Guard. "Most of the students were standing between 80 and 125 feet away from the guardsmen." A small board was flung, missing the troops. A protestor jumped up and down waving the black flag of anarchy in front of the students. He was shouting.

Carter saw three or four students picking up stones in the parking lot about two hundred feet from the practice field.

Alan Canfora was in front of the students waving his black flag. He noticed the rocks being thrown were falling short of the Guard. "I did not see one rock hit a single soldier," he said. "At least once I saw a soldier throw rocks back."

Sergeant Russell Repp said he was hit ten times by stones. "They were just having a good time. They thought we were a bunch of nobodies. A good-sized kid kept coming up behind me and stoning me from behind, then laying down about five yards away. I picked up a rock and threw it back."

Sarah Terhune, a student, saw a piece of wood, "a dead branch," thrown from the crowd. Michael Erwin saw students in the parking lot gathering stones. The lot was unpaved and it provided rocks "about the size of golf balls." He estimated that twenty-five to thirty people were throwing rocks. "Most were falling short by fifteen to twenty feet," he said. "One soldier staggered. I don't know if he was hit with a rock or if he just tripped." John Barilla, another student, saw four or five people throwing rocks.

"A half of a brick almost knocked me down," said Major Harry Jones. "Some [men] were knocked down with rocks but scrambled up," said General Canterbury.

Joseph Carter saw no guardsmen go down from a stone. "It was too far to heave a rock with any accuracy or force. A couple of the troops picked up stones and threw them back," he said.

Jim Minard, a student, said, "I was really mad. And we were throwing stones and we were yelling at them to get off campus. Some students had kidded me about my good arm because I had thrown a lot of tear-gas canisters back."

Michael W. Hill, a senior, saw a guardsman get hit in the foot. "They were all fired up and it's sort of easy to tell when somebody gets hit because you sort of move out of formation and jump back."

Suddenly, some of the guardsmen in the practice field dropped back, took a kneeling position, and pointed their M-1 rifles at the demonstrators. Greg Benedetti, a campus radio newsman, watched the Guard back off. "The protestors would retreat, then charge, throwing things and shouting," he said. "The Guard kept moving back and the protestors kept coming forward."

Students began to yell, "Shoot, Shoot, Shoot."

John Filo, a student photographer, saw a stone the size of a golf ball bounce off a guardsman's helmet.

"The tear gas wasn't doing any good," said Sergeant Russell Repp. "We didn't run out. I still had eight canisters on a bandolier."

"We exhausted every tear gas round," said Canterbury.

From his vantage point atop Taylor Hall, Jerry Stoklas looked down on the practice field and saw a guardsman with a .45 pistol fire in the air. He appeared as "a guy who looked like an officer." Richard Schreiber, a journalism professor, saw the same thing. "He aimed over the rock throwers and fired at least one round over their heads," he said.

"Those guardsmen who had not assumed the kneeling position seemed to be milling around in no particular formation and began to take a few steps toward Taylor Hall," said Joseph Carter. "Some interpreted it as a withdrawal."

The Guard assembled in a formation and started toward Blanket Hill, away from the crowd. "They walked at a pretty fast pace," said Ben Parsons. "Then they started running. Everybody started screaming because it was like we'd won."

James Dawson saw students throwing rocks and bottles more heavily as the Guard left the practice field. "It seemed to almost panic the guardsmen," he said. "They almost seemed to start running. Which I thought did nothing but give more impetus to the students and the students started to move quickly toward them."

The troops were ordered to return to their original position at the bottom of the Commons. "The behavior of an estimated seventy-five to one hundred members of the crowd was illogical, they appeared to be frenzied and frantic during the period when the troops were being attacked when returning to the original positions," a Guard report said.

Sergeant Dale Antram said, "We were walking up the hill but we were thinking behind us. We were always glancing over our shoulders and guys were saying, 'Back there, watch it, here comes a rock.' I couldn't wear my glasses because of the gas mask."

"It was hard to see through the plastic," said Private Paul Zimmerman. "To look behind you, you'd have to turn your head all the way around. I was hot and sweaty."

"Those people were closing in on three sides," General Canterbury said.

The Guard's withdrawal up Blanket Hill drew cheers and hoots from the students. Jim Minard described the scene, "People were just going everywhere, going crazy." Jerry Stoklas watched the Guard climb the hill and saw a "bunch of kids further back in the parking lot, throwing stones at them over the others' heads."

"There were some kids coming up the hill who had been down at the bottom before and there was a lot of yelling," said Cheryl Birkner, a student. "People were yelling and screaming."

Jim Minard was moving up the hill behind the Guard when he began what he called an "eye and verbal" battle with an officer. "I was yelling at him to get off the campus. And actually, maybe three or four times, he pulled his .45 out of his holster and pointed it at me. And one time he did that and said, 'Come on, come on.'"

Watching from a window on the second floor of Taylor Hall, Donald Ross, a janitor, said he saw "this guardsman with a .45 behind the rest of them pointing his pistol at a couple of the kids."

General Canterbury said, "Every guardsman up there was hit by rocks."

Bruno Speco, a junior, saw a two-foot-long stick thrown. Steve Tarr said students were right behind the Guard throwing stones, "hitting them because they were at close range."

"I heard the students yell, 'Kill the pigs!'" said Bill Resch, president of the Graduate Student Council. "The intensity of the yell surprised me."

"The situation was extremely dangerous," said General Canterbury. "I felt I could have been killed."

"I didn't feel danger and I was right in the middle of it," said Captain Raymond Srp.

"There were only two ways out of there," said Private Paul Naujoks. "To run down the hill or shoot and turn them back." The guardsmen now were a few steps over the crest of the hill.

"Suddenly a small group of students raced within close range of the Guard," said Al Thompson, the reporter. "They were throwing more rocks."

"I could see a kid run close behind the Guard," said Donald MacKenzie, a senior. "He had a rock and he threw."

A reporter from the Akron *Beacon Journal* saw "a civilian with a large rock run up behind the Guard." There were more students behind him. "I saw this one in front throw the rock."

"I saw the guardsmen stop and turn," said Alan Canfora. "I had my flag in my hand. They were aiming their guns into the crowd. I turned and started to run."

"They turned toward us," said Barbara Neff, a sophomore. "We were expecting tear gas. We knew they were going to fire. We knew they were going to fire something."

"One of the guardsmen turned and fired and then I heard the volley," said Donald MacKenzie. As the Guardsmen turned, they rushed a few steps back up the knoll, firing, led by a guardsman with a .45 pistol.

"One guardsman with a pistol shot first," said Rick Levinger, a freshman, "and then the others opened up."

"All of a sudden," said Bill Reymond, a senior, "everything just blew up."

"I heard a single shot precede the volley," said General Canterbury. "I did not identify the kind of weapon. It was a split second before the volley."

"Everything happened so fast," said Private Paul Naujoks, "it was like a car wreck."

"I heard no single shot," said Jackie Stewart, a university secretary. "They turned together. They just started shooting. I stood there."

It was a long, irregular volley that snapped and crackled, partially obscuring the men on the firing fine in a cloud of smoke and dust.

"It sounded just like the Fourth of July," said Jim Nichols, a junior.

Those being fired at could not comprehend the hail of bullets. "I thought," said Mike Erwin, "that only blank rounds were being fired and I thought that until the bullets started kicking up dust at my feet." When he heard the volley, Chaplain Simons "knew better, but I thought they were blanks." Cleveland Press reporter Al Thompson thought, They must be firing blanks, those can't be real bullets.

"Everyone was up tight," said Sergeant Russell Repp. "No one was thinking of firing. Then I heard small-arms fire, three shots, it might have been an echo, and the guys returned the fire."

"One guardsman was raking the area," a student said. "He wasn't aiming. Others had their guns in the air. The guy I was watching was cutting an arc with his rifle."

"I thought I heard the command to fire," a guardsman said. "I was approximately in the center of the line formation. The students were throwing rocks and were too close for the safety of the men."

"I was laughing," said Walter Zimny, a junior. "I thought, Those jerks are firing a machine-gun over everyone's heads."

"Others in my unit fired," said Private Duane Raber, "and I tried to fire but I couldn't. I extracted the first round and then fired three rounds over their heads as warning."

"I was watching the firing line," said Ben Parsons, a sophomore. "I saw at least a couple spin, lock the butts of their rifles against their hips, and fire straight into the air, and I saw some spin and fire without looking."

"I heard the first shot," said a guardsman. "I had my rifle at my shoulder, not sighting, just at my shoulder. I had my finger on the trigger and fired when the others did. I just didn't think about it. It just happened. How can you think at a time like that? Right after the first shot, it sounded like everyone squeezed off one round, like at the range, drawn out. I fired once. I just closed my eyes and shot. I didn't aim at anyone in particular. I just shot at shoulder level toward the crowd."

"A few guardsmen just didn't let up," said freshman Steve Tarr. "They just emptied their rifles."

"I heard the men fire," said Private Lonnie Hinton. "So I fired one .30-caliber round straight into the air. The reason was they were all around us and I thought it the most suitable thing to do at the time."

"I turned, and when I saw all those guys falling in front I knew we were safe," said Private Paul Naujoks. "They wouldn't keep coming. It was a relief. I felt it was our only way out."

"Each man made a judgment on his own that his own life was in danger," said General Canterbury.

"I didn't feel threatened," said a guardsman. "I didn't feel trapped. I didn't think they'd try to take our rifles, not while we could use the bayonets and the butts."

Major Harry Jones said he gave no order. He had a baton in his hands and he brought the stick down so hard after the firing began that he broke it. Some students, confused in their timing, thought the stick came down before the firing and constituted an order.

"I had my stick in my right hand," Jones said, "and I started beating the men over their helmets. I had to run out in front of the line, in front of the fire. If I wouldn't have, they never would have stopped. And I yelled, 'Cease fire! Cease fire! Cease fire!' And General Canterbury was yelling too at the other end of the line."

One Guard official said some of the soldiers may have misunderstood the "Cease fire!" order, thinking the order was to "Fire!"

Private David Rogers was struck by Major Jones' stick. "The major hit me so hard it made my ears ring. I could see the kids fall. I saw this one. I don't know if it was a boy or girl. It didn't bother me at first, either. I've been with my brother's wrecking truck out on accidents and things. The major was out there waving like crazy."

Twenty feet to his left reporter Al Thompson saw a student, long hair flying, pirouette as he was hit in the chest. Blood flowed through his shirt. As he twisted, head bowed, one shoulder wrenched high in the air, the student had a look of "utter disbelief" on his face.

Robert Stamps, a sophomore, was standing seven hundred feet away. He had a pretzel in one hand and a notebook in the other. He heard the shots. "Something hit me in the ass. I thought it was a rock, and then I put my hand back there and felt the blood." If another bullet hits me, he thought, I'm going to die. He leaped down on top of two girls in the parking lot. "As soon as it stopped, I jumped up and started running again." He ran into another student, threw his arms around him, and said, "Brother, I've been shot, help me."

On top of Taylor Hall, photographer Jerry Stoklas saw a boy "jerk like a puppet," then twist and fall, "like he got broken into pieces."

In the parking lot, photographer John Filo was looking through his viewfinder and saw the guardsmen point their rifles directly at him. He heard a bullet bang through a metal sculpture near him. He dropped his camera and fell flat on his face.

Sophomore Douglas Wrentmore, a conscientious objector, heard the noise, took a few steps, and found he couldn't walk any more. "I was on the ground. I crawled behind a car. Bullets hit the side of the car. I tried to get up and walk. I had to hop."

Greg Benedetti was running toward Taylor Hall. As he ran he looked down and saw blood on his hands. Five feet from him a student had been hit. "The wound sprayed blood over the area."

Four or five seconds elapsed in terrible stillness after the shooting stopped.

Then junior John Dienert got up and yelled: "MURDERERS!"

Freshman Danny Herman got up and pointed to a wounded student. "Look what you did!" he yelled.

Michael Erwin saw a boy holding a rag over a girl's throat, "only there wasn't much of her throat left."

Robert Dyal, a philosophy professor, couldn't hear any voices "except screams."

Earel Neikirk, the Elyria reporter, thought, I have seen this all before, in the service, during the war, on a beach in the South Pacific. Now I have to see it again? Here? At my alma mater?

Graduate student Joseph Carter thought, Where am I? Is this a battlefield? Is this a nightmare? Is this a campus? Is this America? Is this a war? Who is fighting? Who is the enemy? Who won?

Greg Sbaraglia, the reporter, looked around and couldn't comprehend it. He thought, Campus radicals have used animal blood to give the impression of injury. This is guerrilla theater, a bad joke.

Bobbi Moran, a freshman coed, saw the blood and couldn't "fathom" it. She thought it was fingerpaint.

Jerry Geiger, twenty-four, a junior and a Vietnam combat veteran, thought, There is a helicopter up there and there are people bleeding all around. I'm back in Vietnam.

The Guard contingent that had fired from Blanket Hill withdrew. Twenty-six men had fired fifty-nine shots.

"We felt we had accomplished our purpose," General Canterbury said. "The crowd was dispersed at that point."

The guardsmen went cautiously down the hill. Junior Jim Nichols noticed how each guardsman covered a different angle with his rifle. As they neared the bottom of the hill, they broke into a dead run to reach the Guard compound by the ROTC building.

"We didn't know anything was seriously wrong," said Sergeant Mike Delaney, who was on the Commons, "until we saw the guys coming over the hill and the officers yelling for help."

Chaplain Simons ran toward the men as they came off the hill.

They didn't want to talk to him. "They were already withdrawing," Simons said.

When Sergeant Dale Antram got to the bottom of the hill, he felt like crying. "I couldn't believe it. My first thought was, I'm getting out of the Guard, I'm a conscientious objector, baby."

When the guardsmen left the hill, the students were clumped around the dead and wounded.

Michael Stein, watching from Blanket Hill, saw a coed run toward the guardsmen on the Commons with her hands over her head to make sure she wouldn't be shot. She was Pam Holland, a sophomore. An ambulance stood next to the guardsmen.

"As I ran down," Pam said, "I was screaming obscenities. I wasn't in any way to be talked to." She screamed, "People are dying, get the ambulance up there!" One of the guardsmen came up to her, shoved her, and said, "Where's your identification?" She kept screaming, "Get a doctor!" They finally sent the ambulance up.

As the guardsmen stood on the Commons near the ROTC building, General Canterbury asked Chaplain Simons to talk to the men who had been on the firing line. "He wanted to know whether they fired up or down," Simons said.

The first guardsman Simons talked to said, "I fired right down the gulley." The chaplain noted "there was hate on the guy's face" and he thought, You just can't get away from it. This guy placed one exactly where he wanted to.

Simons talked to another guardsman who said, "I didn't realize the guys were shooting at the kids until I saw this kid's chest break into blood." The guardsman said he had fired into the air.

Joseph Carter was inside Prentice Hall, the dormitory behind the parking lot. "The lounge was a scene of terrible shock and confusion." Coeds screamed in hysteria.

In the parking lot Dan Smith, a photographer for the Kent *Record Courier*, heard a coed scream, "Get mattresses, the pigs shot them, help us." The wounded were carried from the parking lot. He saw a girl, her face waxen, her clothes and those of the students carrying her bloodstained. He saw a boy whose headband had slipped below his eyes. It was soaked with his tears.

In the administration building Leona Wright, the university's chief telephone operator, saw the Centrex system go dead. She thought of one thing: Dallas.

A wild rumor spread among the students that the Guard had ordered the phone line closed down so nobody would find out what had happened.

A group of guardsmen who had stood between Taylor and Prentice Halls at the time of the shooting moved toward the parking lot to look at the wounded and the dead. They were led by Captain Ron Snyder, an investigator for the Summit County coroner's office.

Freshman Steve Tarr saw a girl approach one of the guardsmen and yell, "You killed him!" and "Fuck you!" The guardsman got about six feet from a body and turned around and went back.

"I saw a boy in the road," said Captain Snyder. "I tried to make a recovery of him. They were calling us goddamned murderers." He made the decision to "forget the bodies" and moved his men from the parking lot toward Blanket Hill.

When the new contingent of guardsmen were on the hill, Snyder saw "a kid was yelling trying to get another crowd together." He threw a tear gas canister at him. The student ran away. It was the last canister fired that day. Those clumped around the bodies couldn't believe it. "Here was all this blood," said Steve Tarr, "and they were still shooting tear gas."

Dan Smith, the photographer, was numb. He walked inside Prentice Hall. He wanted to cry but the tears wouldn't come. He saw that a window screen had been removed from the lounge's big front window. Two of the injured were brought through the opening carefully on couches. He saw a tall, dark-haired girl strip the mattress from her bed and, despite its bulkiness, throw it through the corridor outside.

Greg Sbaraglia walked around the parking lot and saw rocks, bricks, and cartridge shells on the ground near the fallen students.

Dan Smith, back in the parking lot, was still waiting for the ambulances. Students were screaming for help. The only ones quiet, he noted, were the wounded and those in shock. When the first of the red-and-white Kent ambulances got there, a crowd gathered around it. They began yelling at the ambulance attendants. "You goddamn pigs!" they yelled. Seconds later, Smith saw, students were helping the attendants with the wounded.

Steve Tarr watched in the parking lot as a faculty member checked the pulse of a student who'd been hit. "He had no coloring on his lips. His face was completely pale. I knew he was in shock then because he said, 'I have to take a piss bad.' We unbuckled his pants and he started to kick his legs aloft and I held both legs down.'

As the ambulances were picking up the dead and wounded, a helicopter hovered overhead and a voice from a loudspeaker ordered everyone back to the dormitories. Junior Scott Varner thought, It sounds like a voice from heaven.

Dan Smith, standing next to an ambulance, was loading his camera. Why should I shoot? he wondered. Almost subconsciously he threaded the film. He shot through the ambulance window at the wounded. He was half ashamed of what he was doing but he was too shocked not to do it.

Gene Pekarik, a sophomore, saw a student in a sport coat running around near Blanket Hill "like a wildman." The student had a gun. "He looked like he was going to shoot somebody." He was three feet from Pekarik. He was pointing the gun at him. "He was so close to me I could see the gold bullets in the chamber." Pekarik thought, I am going to die.

The student was junior Terry Norman, a sometime undercover photographer for the campus police department. "I was up on the hill after the shooting and I stopped to help one of the students who'd been hit and some of them surrounded me and yelled, 'Get the pig! Get the pig!' They took my camera away and beat me. I heard someone yell 'Stick the pig!' " Norman said he saw a student reach for a knife. "I pulled my gun and scared him off."

Chaplain Simons saw Norman race down the hill toward the Commons chased by two or three people. Norman ran to a guards-man.

Sergeant Mike Delaney took the pistol from Norman. He had issued press credentials to him earlier. A campus policeman told him Norman would be taking pictures of the demonstration for the FBI. Delaney gave the gun, a .38, to campus police detective Tom Kelley. Kelley examined it and determined that it had not been fired. Campus police chief Schwartzmiller said Norman "definitely" was not on assignment for his department that day.

In Lowry Hall, not far from Blanket Hill, a girl with a pony tail ran screaming to Mrs. Darlene Mack, a secretary. The girl screamed, "I killed him, I killed him." She blamed herself for the boy's death because, she said, she had taken part in the demonstration. Mrs. Mack tried to comfort her. "She told me to please leave her alone."

In the parking lot a student tied a bloodied white cloth onto his purple anti-war flag and walked away.

Another student, eyes glazed in hysteria, dipped a black flag into a pool of blood, staining it red. "Here, here," the student cried wildly, whirling the bloody flag in the air.

Dan Smith inspected his dusty '61 Volkswagen, which had been parked in the lot behind Taylor Hall. The back window was completely shattered. The same bullet hit an adjoining car, shattering a side window and ripping through the driver's window. "At that moment I felt very close to that oil-burning heap of mine," Smith said. "I photographed its wounds."

Captain Ron Snyder saw a student ringing the victory bell again. He went over to the student. "I flailed him a few times with a big stick."

On the Commons, Guard private Richard Parker, a Wooster patrolman, saw some of the men who had been on Blanket Hill "throw down their weapons and start to bawl." Private Mike Chizmadia noticed that "no one wanted to talk about it."

General Canterbury told Chaplain Simons to tell every man not to fire again unless an officer "tapped him on the shoulder and told him to fire." Simons tried to console the men. Should I go up there to help the dying and the wounded? he thought. "It sounds awful crass to say let them bury their own dead."

In the emergency room at Robinson Memorial Hospital, wounded Doug Wrentmore watched as "the kids came in, stretchers and stuff. Most of them were a lot worse off than I was. It is really something when you see a girl lying on a stretcher, her face is all contorted and swollen and then, you know, they pick up this sheet and slowly lay it over her."

President White, eating lunch with university vice presidents Matson and Roskens, got a phone call telling him of the shooting. Matson and Roskens raced to their offices. White rushed to his home, on campus, overlooking the Commons. He saw that two or three thousand students had massed again on the Commons and made an immediate decision to close the school.

Around Blanket Hill and on the Commons the mood had turned from shock to fury. "Everything really turned ugly," said student Dick Woods, an ex-Marine. "I really wanted to hit one of those clowns. We started shouting and screaming.

Gene Pekarik also noted the wild anger of the students. "There were a couple thousand kids milling on the Commons and the hill, not going past the victory bell. The guardsmen stood around the ROTC building." To Pekarik, it looked like two camps, two sides grouping before a big battle. He thought, God, again? Is it going to happen again?

Standing with the guardsmen by the ROTC building, sensing the building fury in the crowd, Chaplain Simons heard one of the soldiers say, "Gee, if they come down again, we've got no alternative except to shoot."

General Canterbury said, "If they come down again, we'll give them the Commons."

Simons was afraid. He foresaw horrible possibilities.

Geology professor Dr. Glenn Frank, voted the university's outstanding professor the previous year, went to Canterbury. "Don't do anything; give us time to get the students away," Frank said.

Canterbury told him, "You've got five minutes."

Frank was desperate. He began to cry. He ran back to the students on the Commons and begged them to disperse.

As Frank walked away, Captain Ron Snyder heard Canterbury say, "They're going to have to find out what law and order is all about."

With tears streaming down his cheeks Frank stood in front of the crowd and begged, "Please, we can't do anything here. They're going to shoot us again. We're going to get slaughtered. They've got guns and the guns are at our throats. People died here, but please, because of their martyrdom, let's not have any more martyrs. I beg you, let's move."

As Frank spoke, General Canterbury got the reinforcements he was waiting for. "He got all cranked up to clear the area again," Chaplain Simons said. "He wanted to start the sweep again."

Simons thought, No. No. No.

Canterbury was picking up the bullhorn, ready to tell the crowd to disperse. Simons went up behind him and tapped him on the shoulder.

"Come on," the chaplain said, "you told him five minutes."

"Oh, all right," Canterbury said. He shrugged his shoulders.

The crowd on the Commons began moving.

"Almost beyond reality," Frank said, "they started to leave the

Commons. I could barely walk I was so weak. I could hardly see because of the tears in my eyes. They moved up the hill overlooking the Commons and sat down."

Dr. Seymour Baron, chairman of the psychology department, went down to the Commons to speak to Canterbury. The two had a long conversation. Baron told Canterbury he was involved in a situation of mutual escalation.

"The general had no comprehension of the idea," Baron said. "He did not want to lose his advantage."

Baron asked for a gesture.

"If you could put your guns down," he said, "the kids would see that and listen to me."

Baron looked at the guardsmen around him. "They were a bunch of young men with dry mouths whose fists were clenched up so tight to their rifles that their knuckles were white. They were benumbed."

He kept talking to Canterbury.

"He kept telling me he had his job to do, which was to clear the kids away. He did not want me to tell him how to do his job."

Baron asked that the guardsmen's rifles be placed behind a truck.

"Canterbury was unimpressed. I kept on talking."

He begged that the rifles be put down at parade rest.

"Canterbury thought about it, finally he said, 'Oh, all right.' "

Baron went back to the crowd sitting on the hill. He was scared to death. He had spent his life studying psychology. If you know anything at all about it, he thought, now is the time to show it.

He yelled, straining to be heard:

"Listen," he said, "if there's one thing those guys are taught, it's not to take their hands off their weapons. So for crying out loud, I've got them now, they've got their guns at parade rest. Look, in the meantime, there's one thing that we can do, we can sit. It's a nice sunny day. I'll be glad to join you. Let's talk about the issues, let's talk about the problems, and for God's sake let's not charge them, they've got live ammo. Now listen, has anybody done the smartest thing yet, go to see if we can get some sandwiches? Who's got a bottle of beer? I don't think it's a bad thing to ask about food when guys have got killed. I say there are three ways I know of to settle a man's stomach—women, whiskey, and food."

A coed interrupted him. "How about rationality instead of women?"

"Okay," Baron said, "rationality too if it helps anybody. Now listen to me, if you go down toward them, they'll kill you. Now the reason they'll kill you is because they're scared to death. They're a bunch of summertime soldiers. They have no idea about what soldiering is or what war is about. Those guys are scared kids. Now I'm telling you, you can yell all kinds of things at me, but I just want you to stay alive. I don't want you going after them. Some of you guys feel that you have to be heroes, well, you can be heroes, but remember, the girls and people here don't want to get shot and that includes me."

A student leaped up and tried to take the bullhorn from Baron. Another student told him to stop. "Let him speak," the crowd yelled.

"He says not to take it away from me," Baron said, "and I surely, surely am not going to stop anybody from making any kind of speech. I have no authority of any sort, whatever. I just want to say this: Please don't, don't let anybody start you going across this Commons again. We've had bloodshed and it's a terrible thing what happened here today. This campus will never forget it. Don't, don't, don't start chasing across this field again. I'm a faculty member. I want you to understand that the faculty is with you in regards to this stinking war."

The crowd cheered.

Red-faced, at the top of his lungs, Baron yelled, "We're with you, we're with you, we're with you and I mean it, we're with you all the way!"

After twenty minutes the students began breaking up and headed for their dormitories. A sound truck blared that the university had been closed.

Seymour Baron dripped with sweat. When the crowd broke up, Glenn Frank threw his arm around him and, helping each other, the two professors climbed Blanket Hill and disappeared over the rise.

General Canterbury sat on a jeep and watched.

Earel Neikirk, the middle-aged Elyria reporter, walked around the ROTC building. He saw a guardsman huddled in a jeep. The soldier pushed his helmet down over his face to cover his tears.

"My God," the guardsman said, "they were just lads."

Yeah, Neikirk thought, and you, you too, you're just a kid too.

General Canterbury walked across the Commons. A newsman stopped him.

"General, how can you be so calm?"

"You can't see the inside of my stomach," the general said.

Captain Don Peters watched from the hulk of the burned-out ROTC building and thought, It is just like another Kennedy has been shot.

"Even if you are directly involved in such a horror," Chaplain Simons said, "life has a weird way of going on, as if nothing happened."

By five o'clock most of the campus was deserted.

At Johnson Hall near Blanket Hill, dangling from the windows, were several bedsheets that had been tied together. One word was scrawled there, in big red letters:

WHY?

10

The Chaplains

Afterward, after he went home that night and got drunk, National Guard chaplain John Simons thought, We have found the new enemy. The kids have replaced the blacks.

He got to Kent on Monday morning at nine o'clock and as he drove off the Ohio Turnpike the toll maid had said, "I hope you guys bust some more heads today." He was wearing his fatigues and he had a cross on his helmet.

For the chaplain of the 107th Armored Cavalry Regiment, the thirteen seconds were beyond comprehension. Thirty-nine-year-old ashen-haired, crewcut John Simons is a unique mixture of a man. Intensely human, the father of four, he comes from an extensive military background. His father was an army career officer. In the early fifties he spent three years as a military policeman in Germany. As the minister of Cleveland's St. Phillip Episcopal Church on the near West Side, he has worked among poor whites for eleven years. He is devoted to helping the poor, the disenfranchised, the alienated. He is a totally candid man.

"Those silly asses from Columbus," he was to say later. "What is a brigadier general doing screwing around those troops? What are Canterbury and Del Corso doing throwing rocks? Canterbury is a general, yeah, but he is no more general material than I am."

And, "One of the effects of the shooting was that in Guard actions after Kent, you didn't find Del Corso or Canterbury on the scene."

He became a minister after an overwhelming religious experience on a Sunday afternoon in Germany in 1950 when, touring, he went to see Dachau. "I'd been in Germany about two years and I'm glad I went to see Dachau then and not right after I got over there. Had I gone right after I got there and seen the relics of that horror, I would have thought, Those inhuman Krauts! Now, though, I knew. If I were a German and Dachau would have been around, what would I have done about it? Anything? I learned something that day about suffering and evil and good that changed my life."

It was that kind of concern for society which prompted him to become embroiled in controversy in November 1969 when he, a National Guard major, sent a blistering letter to General Del Corso and threatened, publicly, to sue him. The issue was the Moratorium and the War in Vietnam. Del Corso had urged guardsmen to support the Nixon Vietnam policy and sent forms for the men to sign and send on to the White House. To John Simons, this was a political issue and, he felt, the adjutant general had no business urging anything of the kind. Besides that, he thought the Vietnam involvement "ludicrous" and felt the general's action was a low-blow tactic to stir support for a sagging policy. "The general had a captive audience," he said.

"Del Corso asked me to go down and talk to him in Columbus and I did. He said he had done this as an individual and at his own cost. Then why, I asked him, did he use Guard stationery and Guard letterheads? He said he wasn't ordering anybody to do it, he was just giving the men an opportunity to show their support. Then why, I asked, weren't the men given an opportunity to show their dislike for the war, too? Why weren't anti-war forms provided as well? The general didn't have too much to say. Our dialogue had ended."

The men like Major Simons. He speaks to them on a gritty, down-to-earth basis, using four-letter words with beautiful originality. He radiates a crusty, uninhibited warmth.

When he got to Kent that Monday morning, he went to the 107th's headquarters and found himself consoling a guardsman who would have to take his law exams soon and who said the campus activity wasn't doing anything to promote his understanding of the law. He walked by the gymnasium and lingered when he saw a group of coeds fencing. Some of the coeds were very pretty and he hadn't seen any fencing since he left Germany.

He didn't expect serious trouble. He had seen a vicious race riot between black and white GIs in Frankfurt in 1952 and he didn't think he would ever have to see that kind of senseless horror again.

Afterward he walked down the line talking to the men who had been on the firing line and found a guardsman who had been graduated from Kent two years before. "This is unbelievable," the guardsman told him. "Here I am back on my campus, here, two years later, like this, involved in . . ."

As he walked down the line, he noticed, "Everybody was hoping for a sniper, just like Nixon was hoping to find the VC Pentagon in Cambodia and neither were to find what they were looking for."

He went to see a guardsman in the hospital who had collapsed from hyperventilation. The guardsman told him, "I'm supposed to be getting out of the Guard tomorrow. Can you imagine that? Tomorrow. And this has to happen on my last day."

Major Simons went home that night at seven-thirty, sat down with an old friend from seminary days, and talked. "The more I talked, the madder I got. The madder I got, the more we drank. There was no reason for what happened. It should never have happened."

He went back to Kent at seven o'clock Tuesday morning, hoping, once again, to see the turnpike toll maid, wanting to ask, Has there been enough blood for you now? But she wasn't there.

When he got to headquarters, the guardsman manning the phone was visibly upset. "Calls are running seven to one in our favor," he told the chaplain. "A lot of callers are telling us to go ahead and kill four more kids today."

The chaplain saw the guardsman again late that afternoon. "The kid was really down by then. It really began to dawn on him that a lot of bloodthirsty Americans thought we were their hired killers."

He drove back to Cleveland to vote and as he walked out of the voting booth he was stopped by a big, beefy man who said he was enraged by the Guard. The man said he resented it as a human being, as an American citizen, and thought Del Corso should be jailed.

"I'm a Teamster," the man said, "and what the Guard did during the Teamster strike was unconstitutional." The man thought a minute, then said, "But as far as I'm concerned, you guys can sure go back to Kent and kill some more students, that's what this country needs." The man slapped the chaplain on the back.

John Simons went back to Kent on Wednesday and saw Canterbury again.

"I can't understand what's going on, John?" Canterbury said. "What's gone wrong with this country?"

Later that day Simons wrote out a statement, critical of both Del Corso and Canterbury, and the next day, when a newsman called to set up an interview, he agreed.

A half hour later Canterbury called him and said, "John, I'm not ordering you, but with all the investigations and the publicity, do you think it would be wise to talk?"

Later that day a friend in Columbus told him that when Del Corso and Canterbury found out that John Simons might speak to the press, Del Corso said:

"For Christ's sake, let's get to Simons. If he talks, it's going to be disastrous."

Disastrous? the chaplain thought. The truth?

That Sunday, talking to his parishioners, to people he loved, lived among, and seldom agreed with, he said, "On the edge of the Commons at Kent State, American troops fired into a mob of students and four students are dead. As tragic as their deaths are, that tragedy will become magnified if it becomes one of a series of events leading to the loss of our freedom. We will not lose that freedom because there is a Commie under every rocky event, as many of our elders believe. Nor will we lose that freedom because every person over thirty is a fascist, as many of the kids believe. Rather, we will give up our freedom because it is too expensive. By 'we' I mean those of us who are the so-called Middle America—middle-aged, middle-income, middle-education. We will give our freedom away to whoever promises us law and order."

A week later the chaplain was involved in a confrontation of his own, speaking to the Kiwanis Club in Parma, Ohio, a middle-class suburb where most people wear white socks and keep construction helmets on the dashboard, where George C. Wallace got his heaviest vote in the Cleveland area in 1968.

"I am sure," the chaplain began, "that some of you in this room wanted us to kill more." Later in his speech he said, "It seems to me that one of the faults of the older generation is their tendency to duck crucial issues for all generations. The younger generation is naive, life is not that simple, but the elders run from change by placing the responsibility for every rocky event on some Communist conspiracy. The older generation that wields power now has sold out to its fear of Communism. Perhaps the middle generation can gain the power and achieve the maturity which is not afraid of criticism or change. If we do not, life will go on as usual—there will be more Kents and Jacksons and Vietnams and Cambodias and with each new horror the solid middle America will become smaller and smaller until there is nothing left but two unspeaking and unspeakable extremes tearing the guts out of this great country. If you are part of those extremes, get lost. I hope that you see Kent as an avoidable tragedy, not something you secretly longed for. Four young lives were lost that day and for a while one of our four freedoms was lost. Those lives are irretrievable. That freedom of assembly is retrievable."

When the chaplain finished his speech, there were a few moments of startled silence followed by scattered polite applause. And then, John Simons noted, the Parma Kiwanians walked out, getting to the door as fast as they could.

Afterward, Bill Reinhardt stood across the no man's land of the Commons, comforting one of his men who had been on the firing line. "A time to weep," he said, "a time to mourn. This is the time."

National Guard Captain William B. Reinhardt, forty, chaplain of the 145th Infantry Brigade, would staunchly justify the shooting later, talking about Maoists, outside agitators, and the guardsmen who were hit by rocks. A conservative, known as a church traditionalist, pastor of the Lutheran Church of the Good Shepherd in a middle-class, semi-suburban area of Cleveland, he would say, "There were seven kids killed in California in campus demonstrations over a period of years and there was nothing made of it. Four kids are killed in one place and it becomes a big national issue."

Baby-faced Bill Reinhardt, who looks nowhere near his forty years, comes from a long ministerial background—his grandfather was a minister, so was his father, so is a brother. He became a minister this way: "My father died and I was living at home in New Orleans with my mother. I couldn't get along with my mother, we never got along. She sent me to Tulane and I flunked out of Tulane purposely so she couldn't send me back there again. I desperately wanted to get away from home and I did it by going into the ministry. Now, of course, I wouldn't trade my job for any profession in the world."

He became a National Guard chaplain while he was living in Savannah, Georgia. "I was asked to join the Community Chest, the Welfare League, etcetera. As a minister, it was my responsibility to shoulder a civic duty. I opted for the Guard. There was, too, to be honest, a second consideration. I'm a full-time clergyman and being a Guard chaplain is the only way I can moonlight and earn a salary supplement."

He has consistently supported military positions. "There is no greater thing one man can do for another than to give his life for his fellow man," he said. "What's wrong with serving in the armed forces of the United States? Our friends and relatives did so in the 1940s and the 1950s. They were citizen soldiers who did not want to go to war any more than we do, and yet I cannot help but say it is a privilege and responsibility to serve in the nation's armed forces, a privilege and responsibility given to us by God in this, the finest and most blessed country that has ever existed."

A chaplain's task, says Bill Reinhardt, is much like a doctor's. "You don't know how much you're needed until the patient is in pain. In eleven years as a Guard chaplain I have felt myself realizing my responsibility only three times."

One of those times was on assignment with the 145th on Wooster Street, during the Akron ghetto riot of 1968. "I stayed up for three days going up and down the line, talking to the guys, telling them, Don't shoot for Christ's sake, don't shoot, stay cool."

The second was at Camp Grayling, Michigan, during the 145th's summer camp, when a forty-eight-year-old guardsman suffered a heart attack while on a maneuver and died with his head in the chaplain's lap.

The last time was at Kent State.

Minutes before the noon rally was to begin, Bill Reinhardt was in his company's headquarters area. "I could tell something was happening because of the movement of people. Our companies had pulled out and were going toward the Commons. I started after them, but then I changed my mind and stopped. For two reasons: One, it could have been an emergency. Two, the company commanders didn't know I was going with them and I didn't want to get in the way." (Afterward he would think, Did I not go because I was afraid?)

He heard the volley and thought it a combination of shotgun fire and tear gas. "My reaction wasn't surprising to me. I've never been in battle. I don't like the Army's regimentation. I don't go out on the range. I've only fired a .45 once and even then I missed the target. I fired a machine-gun once and hit the bull's eye every time."

The chaplain and his driver drove to the administration building and stood by the burned-down ROTC building, far from the scene of the shooting.

"I did see one kid who'd been wounded. I saw a kid with a tear-gas canister sticking out of his back pocket. He was with his girl and I told a major about it and the major stopped the kid. When the kid turned around, we saw a shotgun pellet had hit him in the forehead. We wanted to give him medical help, but he wouldn't hear of it. We asked him what he was doing with the tear-gas canister and the kid said, 'I picked it up because you're littering our campus with it.' "

In those moments of shock, as he stood on the side of the Commons away from the shooting, a chaplain's cross marked on his helmet, in fatigues, a group of fifty students gathered around him.

"For the next hour and a half I talked to those kids. It was a miracle to me. One, because I'm a chaplain. Two, because I'm forty years old. Three, because I was in a military uniform."

Every now and then a student would approach him and scream an obscenity, "blaspheming in my face," and the chaplain remembered the time on Akron's Wooster Street when a woman yelled, "Hey, you mother-fuckin' preacher, how come you leadin' those troops to hell?"

"I attempted in that hour and a half," Reinhardt said, "without making judgments or pronouncements, to ask questions."

A middle-aged woman said, "Why doesn't everybody go home?"

"Yes," he said, "why don't you go home?"

"Why did you do that? Why did you kill?" a girl asked.

"Yeah, why do people kill?" he replied.

"You shouldn't kill," the girl said.

"I tried to get her to see," Reinhardt said, "that there were no simple answers to anything."

"We can't afford to judge now," he said. "We can't judge and condemn. It's not enough."

"I realized, too, that some of those kids were trying to make me feel guilty, trying to make me feel at fault. They said, the blame is there, there, there, but never here."

"These kids who are guardsmen are your brothers," he said. "They don't want to kill you. It was a complete tragedy, it was like Oedipus Rex, they had no control over what happened."

At the end of that hour and a half, the chaplain said, "I was crying and a lot of the kids were crying, too."

About an hour later he gathered the men of the 145th around him, many of whom had been on the firing line. "I talked to many of the men and they were horror-stricken. Many men cried. I tried to talk to them as their chaplain.

"I started with the idea that we're not as perfect as we would like to be. We're not as perfect as we would like others to think we are. We're not as perfect as we would like God to think we are. We are human beings and we are imperfect.

"I reminded them of God's love. While we were yet sinners, Christ died for us.

"Even though they had been called fascist pigs, I stressed that we must love those who were on the other side that afternoon, that we must, in some way, be reconciled with them."

The men kneeled down and he read them, three times, a psalm. Many men still cried.

> Relieve the troubles of my heart,
> And bring me out of my distress.
> Put an end to my affliction and my suffering
> And take away all my sins.
> Behold, my enemies are many,
> And they hate me violently.
> Preserve my life and rescue me,
> Let me not be put to shame,
> For I take refuge in you.

Since the shooting, he has spent much of his time talking to his men.

"Every now and then, that day, and in the days afterwards, one of them will come to me and say, 'Talk to so and so, he really needs it now.'

"Two guys had very serious troubles of conscience. It would be very easy for me to sit down and philosophize. I don't say, 'Don't feel guilty.' I ask questions. I try to shed light."

That afternoon the chaplain told his driver, "Don't carry a weapon. Don't you ever fire in defense of me. If you're going to be a chaplain, you can't be a killer. You can't be both."

That Sunday he told his congregation:

"Those National Guardsmen are not monsters, as many would have it, and as many have written it. They are husbands, sons, and fathers, neighbors of yours. We were called to Kent State after two days of violence there, and please don't forget that. When the local authorities can't control a situation, then the National Guard is called into duty. When we arrived, the order to the students was that there were to be no assemblies, peaceful or otherwise.

"We are all guilty because we are all sinners but the massive guilt will be, if, as Christians, we now do nothing. There must be an overwhelming move at this time to find a different way to solve our problems. There must be some way in our modern society that we can find better methods as Christians, as Americans, to solve our differences other than inhumane, animalistic behavior."

Not long afterward the chaplain was informed he had been promoted to the rank of major.

11

Allison Krause

On weekends in the spring and fall, the best of seasons in Ohio, Arthur Krause would assemble his family—his wife, Dorothy, and their two daughters, Allison Beth and Laurie—and drive out of Cleveland. Sometimes they would visit a restaurant called the Robin Hood in the college town of Kent and enjoy a meal away from home. The restaurant was on the corner of Lincoln and Main Streets and if you looked from its front window the rolling green of the Kent State campus seemed to give the afternoon a comfortable backdrop for young dreams.

"You know, Mom, I'd like to come to school here when I'm old enough," Allison used to say. She was still in junior high and there was plenty of time yet.

Arthur Krause worked a peripatetic job with Westinghouse. He was born in Youngstown and among the places he has lived are Cleveland, Ohio; Silver Spring, Maryland; and now Churchill, Pennsylvania, a neat and expensive-looking community fed by Interstate 79 as it empties east of Pittsburgh. At forty-six Arthur Krause is an intelligent and emotional man who voted for Hubert Humphrey. He has been against the war in Southeast Asia and used to agree with his daughter Allison when an infrequent discussion of the war developed in the family. He would caution, though, that withdrawal from Vietnam was not as easy as it sounded.

Allison Krause did go to Kent State University and enrolled in its Honors College. She was a tall girl, five feet eight inches, and attractive in an unusual way. "She looked European; she just had the most interesting face," said a friend. Her dark brown hair was long and her brown eyes sparkled with the curiosity and anticipation that life holds for a nineteen-year-old.

One of Allison's high-school teachers, Richard R. Jaworski, wrote:

> I recall a composition written with the hard sense of a man who had suffered, who had a tough and disciplined mind. When I matched the paper to the face, I was surprised to find a strong but feminine face. I saw a tall girl with deep black hair and very white teeth, soft full cheeks and a finely shaped nose, suggesting Mediterranean beauty with all the repose and richness of that sea.

At John F. Kennedy High, an experimental education school in Wheaton, Maryland, Allison Krause maintained a high B average. Leah Cutler was her adviser at JFK and although she has advised hundreds of students, Allison was not difficult to recall. "She did well in social sciences and the humanities," Miss Cutler said, looking up from a folder that contained the stark, academic abstract of Allison Krause. "Average I.Q. A year of typing. A year of shorthand. She used her high school well. A summer job in the tenth grade. She worked with retarded children. In 1968 she worked as a volunteer at St. Elizabeth's."

Among the papers in her file was a recommendation from the principal of JFK alerting the admissions office at Kent State that Allison was a student who could easily qualify for its Honors College. There was one final note of interest in her file—a letter to Miss Cutler explaining that she intended to transfer from Kent to Millard Fillmore College at the University of Buffalo, in Buffalo, New York, the next fall.

When word came to John F. Kennedy High School on a May afternoon that Allison Krause had been killed by a National Guard bullet, the school slowed and then stopped. There was some meditation among the students and then someone suggested that the flag at the school be flown at half-mast. No, said other students. The flag would remain. Finally, to avoid violence at the high school, one flag was lowered to half-mast for Allison and another was raised to the top of a second pole in remembrance of the Vietnam War dead. Allison's flag was later burned by a student in a second-floor trash basket.

A reporter wandering the halls at the school could not find a student who knew Allison Krause personally. She had graduated the year before and some said they remembered seeing her, but there were few who knew her well. Some students called for a strike. The opposition vehemently talked down such a gesture and the school officials allowed those who wanted to strike to leave class and those who wanted to remain to continue. Some teachers brought in outside speakers. Some of the speakers had long, shoulder-length hair and floppy felt hats on their heads. The polarization and disorganization of the school that week was coldly symbolic of the entire nation.

Allison was not the kind of girl who had many close friends. She was intensely interested in things and people, but there was a certain aloofness about her, a quality of detachment, observation, analysis. Leah Cutler remembers that she did not take a large part in any argument. She was not a joiner and she was not coquettish with boys. There was a smooth maturity about her, not the kind of maturity that is imposed by adults who seek to create an image, but a maturity that was seasoned with personal wisdom and propriety. She possessed imperfections; she was stubborn and sometimes her anger rose to heights, but she cared about people.

"She used to help on a volunteer basis at St. Elizabeth's Hospital there in Washington," said Dorothy Krause. "So few people could do it. She did it so well. As a mother, it was something I liked to see her do."

Allison would go off to St. Elizabeth's, a mental hospital, and visit with the patients. Often she would play basketball with the men. They were patients that society had long forgotten. They sat there in forlorn gloom, waiting for nothing, their eyes glazed, their lives a sea of silence. Some had not had visitors for as long as thirty years. Richard Jaworski would ask Allison to speak of her experiences at the hospital. She told the class that the inmates would let her shoot during the basketball games, leaving her undefended with the delight of her presence and interest. When a boy in class asked if it was not dangerous to work with the patients, she replied, "Love, they sense it. It calms them." The inmates were so grateful for her attention they never considered harm, she said.

One day Allison returned home unusually happy; her eyes were aglow and she could not wait to tell her mother the wonderful thing that had happened at St. Elizabeth's that day. A man had spoken to her! A man who had never spoken to anyone else for the longest time had spoken to her. It was one of the most exhilarating moments of her life. "She felt that she had personally accomplished this," Mrs. Krause said.

Her work in the hospital and her instincts began to come in conflict with another interest, art. She had often spoken of studying special education in college and going on to help the handicapped. In her senior year at JFK she began to take a greater interest in art and hoped to combine it with special education and use it as a method in working with retarded children. She drew, sculpted, occasionally painted, and experimented with other art forms.

In the spring of 1969 Allison graduated from JFK in the top quarter of her class. In many ways her simplicity caused her to go unnoticed. The school's yearbook, *The Legacy*, showed her picture among the 249 graduates that year but beside her photo not one activity was listed. She bid goodbye to her friends in the Washington area when Arthur Krause had to move his family back to Pittsburgh.

Prior to graduation Dorothy Krause and Allison went to Kent State to participate in a seminar dealing with the Honors College. There, for the first time, they learned of the trouble the campus had experienced earlier that spring.

"Somebody asked a question about the troubles on campus," Dorothy Krause recalls. "There was a panel of people in the Honors College and somebody asked them that question. I hadn't read anything about it in the Washington papers. One of the boys told everyone in the audience that he was a photographer and he had gone around with someone from one of the Ohio papers. He said he had spent the evening with the man and when he read the article the next day he didn't recognize anything in the article. He just played up what he wanted to, what was sensational. He said it was distorted and he said it was much less than what the papers made of it. That was the answer we got."

That fall Allison began her studies at Kent. She lived in a room with four other girls and school had barely begun when she met Barry Levine. Levine, also a freshman, was from Valley Stream, New

York. He is an almost frail-appearing youth with long hair, a beard, and a soft, wandering voice. They talked and Allison urged him to join the Honors College. From the start Allison Krause and Barry Levine had one of the best things going on the Kent campus. Everyone who knew them said so. Allison called her mother, who took the news of meeting Barry Levine with a shrug. She had met other boys before and nothing much had ever come of it.

"It was just beautiful," a friend said. "Barry and Allison together . . . it seemed so good . . . so good for them . . . so good for the rest of us who knew them."

"I don't know," Barry Levine began. He spoke with a reluctance that was a combination of shyness and fear. The long hair and his slight build give him a wispy, fragile appearance. His eyes dart and sparkle with suspicion and apprehension. He wore a braided leather cord for a bracelet and on this day he had a limp-brimmed bush hat. His back pack was next to him, for he was on the road, and his destination was California. Levine sat in front of the Cleveland Art Museum and talked of Allison Krause.

"Like, we were both from the East and there weren't many kids at Kent who were from the East," Levine said. "I felt comfortable with her. We had a lot in common. Allison and I always had a good time together, always."

Allison met Bonnie Henry, a freshman from Cincinnati, early in the school year and soon the two were fast friends. Bonnie remembered her first impressions of Allison as being a pretty girl who avoided makeup and who was serious about an education. It struck Bonnie that Allison had an odd, almost foreign appearance about her face. Her legs tended to be a little thick, but she was shapely. "Allison was not a knockout, but she was nice looking," said Bonnie. "I know a lot of boys who would've liked to date her."

"Allison Krause was a really cool girl," said Gene Pekarik, a friend of Bill Schroeder, who was killed that day, too. "You'd see her around campus barefoot, carrying her cat. Every time I saw her she had that cat. She really was nice."

"They were both very intelligent," said Bonnie Henry in reference to Barry and Allison. "I think the first time I saw that they really dug each other was at a Donovan concert. You could just see it in their eyes and it was wonderful. She was really a gay, happy girl. I remember the time she got up and danced at this free concert. She was dancing, waving her arms, and really being festive. Oh, she was so happy that night."

Her year at Kent State was not a time that could be written apart from the year that Barry Levine spent there. They were always together. Unequivocally, Bonnie Henry calls them the nicest couple she has ever met. She thinks she may never see the same kind of relationship again.

"Barry Levine is absolutely unique," Bonnie said. "He's so good-natured. He never gets upset. When there would be a discussion about something he would talk logically and slowly."

With his hat and long hair Barry Levine appeared as some diminutive cavalier. At Kent he had not picked a major study but tended toward sociology. He and Allison had never talked of marriage, he said. "We just never talked of it. Like, we were just going to go on and on and later maybe live together. We thought we had plenty of time to think about it."

"I know I'll be with him for a while," Allison once told Bonnie Henry. "I'll stay with him forever."

Allison moved away from her room into a single in Engleman Hall. Her father remembers her commenting on the difficulties of living four to a room. Her new room was on the third floor and Bonnie Henry used to climb the stairs almost daily to see her or to get help with studies. "She helped me on the psychology exam," Bonnie remembered. "Boy, we stayed up almost all night and if it had not been for Allison I wouldn't have passed."

Bonnie remembers the time she and Allison attended a Students for a Democratic Society rally early in the year. "She listened for a while," Bonnie said, "and then she started to argue with one of the boys. I don't remember what it was about, something about them not understanding or something. I forget. Anyway, Allison didn't think they were too cool and we left. She kept saying that while you were in school you had to learn. You had to learn and to do that you had to study. She seemed to have this motherly concern about her friends. Always encouraging, always willing to help. I wish I could be like her."

"She told us about the SDS meeting," Arthur Krause said. "She said she couldn't make sense out of what they were talking about."

"She said they wouldn't give her a straight answer," Dorothy Krause said. "They kept hemming and hawing when she asked questions."

There was one friend of Allison's, a boy who was having difficulties. "This boy kept tripping out on LSD," said a mutual friend. "He had problems with school and things. Allison kept telling him to be careful and give it up because she had worked in this mental institution and she used to tell him what it would be like if he tripped out completely. Wow! She told him so much he didn't want to hear it any more."

Allison and Barry drove to Washington with friends in November 1969 for the Vietnam Moratorium. Allison marched with a small American flag and shivered in the shadows of the government buildings that hid the sun.

On occasion she would get angry at Barry. She could rise to anger and once she told him he was lazy because he was slow to awake when she came to meet him at his dormitory. Barry's mother once told Dorothy Krause how much Allison had done for her son, lifting his grades and his spirits.

Even though she had wanted to attend Kent State for years, the school was in some ways a major disappointment as far as she was concerned. Allison began to feel tied down by the requirements. Some professors seemed unconcerned and oblivious.

"She was getting 'D's' on her papers in this honors English course," Barry said. "She went to the prof and asked why. She wanted to know how to improve. He talked with her and she worked harder but she still got 'D's.' She dropped out after the first quarter. A third of the class did too."

After the freedom and stimulus of John F. Kennedy's experimental atmosphere, Kent seemed mediocre and stiflingly regimented. She complained to her parents that there were too many requirements and that it would take an extra summer of studies in order to graduate in four years. Therefore, she proposed to transfer to a school in Buffalo where freedom and challenge beckoned.

"I was going to transfer, too," Barry said. "I know that Allison's parents thought that I had influenced her into making the change, but it was her idea in the first place. We liked the programs there. We were going to start in night school because we applied too late for day school. Jeff Miller was thinking of transferring with us." Jeff Miller died across the parking lot from Allison.

Bonnie Henry remembered that Allison was happy with the decision to go to Buffalo. "She was going to live in an apartment with some friends of Barry," she said. "Barry was going to live nearby and they were going to get some of the classes they wanted."

Allison had always been an avid reader. Dorothy Krause recalled that she shied from ordinary fiction, calling it a waste of time. She preferred books with substance. "She liked modern classics," Mrs. Krause said. At Kent the academic atmosphere and Allison's searching curiosity pushed her deeper into the world of books. She read Kafka, the present Tom Wolfe, and *Catch-22*. Slowly her reading began to widen into the current political trends. She and Barry shared a political-science class that friends say absorbed her. When the Black Panthers emerged in controversy, Allison applied her energies to satisfying her need to know. She began to believe that political repression was real and it frightened her.

"She wanted to go to Canada and open an art gallery after school," Barry said. "We wanted to go there because of the growing political repression that we felt was increasing in this country. Things like the Chicago Seven, the Panthers, and the ineffectiveness of the Moratorium all led to her feeling of the coming and existing repression."

Barry said they would watch President Nixon on television and Allison would comment that he sounded so believable but when she read commentary and took a look at all the information she reached her own conclusions. As time passed, her conclusions became more definite: the war was wrong, very wrong, and had to be ended at once.

Her concern for politics and the course the United States was following in Southeast Asia were hardly predominant in her life at Kent State. There were the usual youthful distractions. When a girl was discovered to have broken dormitory rules by possessing a cat, Allison offered to take the animal and harbored it in her room. Its name was Yossarian, after the hero of *Catch-22*. She called it "Yo-Yo" and carried it around campus with her. Allison loved to cook and when she got her single room she brought pots and pans from home.

She played records in her room; "All in All" by Melanie was one of her favorites. She listened to the Beatles, the Rolling Stones, Crosby Stills & Nash, Donovan, and the Jefferson Airplane.

Allison, Barry, and Bonnie Henry were often together. When Bonnie Henry would go to lunch with them, Allison and Barry were sure to bury their faces in a copy of the *Kent Stater*. "That was the trouble with Barry and Allison," Bonnie said. "They'd always read at lunch." Sometimes when she was particularly lonely, Bonnie remembers how nice it was to have Barry and Allison stop by for her on their way to town or when they went for a walk. When spring came, Allison expressed her desire for the woods. She had gone camping with friends when she lived in Silver Spring and had a yearning for the silence and fragrance that nature offers. "I wish there was some place where we could go and walk, some place with trees and flowers," she told Bonnie. "Some place away."

Allison was frugal with money, but she would call home instead of write. Sometimes the Krauses would get two calls a week, on her progress, or a minor obstacle, or simply on her sense of well-being. Like many students at Kent and across the country she tried marijuana, but she cautioned others on the possible effects of acid and other drugs. Her experience in the mental hospital had been indelible. She planned to work that summer at a camp for mentally retarded children in Connecticut. Things seemed to be going marvelously for Allison on her nineteenth birthday, on April 23. She was set for the summer and for Buffalo in the fall, and most important, she had Barry. Her fifteen-year-old sister, Laurie, came up to visit her on her birthday and the following Sunday Arthur and Dorothy Krause drove up. Together with Barry, they ate at the Brown Derby Restaurant a few miles from campus.

"She was so happy to get out for a meal," Dorothy Krause said. It was the last time they were to see their daughter alive.

A week after her birthday Barry and Allison crowded into the television room at Moulton Hall to hear Richard Nixon explain why American troops had been sent to Cambodia. She watched the flickering screen and commented to Barry that the President always seemed so believable. There were a few jeers in the room in response to the rationale behind the new expedition. The whole thing had a familiar, ugly ring to it. Allison laughed at Richard Nixon when he seemed to fumble with his speech and stutter in a couple of places.

Bonnie Henry remembered that a week before the shooting Allison began a discussion about the hereafter and talked about the differences between the Jewish and Christian funeral services. A few days later she turned to Bonnie and said, "You know, I've just written people I haven't sent a word to in years." Bonnie remembered it later as an ominous portent.

The final weekend of her life began on Friday evening when she, Barry, and Bonnie Henry walked from campus to town. Earlier, she wanted to send a telegram to President Nixon calling the Cambodian invasion an "outright crime." The Western Union office had been closed when they got there. The evening started as the usual Friday-night scene in Kent, the college kids down from the campus, the townies humming up and down the streets in cars loaded with horsepower, the rural folk in from outlying farms in dented and muddy pickups, and the fierce-looking motorcycle gang with their mottoes, tattoos, and chains. The bars were filled and the spring night settled like a narcotic.

"I'm getting a headache," Allison said to Barry. Already he was getting bad vibrations from the crowd. "Yeah, let's go," he said, and along with Bonnie Henry they returned to Engleman Hall. It was still early and the crowd had yet to combust into the window-breaking, stone-throwing mob that would signal the beginning of three days of violence.

The next day Barry and Allison encountered a student on the street who promised the beginning of the Revolution. Barry smiled at the youth's earnest talk and began a mild and logical argument against further turmoil. It would do no good to attack the City of Kent, he explained. Breaking windows would not solve anything and besides the iron fist of repression would follow.

Barry Levine has an almost overwhelming fear of repression. Months after the shooting he would ask if it was not true that two additional students at Kent had been killed in the shooting and the deaths covered up by the authorities.

On Saturday afternoon Allison called home and told her parents about the trouble the night before.

"I hope you weren't involved," Arthur Krause said.

"I was not involved," Allison answered. "It's bad to destroy property the way they did. I'm not sure who was responsible, the students or someone else."

"Just stay away from trouble."

"I will. The kids seem to be upset over the Cambodia thing."

"Be careful of the National Guard, Allison," Arthur Krause warned.

"Dad, there's no National Guard here."

That evening Barry and Allison decided to attend a free movie at the college administration building. To get there they had to cross the Commons, where they encountered a growing crowd of students. Curious, both Barry and Allison decided to watch what would come of it all. "I couldn't see any purpose to what they were doing," Levine said later. "We wanted to see what would happen."

Bonnie Henry joined them and together they all climbed Blanket Hill. An air of spring and expectation permeated the evening. It was a strange time. There was the excitement of the season and the excitement of the crowd. On the hill Barry and Allison began to wrestle playfully on the ground. Bonnie was thrown into the joyous melee of arms and legs. They shouted and laughed and applied make-believe holds of submission as the evening sky began to fade to black. Child-like in the twilight, they tripped and rolled over the patch of ground on which the National Guard would stand and fire less than forty-eight hours later.

Bonnie Henry remembers the way Allison always joked about going to jail. Allison would say that it was Bonnie's responsibility to bail her out and together they would laugh. That evening Allison said:

"Bonnie, remember, you have to bail me out. My checkbook is in my desk."

"No, Allison, I'll just have to send flowers," Bonnie said with a laugh. She hated herself for saying that later. To Bonnie Henry it seemed to be a terrible prophecy.

"With the crowd and all I was afraid that I'd fall down," Bonnie said. "I held on to Allison and she told me not to worry."

"We're not going to get killed," Allison Krause said.

When the crowd began its assault on the ROTC building that night, Allison and Barry were watching from a dormitory. They heard the anti-war chants, they saw the flames in the building flicker, die, and then blaze again.

"She watched the fire and objected to it all," Barry said. "She was against the war but she was against this, too. She said it was not right. This solved nothing."

On Sunday, Barry and Allison walked to town and bought a newspaper. The National Guard had moved in and together with the rest of the curious campus they looked over the troops.

"Allison told me she could understand why the Guard was on campus," Bonnie Henry said. "There had been too much destruction. She said the kids should have expected the Guard."

In the afternoon Allison had her confrontation with the Guard officer and called after him "Flowers are better than bullets." Yevgeny Yevtushenko, the Soviet poet, memorialized the line with a poem:

Don't give flowers to the state, where truth is punished
Such a state's gift in return is cynical, cruel, and
The gift in return to you, Allison Krause,
Was a bullet that rushed the flower back
As the President said about you, you are "an idler."
Everyone dead is an idler, but the fault is not his
You were a student You studied fine arts.
But there is another art—bloody, terrible.
That hangman's art too has its geniuses.
Who was Hitler?
A cubist of innovative gas chambers.
On behalf of all flowers
I condemn your creations,
Architects of lies,
Directors of murders
Rise murdered Allison Krause
Like an immortelle of the epoch
A thorny flower of protest.

Sunday night, while students were confronting the authorities at the corner of Lincoln and Main, Barry and Allison were on campus, walking on the practice football field. "We were there just walking when a rank of guardsmen came at us," Barry said. "We were kind of trapped because there is only one small entrance in the fence and the kids were going out while the Guard was firing tear gas at us. We got out of there and went to Tri Towers and they had the doors locked."

One of the dorm's resident directors had locked them. Kids were pounding on the doors, begging to be let in. The gas was painfully effective, but worse, the Guard was coming. The kids had no place to go. Allison Krause was crying and screaming for the doors to be opened. Finally, a student in the hallway brushed past the director and flung the doors open.

"You can't stay here," the director yelled. "You'll be arrested." The students poured in and sought refuge in a hallway. Their eyes were burning from the gas and many felt a deep, burning sensation in their throats.

In an hour or so the director relented. Students who were not living in the dorm could stay. Rooms would be provided. Allison was still crying when she and Barry and several other friends found the room of another friend. "We were told that the Ohio State Patrol would arrest us if we went outside," Barry said. "We didn't want to go outside. It was very bad out there. Someone said that the administration was sending a spokesman over to talk to us. We waited for a while in the lounge but no one ever came."

Outside, the Guard and the police were patrolling. At 11 p.m. the kids in the lounge watched the news on television. The situation at Kent was mentioned.

About thirty guardsmen, led by a man in an orange raincoat, marched up to Tri Towers and called the resident director out. The students could see him talking with the Guard.

In a few minutes an announcement was made over the dormitory's public-address system. The message said that the National Guardsmen outside the dorm would go away if the students kept away from their windows. Sniper fear. "You know, it's funny," said Barry Levine. "If there was a sniper there he wouldn't have had anything to shoot at until the Guard came up to warn us to stay away from the windows."

Late Sunday night Dorothy Krause was aroused from sleep by a call from Allison. The girl said there had been more trouble at the school and she called to set the family's mind at ease in case they had heard anything on the news. Otherwise, she was fine and don't worry.

On Monday, Allison cut her 11 a.m. art class so she could go to the rally. All morning there had been talk of this rally. Just before noon Allison stopped by to see Bonnie Henry. "I'll see you outside," she said to Bonnie, and before she left she turned and patted her on the head. "One good thing is that we're really good friends, Bonnie," Allison said. And then she was gone. Bonnie later saw her from a distance at the rally, but lost her in the crowd before she could join her.

At noon Barry Levine and Allison were in the crowd near Taylor Hall when the National Guard began to come across the Commons toward them. A student photographer, Howard Ruffner, took a photo that shows Allison on the crest of Blanket Hill as the Guard is moving forward. There are clouds of tear gas in the air and Allison is carrying a rag.

"She was crying," Barry said. "But not from the gas. It was emotional."

The next few minutes are enigmatic. Barry Levine will not talk about them. "I did not see Allison throw any rocks," he said. "But I wasn't watching her all the time." One student who had talked to her the previous day, Robert Roepke, told a newspaper he was only fifteen feet from her. "She was one of about a hundred kids who were throwing stones at the Guard," he said.

It seemed strange. Arthur Krause said that it was always his impression that his daughter avoided confrontation. "She would just walk away." Was it her anger? Was it stubbornness? Was it her disgust at the repression Barry spoke of? One thing is clear, at the moment of the shooting Allison Krause was not throwing rocks. She was too far from the Guard and her back was turned.

The main reason for Barry Levine's reluctance to talk of those crucial fifteen minutes was an interview he gave a reporter which resulted in a story that mentioned that he was throwing rocks at guardsmen.

Barry Levine continues his narration of the events. "It was getting ridiculous. It just couldn't keep on going like that. I grabbed Allison by the arm and I think we took a couple of steps. I'm not sure. We were not facing the Guard. I wanted to leave. I was holding her right hand when the Guard fired. We sort of jumped toward a car on our left. . . ."

Allison Krause fell on her knees and elbows. The bullets were cutting all around but Barry Levine was oblivious to them.

"Barry, I'm hit," Allison said. She fell on her back.

"Where? What?" Barry cried. ("I couldn't see anything. She looked all right.")

"Barry, I'm hit," she whispered again.

"I saw it then. I was kneeling over her and I saw that there was blood under her left armpit. She must have been hit as we were going for the car. I don't know. I looked down and she was in shock."

Barry was yelling, nearly hysterical, screaming for an ambulance.

"It's on the way, it's coming," somebody called from the crowd that was gathering.

Allison appeared to be losing her breath. Barry bent and applied mouth-to-mouth resuscitation. "I used only one breath. I could see that she was breathing. I wanted to lift her, but I knew she shouldn't be moved. I was crying. I lifted her feet and then I stroked her cheek. There was nothing to do. It took such a long time for the ambulance."

Someone brought a metal stretcher and Barry saw an ambulance on the hill. Together with several others he lifted Allison on the litter and carried her up the hill to the waiting ambulance.

"No, this one is filled, get another one," somebody yelled as they reached the top of the hill. By now there was another ambulance near Prentice Hall, to the left of Blanket Hill and above the parking lot.

"Don't worry, she'll be all right," the ambulance attendant said as they lifted Allison into the back of the vehicle. Barry got in behind the stretcher. Another casualty was already in the ambulance. It was Jeff Miller. He was already dead and Barry Levine did not look over at him; he was too busy holding the stretcher still as the ambulance moved off campus toward Robinson Memorial Hospital. His tears were falling upon Allison, who was still breathing. The ride seemed interminable. Allison's breathing became more labored.

"Jump off when we get to the emergency room," the attendant in the ambulance said as they pulled into the hospital. Allison was still breathing when Barry stepped from the back and wandered almost aimlessly into the waiting room. He was still crying.

People in the waiting room seemed to ignore what was happening. Two men sat and talked business. Bloody bodies were being hustled by them, and the walking wounded stumbled by. A little girl who had fallen from her bike cried while her mother soothed her.

Alan Canfora, who had been wounded in the wrist by a bullet, came out of the emergency room and stopped to talk to Barry Levine.

"Do you know anything about the two girls in there?" Levine asked. Barry had heard that another girl had been brought to the hospital.

"I heard some bad things," Canfora said. "Is that your chick's blood on your shoe?"

"I don't know," Barry said. He had not noticed the blood.

After what seemed an hour a nurse approached Barry and asked him who he was waiting for.

"Miss Krause."

The nurse left and returned in a few minutes. "Is that Allison Krause?"

"Yes."

"Allison was dead on arrival," the nurse said.

"She couldn't be," Barry blurted. "She couldn't be. She was still breathing . . . ." He sat back stunned. As the nurse passed him again, he called to her. "I'd like to see her in the morgue."

"You'll have to get permission. I'll check with the doctor." An hour later the nurse returned. "It'll take a couple of hours." He waited. One, two hours. He waited and the call came back from the morgue. "You can't come in."

The doctor in charge of the morgue came past and told him he was too busy to allow him to view the body. Maybe later.

Finally, a state patrolman saw him sitting there and asked him what he was waiting for?

"To go to the morgue."

"You won't be allowed," the officer said. "You can't wait around here. You'll have to leave."

"I have no place to go. The school is closed."

"You can't stay here."

A nurse overheard the conversation and offered Barry a place to stay that night. She lent him money and the next morning he flew home.

Arthur Krause was in a meeting at work when his secretary called him out to answer a telephone call from his brother, who lives in Cleveland. His brother said there had been trouble at Kent and the radio was reporting that Allison Krause had been killed. Immediately, Krause called his wife, who was working part-time. What was Allison's telephone number? There was some trouble at Kent and he wanted to get hold of her and drive up and bring her home, he told his wife. "I didn't want to tell her over the telephone," Arthur Krause said later.

Laurie Krause was on her way home when a neighbor stopped to tell her there was a message for her mother to call KDKA, a Pittsburgh radio station. Dorothy Krause called home. Then she called KDKA and heard that her daughter had been shot.

Meanwhile, one of Arthur Krause's fellow executives at Westinghouse got a call through to the Kent police who told him not to worry. "Just a couple of kids got shot in the leg."

Dorothy Krause had been frantically trying to get a call through to Robinson Memorial Hospital. The radio station said this was where Allison was taken. She still did not know her daughter was dead. Finally she called the operator, who put through an emergency call. She was switched to the hospital administrator.

"Oh yes, Mrs. Krause," he said. "Allison arrived DOA." At that moment Arthur Krause walked through the door.

A friend drove them to Kent. They took Laurie and the family dog and set out on their sorrowful journey. The car radio was broken and Arthur Krause later called it a blessing that it would not work. By 7 p.m. they arrived at Robinson Memorial. The doors were locked and they had to identify themselves to get in. "I never saw so many people with guns in my life, never," Arthur Krause said.

"The first thing we heard was that two guardsmen had been killed," he said. "We heard about snipers. We heard about a cross-fire. We heard everything but what had really happened. A young television reporter told me I was getting a snow job from these people. He was there and said there was no such thing as a sniper."

After they had been taken to the morgue and identified the body, Dorothy Krause asked a doctor if he could determine whether the bullet that killed her daughter had come from a military weapon? The doctor said the bullet had fragmented. It broke into four pieces as it tore through the left lower lung, spleen, stomach, duodenum, liver and vena cava, the major vein leading to the heart. There was a large wound where the remainder of the bullet exited. The doctor told Dorothy Krause that the fragments were being sent to the laboratory to determine where it had come from.

In a hallway at the hospital reporters gathered around Arthur Krause and in his grief he talked:

"All I know is that my daughter is dead! I'm not on anybody's side. We were so glad we had two daughters so they could stay out of Vietnam. Now she's dead. What a waste. What a horrible waste."

His sorrow turned to anger as he lashed out at the National Guard: "I'd like to know who the boys were who shot my daughter. I'd like to meet them. "They're young, immature guys who joined the National Guard to stay out of Vietnam." He shook his head and said quietly, "They've got a miserable job to do." The Krauses waited until a funeral home came for Allison's body. Then at 10 p.m. they began the long ride home.

A few weeks later the university sent them a check for $514. It was a refund of Allison's spring quarter tuition.

12

Sandy Scheuer

Youngstown, Ohio, has always been a volatile place. A few years ago they called it Bombtown, U.S.A., when feuding gangsters took to blowing apart each other's automobiles, preferably with someone behind the wheel. Television produced a special on the bombings and the U.S. Justice Department considered opening a branch office in Youngstown. Then, for a change of pace, the mob gunned down one fellow while he putted golf balls on his front lawn.

Youngstown has always been a tough, sooty steel town where industrial strikes have all the amenities of war. Well-scrubbed athletes from Ohio's small middle-class colleges can count on University of Youngstown fans to spit, curse, and threaten violence. Cut it any way you like, Youngstown is a mean, gritty place and when the National Guard shot twenty-year-old Sandy Lee Scheuer the city could hardly restrain itself.

"Heard that the Scheuer girl organized all the trouble in Ohio," the talk went in a barber shop on Market Street. "Yeah, she traveled around the state, sold drugs, and stirred up the kids. She deserved to be shot."

Even official Youngstown could not remain silent. The Youngstown City Council minutes for June 3, 1970, carried this exchange between two councilmen.

Councilman John Knapp, a poultry store owner, said:

"Today, when I left Council Caucus I go downstairs and as I leave City Hall I see guys marching up and down the street. And, it is a little perturbing when you see guys walking up and down the street and they have signs on their backs: 'Mississippi Yesterday—Georgia Yesterday—Youngstown, Tomorrow.' This to me is getting sickening, believe me. I think we should have some kind of city ordinance that this kind of demonstration should be curbed, not only in the city of Youngstown, but in the whole United States. Thank you."

Councilman Herman Starks, black, replied:

"Mr. Chairman, I think some Councilmen better go back to school to be able to read, to find out what people are doing. I don't know how familiar some individuals are, but I happen to go out into the street this afternoon after I got out of Council, and I, for one, will go on record, that I can't see what transpired in Mississippi. I cannot see what transpired in Kent State University. But, Youngstown is not Germany. And we have no 'Hitlerism'. I believe that all men are created equal and all men are subject to go before a court and trial. When there is a peaceful demonstration, I would rather see a peaceful demonstration, than rather somebody getting shot."

Councilman Knapp:

"Mr. President, I'd like to make one remark. I've heard a lot of people say that they're sorry to hear about Kent State. I have heard our chief of police being asked different questions—the four people getting killed at Kent State. I'm going to make a remark that I know isn't going to help me, but I'm going to talk from my heart and I think instead of four people getting shot down, if 4,004 got shot down a lot of this bullshit would stop. Thank you."

Sandy Lee Scheuer grew up in Boardman, a suburb of Youngstown, where people have worked most of their lives to attain the middle-class status the neighborhood represents. Her father, Martin Scheuer, whose hair is still dark at sixty-two years of age, runs a one-man health and beauty aid wholesale business. He has worked long and hard at the business and his comfortable ranch-style home testifies to some success.

For Martin Scheuer Nazism is not just an abstract idea. He can remember what it was like to be a Jew in Germany as Hitler ascended to power. He had to leave his pre-medical studies at the University of Heidelberg to flee to Palestine, where he lived for a time on a kibbutz and served as a member of the Jewish underground organization, the Hagganah.

"There was no future for a Jew in Germany, then," he said. "I was fortunate to go when I did." He speaks with a Germanic thickness, the remnants of an accent that has not been worn smooth. "I see, today, things here in this country that remind me of fascism."

Martin Scheuer came to the United States in 1935 when he was twenty-seven-years old and worked in a cannery in San Francisco making maraschino cherries. He came to Youngstown in 1937 and met his wife, Sarah, and together they raised two daughters. They were celebrating their twenty-seventh wedding anniversary the day their youngest daughter was killed in her junior year at Kent State.

"Before Sandy was killed, I supported the President," he continued. "I would read the Youngstown newspaper and believe what he said was right. I voted for Nixon, but all that has changed since her death. Yes, I have changed. Today I am against American presence any place in the world."

Around his neck, tied with a piece of rawhide, Martin Scheuer wears a peace symbol. He wears it to work in the morning. He wears it when he goes shopping. He is not afraid to wear it in the neighborhood although people look at him with curious hostility and often comment about the medallion. It was given to him as a Father's Day gift by his son-in-law in Pittsburgh and he wears it as a sign of his grief. One neighbor asked if he was a "hippie." Another asked if he intended to lead a revolution.

"People look at it and think I am some enemy of the U.S.," he said. "I used to think the war was all right, you know, to keep the Red Chinese in check. Now, I see no reason for it at all. We should get our soldiers out immediately. It would be better for the U.S., better for the world."

Martin Scheuer looked out over his lawn and recalled how he never questioned things the government did, until Sandy was killed. "Those bullets, they did not know three of the four killed were Jewish. Sandy had more in common with Bill Schroeder than with the other two. I wanted to talk with Mrs. Schroeder but when I call she does not seem to want to talk with me. I don't know why."

The Youngstown *Vindicator*, the town's only newspaper, did not report Councilman Knapp's statement, but Sarah Scheuer eventually found out about it and went to see the man at his poultry store.

Mr. Knapp was not there, but a clerk told Mrs. Scheuer that all the students should have been killed.

"Not only that," the clerk said. "A lady who was just in here told me your daughter was arrested three times at Kent."

"Listen, whatever you wish on my daughter I wish back on your children," Sarah Scheuer replied with ache and disgust. "I told him that. The grief in my chest is like a rock. What is the matter with people? I don't understand."

On the urging of the Scheuers, Kent State president Robert I. White wrote a letter to the *Vindicator* explaining that Sandy had never been arrested and indeed was a fine student. It said:

> During the past few days, I have been chagrined and deeply saddened to learn that there have been irresponsible statements concerning Miss Sandra Scheuer, the Kent State University junior from Youngstown who was killed on May 4. These rumors allege that the late Miss Scheuer had an arrest record of some kind.
>
> For those who might give credence to these reports, not published to my knowledge, I would like to state that Miss Scheuer never was abused or cited by KSU security officers, the Kent city police, or any other law enforcement officers, according to local and state agencies.
>
> I have said this before, but it appears worth repeating. The public, or at least some segments of it, too quickly and too thoughtlessly draws the same cloak over millions of genuinely distressed college students who hold lofty goals and impeccable integrity, as it does over an infinitely smaller number of committed "burners" or "out-and-out destroyers."

Martin Scheuer wished that White had used plainer language. "Some of the words are difficult for people here to understand," he said.

Sandy Scheuer had a multitude of friends on the Kent campus. If you walked with her to class as her friend Sharon Swanson did every morning that spring, you could see she knew hundreds of people. Some of her friends were straight, their hair short, their clothes conventional. Others were freaks with shoulder-length hair and grass bags dangling from their belts. She could cross the flat of the Commons at any given moment and throw friendly waves and "hellos" almost continually.

"Fred, that beard is really looking good," she would call to a long-haired youth who was forced to smile at her bounding exuberance. "You better watch it, though, one of these days you might step on it."

"Sandy had no enemies," said Sharon Swanson, who, like Sandy, was a junior majoring in speech. It was because the school had such a good speech department that Sandy had gone to Kent State University. Her father had relatives in California and had suggested she go to Stanford, but Kent State was just up the Ohio Turnpike. It was close enough, but yet far enough. She could telephone home each Friday just to say hello and that everything was going fine. Most weeks Martin and Sarah Scheuer would talk with her two or three times. It was easier to phone than write.

"I was always afraid that something would happen to Sandy," Mr. Scheuer said. "I did not give her a car when she asked because of the danger of driving. Every time she used the family car I worried. When she went to Florida during her last Christmas vacation, I gave her money to fly down instead of driving with the girls. I was afraid of something. A father worries."

Sandy worried, too, but not enough for most people to see it. Even though her grades were B-plus she would complain that she was not good enough. If something went wrong in class, she would throw up her hands and exclaim, "See, I'm never going to make it."

"She always had nice things to say to people," said Sharon Swanson. "It kind of, like, made their day, you know. She always treated people like she wanted to be treated."

Occasionally, friends would find her in a depressed mood, but she would wave it off with a shrug and a joke. One of her fears was that she would be an old maid. Sometimes she would complain that she did not have enough dates.

"I think it bothered her that her parents wanted her to meet and marry a Jewish boy," Sharon said. "I mean, I think she had some kind of a hang-up there. Sometimes she talked about going to a school where there were more Jewish boys."

Bruce Burkland and Sandy Scheuer had been good friends ever since they were in high school together. When she went to Kent, he went to Ohio University to major in psychology. They made an agreement that they would date around and then see what happened after four years of college.

When a fraternity brother found Burkland in the Ohio University library the night of the shooting and told him of Sandy's death, Burkland collapsed from shock. He, too, felt anguished over the rumors that spread through Youngstown. "Some people in my church have said Sandy deserved to die," he remarked bitterly.

The last time he talked to Sandy she was frightened. He was home for his semester break when she called him one night from the house she shared in Kent with several other girls. It was late and there were strange noises in the house and Sandy was alone.

"She heard someone at the door and called," Bruce said. "She was really scared for a while, but it turned out to be one of her roommates. Sandy was afraid of things like that. She told me she was afraid of demonstrating crowds, too."

Whenever she and Bruce would get together they would see a movie, bowl, or eat Chinese food. She loved Chinese food and especially liked a restaurant in Youngstown called the Lychee Tree. The afternoon she died an anniversary card she had sent to her parents arrived and Sarah Scheuer read: "Hope you have honorable good time and go to somewhere good to eat like Lychee Tree.—Ah So, Honorable Love."

Being an animated and happy girl, Sandy liked to clown with a Chinese accent and mimic what was known around the Scheuer household as the "diaper walk."

"Stop that, Sandy," Martin Scheuer would scold. "That is not lady-like." But every time he had his back to her she would begin her waddling walk, drawing laughter from those about her and causing her father to shake his head.

Sometimes when Bruce Burkland was eating dinner at the Scheuer home, Sandy would suddenly turn to her mother and announce:

"Mom, Bruce just said that your dinner is terrible." She was always a source of laughter around the dining table.

They have color pictures of Sandy with her thick, black hair in magnificent disarray and Sarah Scheuer recalled how much time her daughter used to spend trying to get the curls out of it. Sandy would wear a wig or fall from time to time, but most recently she let her hair grow to a medium length. Her smooth, round face seemed more oval than it was because she moved it so much talking and laughing and smiling. She was taller than average, about five feet five, and liked to swim, play tennis, and ride her old bike to class. When she was a freshman, Sandy met several boys who would later become active in SDS. Once she brought one of the boys home for a weekend.

"We used to talk about the SDS," said Bruce. "She told me it was really getting big on campus, but later she said she didn't talk to some of the boys who had been her friends because she objected to what they were trying to do."

Sharon Swanson remembers how hard Sandy worked to get one boy's mind off the revolution. She made candles and gave him silly little gifts.

"We knew what was going on around us," said Sharon. "Sandy never discussed it much. She liked to talk girl stuff. She had one friend who was really for the revolution. He didn't seem to have much time for her, but she really liked him and tried to interest him in other things."

"We never talked about the war," said Mrs. Scheuer. "Oh, Sandy would say that she felt sorry about the boys who had to go to war, but she never talked much about it."

"Sometimes I would complain about all these long-hair hippies," said Martin Scheuer. "Sandy would tell me that they were wonderful people underneath their beards. She was right. They are a better generation than mine."

"She was completely non-violent," said Jerry Persky, a friend from Cleveland who cut his shoulder-length hair the day after the shooting. He dated Sandy for a while at Kent. "She was going through changes and sometimes talked about quitting school because she didn't think she was doing well."

Despite the distractions of college life, Sandy remained dedicated to her schoolwork. Although she knew radical students, she did not deviate from the course she had set for herself. Her main interest was education and she would not allow her scholarship to suffer. She had grown up in a family that was work-oriented, a family that was deeply religious, a family that minded its own business. These values had been instilled within her and even the magnetic draw of the times could not change them. If she had had less drive, if she had relaxed and swayed with the tremors, she would not have died. Sandy would have been in Atlantic City with her roommate who was looking for a summer job. The problem was that Monday classes had to be cut in order to make the trip and Sandy was unwilling to make the sacrifice. She and Sharon Swanson had to begin work that week on a paper on organic speech disorders that would examine the effects of cerebral palsy on speech. They had already collected the books from the library.

"Sandy had always wanted to help old people, especially those who were paralyzed and had difficulty talking," said Sarah Scheuer.

The speech department at Kent assigned Sandy a student who suffered from a speech impediment. She told Sharon Swanson and her mother how handsome the boy was and what a wonderful person he was. Later, the boy would see Sandy just moments before she was to die, waving him a cheery greeting.

"Sandy used to say she wouldn't have the heart to charge people ten dollars or fifteen dollars an hour for speech therapy," Mrs. Scheuer said. "She studied to be in a position to help people and this was her first concern."

"Well, she was not being realistic about things," said Martin Scheuer. "Sandy had a lot of idealism. She would have to learn about money."

Sandy was modest in most things, certainly money matters. Bruce Burkland trailed behind her for hours in the shopping plaza near her home while she searched for bargains. At school she dropped out of a sorority because of the expense, and a few days before she was killed she went to a clinic with Sharon Swanson to sell blood.

"If you came in before 11 a.m. they would give you eleven dollars for blood," Sharon said. "After that it was only ten dollars. Sandy told me about it; she had been there before. They didn't take my blood that day, I guess I'm a little anemic. But Sandy sold her blood and she came out with a bandage over the needle mark on her arm. After the shooting I heard there were some stories about her taking narcotics and it wasn't true. I guess maybe it was because they saw the needle mark on her arm."

Friends remembered that Sandy had smoked a little pot from time to time, but at Kent State nearly everybody tried that. The drug scene on the campus was quite active and all one had to do to find drugs was go to town and have the nerve to buy a bag of grass or some acid. It was there and it was not particularly expensive.

"Sandy didn't use dope that much," said a friend. "I remember her trying it but she did not want to become dependent on it. Hell, Sandy never smoked regular cigarettes and she didn't like to drink, not even a beer."

"Sandy didn't dig the scene downtown at all," said Sharon.

Bruce Burkland remembered once when Sandy spit out beer when she tried it, calling it awful stuff. But she never condemned people for drinking or taking drugs or doing what they thought politically right.

"You know, Sandy always worried that people didn't like her," said Sharon Swanson. "Her confidence would waver over the slightest thing. She did so much to help people, like, I would go over to her place to study because Sandy really knew her stuff. In the fall, I broke my back and when I got back to school she insisted on carrying my books and holding my arm when we crossed the street."

Sandy's room at the house was neat and had the usual curiosities that college students collect. Martin Scheuer had given his daughter an inflatable advertising prop from his business, a giant tube of shaving cream. There was a wine bottle brought from France when Mr. and Mrs. Scheuer went abroad the year before and a French soda pop bottle with a funny name. Sandy prized the Omega watch her father had brought her from Europe.

Among her modest collection of records were things from the Beatles. Bruce recalled that she sang along with the words when they saw *Oliver* together. "Ebb Tide" was her favorite song and "Moon River" ranked next.

"The last time we were in New York I gave her liberty to see *Hair*," said Martin Scheuer. "I thought that was very generous of me."

There was probably very little of anything that Sandy Scheuer did that would hurt or offend anyone. Her empathy and sensitivity linked with her streak of insecurity enabled her to understand human feelings. Now and then a professor would stop his lecture and cast an admonishing eye her way, for she loved to talk even in class. She also talked in movies, and Bruce Burkland lost track of the plot of a movie one New Year's Eve because of her chatter.

"She didn't understand the plot of the movie and I tried to explain it to her, but by the time I was finished I got confused myself," he said. "Sometimes she didn't catch on to things like that."

"That was the only thing you could get mad at Sandy for, talking," said another friend. "Sometimes she just bugged you —like, if you were feeling down or something. But you would find yourself getting mad at yourself because you mentioned anything to her about it. She was that good."

Among the hundreds of condolence notes that arrived at the Scheuer home were messages from students who wrote things like "I'm a little better for having known Sandy," or "She had a quiet grace that penetrated even the hardest core and caused a smile from everyone she encountered."

One faculty member wrote to the Youngstown *Vindicator* to help portray Sandy to the disbelievers of that city.

Sandy was our student and we worked very closely with her for the past two years. We supervised her work with children and adults undergoing speech therapy, and we talked almost every day at the speech and hearing clinic.

We found her to be a pleasant, friendly, well-groomed, polite, cheerful young lady. Academically, she was B plus and A in most of her classes. If she was a radical in her political beliefs it certainly was not shown in the clinic or her speech. In fact, her chosen profession was that of helping others, within the existing system, by preparing herself to be the best speech and hearing therapist she could be. We, her instructors, miss Sandy, and the children and adults who would have been helped by Sandy will miss her too.

The Saturday before the shooting Sarah Scheuer brought Sandy's summer clothes up to Kent State. When Mrs. Scheuer reached the house on East Summit Street, she found that her daughter had not heard a word about the trouble that had raged through town the night before. Sandy had been studying. One of her roommates had taken the transistor radio, and the television set did not work.

"If there's trouble on Monday, Sandy, I don't want you going to class," her mother said. Later, Sandy's roommates said there was a test Monday, and Sandy was not going to miss it just because of the trouble.

On Sunday, Jerry Persky saw Sandy sitting and talking about the trouble. The National Guard had been called in and there was an ominous feeling on campus.

"She said something about knowing that this was going to happen here," Persky said.

Another friend, Marty Levick, snapped a photo of Sandy on Sunday. It was a picture of her and the dog the girls at the house had adopted and called "Heavy" because it was well along in pregnancy. *Life* ran the picture the next week in its coverage of the shooting. Levick later sent the Scheuers a copy of the picture with a notation that he and Sandy had had so many laughs together that it seemed impossible she could be gone.

On Monday morning Sharon Swanson could tell that something was bothering Sandy. She seemed pensive and depressed as they met for their eight-thirty class, a two-hour course in childhood art. She was wearing a red knit jersey, blue-jean bell bottoms, and Charlie Brown shoes that morning-

"Sandy didn't say much," Sharon recalled. "She seemed preoccupied and worried about what was taking place on the campus. Her friend, the one that was always for the revolution, I think she was concerned about him because she had not heard from him."

Reports the night before said that sixty-nine persons had been arrested and ten injured in the disturbances. The campus was alive with stories of the bayoneting and violence that had taken place after the National Guard had moved to clear the intersection at Lincoln and Main Streets.

"We peeled and ate an orange in the art class," Sharon said. "We did it behind the teacher's back. But, like, she wasn't really herself that morning."

Sharon and Sandy had another class together at 1:30 p.m.

At 11:30 a.m. Ellis Berns, a friend who lived around the corner, saw Sandy and asked if she was going to the rally on the Commons.

"Yeah, I'll probably be up," she said. Her mood was still unusual and diffident.

Sharon Swanson watched the National Guard make their maneuver on the practice football field. She saw them point their weapons menacingly at student demonstrators who hurled stones at them. The guardsmen began to retreat and Sharon watched from the terrace next to Taylor Hall which is opposite Blanket Hill.

She had been in Taylor Hall trying to get away from the drifting tear gas, but stepped outside and saw Sandy coming from the direction of the Commons. Sandy was walking with a friend, a fellow Sharon did not recognize.

"Hey, Sandy," she called. "Are you going to class?"

"Yeah," Sandy shouted.

John A. Darnell, a student and friend from high school, was on the terrace in front of Taylor Hall. He carried a camera and in a few moments would take a picture that *Life* would spread over two pages. It showed the entire Guard contingent on Blanket Hill in the act of firing.

"Hi," he yelled to Sandy, who waved back.

The Guard had just reached the top of the hill and seemed to be turning.

"I wheeled to take some more pictures of the soldiers," Darnell said. "I didn't see her after that."

"There were shots," Sharon Swanson said. "And suddenly everyone was running. It was panic. My heart was wild. I could see Sandy about ten feet in front of me and she was running toward the parking lot. I ran for the cars and hid behind a red sports car parked in the first row. Sandy seemed to be running for the second row of cars. She was heading for the line right in front of me."

There were screams and the gunfire cracked in an extended volley as Sharon reached her cover, a red MG that offered only meager protection from the high-powered .30-caliber rifles that were being fired down on the parking lot. Breathing heavily from exertion and fright, Sharon had just crouched behind the car when a bullet tore through its windshield, six inches above her head. The firing stopped and students all around her rose in an incredible wail of anguish, a moan that seemed to rise and shake the spirits.

Just before the Guard had turned, Ellis Berns had caught up to Sandy Scheuer, who was trying to protect her nose and mouth from the tear gas with a Kleenex. Berns tore up a rag he was carrying and offered it to her. They were talking when Berns grabbed her. The students were running. He tried to push her to the ground behind a car. The volley exploded.

"I remember there was muscle tension, then all of a sudden it relaxed," Berns said. He had his arm across Sandy's back and they fell to the ground. Seconds ticked by and the air was aflutter with passing bullets.

"Sandy, Sandy," Berns said. The firing had ceased and Berns desperately wanted to get behind better cover. He thought there was going to be more shooting. "Sandy!"

Ben Parsons, a drama student, had been watching the demonstration with a yellow towel over his face to fend off the gas. He ran over with the towel and tried to stop the bleeding in Sandy's neck. People were running by, their panic fanned by fear of another volley. Several nearly stepped on the dying girl as she was being lifted into the arms of Parsons and the others who bent to help her.

Sharon Swanson stood up slowly and looked around. Some of the kids were not getting up. Near the next row of cars she could see a group of boys lifting a girl. The Charlie Brown shoes! She saw the Charlie Brown shoes on limp feet and knew it was Sandy Scheuer.

"I ran over," she said. "I could see her face. Her mouth was open and her eyes were open. Her head was tilted back. I could see a lot of blood on her face and neck. I thought that she was only wounded. How could Sandy die?"

"We carried her to the grass," Parsons said. "We couldn't carry her any farther. She didn't look like she could take any more." He propped his coat beneath her head and turned her head so she could breath better. Ellis Berns tried to give her mouth-to-mouth resuscitation, but she was convulsing.

Sharon Swanson had run into Taylor Hall to call an ambulance. The hallway was a chamber of noise. There were screams of anger and cries from the wounded. Some shouted obscenities and swore oaths of death to the "Pigs." Others just wrung their hands and demanded an explanation. From a window Sharon could see Sandy Scheuer being lifted into an ambulance.

Outside, Ben Parsons knew she was dying. Her face was white and he thought her heart was going. The bullet had struck her on the left side of the neck, exploding her larynx, an organ she had studied often in speech classes. The round passed through, severing an artery or vein that left blood spurting from the wound. Ben Parsons picked up his jacket and found it soaked with Sandy's blood. He hung the jacket on a fence near the Student Union in full view of a rank of tense guardsmen.

In Youngstown a man told Martin Scheuer that there was trouble at Kent State and four students had been killed. Sarah Scheuer was painting the house when she heard the same thing on the radio. Immediately, she tried to call the house on East Summit in Kent. She could not get through. The telephone lines were jammed. It was not until 4 p.m. that she could get the phone to ring in Kent. She was told that Sandy might have been hurt and carried no identification. Her wallet was still in her room. Mrs. Scheuer called the hospital.

"Do you have a girl who has been hurt and has no identification?" She asked an administrator. "She's wearing a red shirt and blue jeans."

"I don't think so," came the reply. "But there is an unidentified girl here."

Together, the Scheuers drove at nearly a hundred miles an hour up the Ohio Turnpike toward Kent, wondering, hoping, praying, and expecting the worst. They were afraid to turn the radio on. When they arrived at Robinson Memorial Hospital in Ravenna and made their apprehensive inquiry, a policeman stepped forward and, not realizing they had not been informed, quietly asked:

"Do you want to identify the body now?"

"Does she have a gold ring with a blue stone?" Sarah Scheuer asked.

The man went into the morgue and returned. Yes, he was afraid the girl had a blue ring. Martin and Sarah Scheuer waited while the bodies of the other three were removed from the morgue and then they were asked to step in. Their daughter was there.

Sharon Swanson did not learn that her friend had died until nightfall.

The telegrams and letters began to come into the Scheuers' home. Mrs. Martin Luther King sent a wire that said in part: "Your America has only herself to blame, because for centuries she has festered and nurtured a climate of violence that has now become ingrained in her everyday fabric." Martin Scheuer blinked and reread Mrs. King's wire. It angered him and he almost sent back a letter until he thought about it. The word "Your" had been pasted over the original copy and he thought that perhaps Western Union had made a mistake. Later, when he read the telegram that Allison Krause's parents received from Mrs. King, he felt sure there was a mistake.

Mr. Nixon sent a letter, and when reporters asked for the contents, Scheuer refused to reveal them.

In Kent the landlord of the house where Sandy lived with the others girls was worried about the remainder of the rent the Scheuer girl owed. He padlocked the girls' bikes to make sure they would pay. Sandy's was among them.

After the funeral the talk started in Youngstown. A man who remembered Sandy as a waitress in a restaurant near the Turnpike one summer nearly came to blows in a barber shop with a fellow who stoked another vicious rumor. When a suburban newspaper wrote a favorable article about the dead girl, it lost subscribers.

Martin Scheuer complained that the mayor of Youngstown had not bothered to send a note of sorrow.

Bruce Burkland wrote to the *Vindicator* in the hope of stilling the slanderous voices.

The funeral is over, I have cried until I can cry no more, but the pain and sorrow are still wrapped inside of me because of the fruitless death of the girl I loved. I keep asking myself why, but that question can never be answered. Sandy will never die in my heart and I will go on living the way she would want me to, but, God knows, I don't want the world to think she was a reactionary student and incited the riots because Sandy wasn't this type of person and would never do such a thing. She felt the same way about the world situation as most of us do today and couldn't understand why there couldn't be happiness and joy throughout the world.

The wound has set in and will in time heal, but the scar that came from that wound will always remain. Those of us who knew Sandy will treasure the times we had with her and those who did not know her, please do not correlate her name with dissent and riot because this was not Sandy. Pray for Sandy's parents and loved ones that they may have strength at this time, but also pray to God that such a senseless and shocking event will never happen again. Please, for Sandy's sake!

13

William Schroeder

The first day he drove down to Kent State, in the fall, as he backed his shiny new Fiat off the driveway, he turned to a friend and said, "You know, I'm not gonna be around that long. I'll go fast and sudden, like Hemingway." And he laughed. He enjoyed life and believed in opening his sensibilities to it: To see, to hear, to feel, to explore, to experience, to discover, to learn, to understand—everything. He had icy blue eyes and a sharply-cut cinematic profile and a look which his ROTC advisor had seen many times before in Vietnam. "He looked like a guy who was gonna die."

At nineteen Bill Schroeder was an existential person; the sum of his contradictions; the victim of an odyssey of self-realization; a mature teen-ager; a man-child. He was not, as they were to describe him, "an all-American boy." "He would have fondled a baby rattlesnake until it bit him," his ROTC advisor said. He was full of love: he loved America, he knew its military history, and he hated war. He had a deep compassion for the poor, the infirm, the retarded, and the black. He did not like learning different ways to kill. He was self-contained, aloof, cool. He was proud, he told his friends, of his daydreams. He was big and muscular and he spoke very quietly and very gently. The last roll of undeveloped film in his camera showed the industrial smoke-clouds of pollution. He admired General Custer, empathized with Joseph Heller's hero Yossarian from *Catch-22*, admired Mick Jagger, the leader of the Rolling Stones. When they undressed him at the morgue, they took: a pair of orange corduroy bell-bottom pants, a black-and-red-striped T-shirt, a pair of cowboy boots, a belt scrawled with peace symbols, and a denim jacket his mother had patched and his grandfather had worn. He owned one suit which he wore three times. "Twice for a dance," his mother said, "once to get buried in."

He lived in an old red-shingled house with four housemates across the street from the railroad tracks, five blocks from campus, at 603 Franklin Street. The night before he died, he went to bed at ten o'clock. He slept on the lower bunk. His roommate, Lou Cusella, a member of the Kent State University debating team, sat at his desk looking through some papers. Shortly before midnight a pickup truck screeched to a stop outside. Bill's reflexes were sharp. Before Lou realized what had happened, Bill pounced awake and shut the light off. The two stood in the dark room and watched. A young man got out of the truck, went to its back, and picked up a bottle. He lighted the rag on the bottle and threw it into the City of Kent's lumber yard. They waited. Nothing happened.

"Now," Bill Schroeder said, "now we've seen it for ourselves."

They both went to bed and couldn't sleep. Lying awake, they listened as helicopters with bright spotlights swept over the house at rooftop level every fifteen minutes. After a while, just before Lou fell asleep, Bill Schroeder said:

"Christ, Looie, I don't like all this. The cops, the trouble, the Guard, God, it scares me. It really scares me." It was the first and last time Lou ever heard Bill refer to fear, and for the first time that night, he remembered later, he was scared too.

It was not Bill Schroeder's style to be afraid. There were times when his mother talked to him about sitting down and making out some insurance forms. He did not tell her, the way he told Lou Cusella, about the Hemingway death. He didn't have time to bother with the forms, he told his mother. He told her not to worry. "Nothing's going to happen to me," he said, "I'll just go rolling along."

He had, in most ways, an ordinary childhood. One of three children, Bill had his father Lou's blue eyes and his mother's awareness. Louis Schroeder, fifty-four, is a superintendent at Fruehauf, Inc., at their Avon Lake, Ohio, trucking terminal. His mother, like his father, came from a German background —she from Cincinnati, he from Detroit. Bill grew up in Lorain, Ohio, an eroded steel town on the shores of Lake Erie usually overcast by steel-plant waste. It is a town filled with Appalachians, Puerto Ricans, Mexicans, and Hungarians, who came to Lorain as cheap labor for the steel companies.

Bill Schroeder never really saw that kind of life, though he may have rubbed shoulders with it in high school. The places in Lorain where Louis Schroeder raised his family were always neat, grassy, middle-class areas where it was always proper, as Bill insisted, to take your shoes off before you came in so the carpet wouldn't get soiled. He learned, too, to take care of himself and his possessions according to the rules of that middle-class ethic. He brushed his teeth four and five times a day. He kept his room meticulously clean. He worked at tire companies, at gas stations, at hamburger stands, and on an aluminum-company assembly line.

In all his boyhood pictures he is smiling: Bill on a big boat in Lake Erie; Bill swinging a baseball bat; Bill with his favorite rocks. He loved rocks and nature. He was an Eagle Scout and enjoyed sleeping out at night on the grass and staring at the stars.

He enrolled at Lorain High School in 1964. In his freshman year, he was too small to make the basketball team, but growing. He loved sports and spent long hours behind the house and at nearby playgrounds stuffing basketballs into hoops. In his freshman year, he played the trumpet in the school band. He was obviously intelligent. He got good grades without working too hard and, from a very early age, he impressed adults with his poise.

He was turning into a take-charge kind of guy. Once, at a nearby playground, when a friend broke his arm on a trampoline, he took command. He called the boy's parents. He called the ambulance. He went to the emergency room and stayed with the boy until his parents got there.

By the time he was a junior, he had grown big enough to play junior varsity basketball for the Lorain High School Steelers. He was also the captain of his cross-country team. He started his first varsity game as a senior and got nine points. In the season's big game he led the team in rebounding and sparked it to a win. He was known as a "workhorse." He was proud of the caption in a local paper. The picture showed Schroeder going up for a rebound. It said: "Extra effort as usual." It was not a good idea, many opponents discovered on the floor, to drive by Schroeder.

He played aggressively and worked at his game relentlessly. He worked out with angle-weights on blacktop courts, and tore his knees up. From then on, his knees hurt much of the time, but he never complained. He began to date and found he was popular. He resented parental discipline, but he obeyed. Sometimes, when his mother waited up for him after a late date, he was resentful. "Why do you have to worry all the time?" he'd say. "Nothing's going to happen."

He was an A student, a member of the National Honor Society. He began to read, devouring everything he could get his hands on. He was fascinated by the fate that befell George Custer, and his intellectual curiosity gradually moved from the Little Big Horn to the Civil War, to World War I, and to World War II. His father had seen service in World War II in France and England. Bill didn't know exactly what he wanted to do with his life when he graduated from Lorain High in 1968, but he knew he wanted to learn everything he could and go to college. He knew, too, that he wanted to do it by himself, independently, alone. He heard of the ROTC scholarships being offered and, at the age of seventeen, made a decision committing himself for the next ten years. He was one of 990 boys—of 15,000 applicants—to get the ROTC scholarship.

His goals were vague, but he talked about money, about having a nice home, nice things. His two big interests were rocks and people, so he thought he'd major in geology and take psychology as a minor. And he wanted, too, like most boys his age, to get away from the hours, the surroundings, and the people at home. When he would go out at night with the guys, to the places in Lorain where they serve liquor to boys like Bill Schroeder without looking too closely at the birthdates, he would notice his parents did not stop him, but of course he felt guilty. He never drove at those times and he never drank when he went out on a date.

When he graduated from high school, he wanted to hitchhike to Florida. "We'd heard about all those Southern sheriffs in those little towns," his mother said, "we didn't permit it. He was out to feel his oats anyway." But they told him he could drive—he could take the family car, an old Corvair, and, in addition, he would have to take his brother, Rudy. Bill was eighteen; Rudy fifteen. He wasn't too happy about taking his brother. The only other condition was that they had to stay with their aunt in Bradenton, Florida. Bill tried to maneuver out of it, but when it didn't work, he agreed. They stayed for a month.

While there, in the form of a letter, he sent a girlfriend a piece of fiction he had written. It was a put-on, done with a sardonic touch. It came in the form of a dying man's letter which had been confiscated by the administrators of an insane asylum:

> here i lay, my body ravaged by a rare tropical disease contracted when i entered the everglades to rescue a little tourist girl got lost and was about to be devoured by ferocious crocodiles when i burst upon the scene in the nick of time to save the innocent child from the jaws of death itself, it is with my last breath of life that i write to you, my sole comfort, of the thoughts racing through my delirious brain, looking back upon my tempestuous past i see with a lucidity and clearness quite contrary to my present state of near death all the mistakes i have made in my rocky voyage through life, i have led a life of sin and shame which has begotten me this tragic and abrupt end. in all of the evil deeds which cover my mind like the eternal cloud of pestilence i see one glimmering light which has been totally pure and clean, unlike my defiled self, it seems this gleam of hopeful glow has appeared too late to save my decadent soul from the all consuming fires of death, as i walk down the pathways of death i have but one wish, that before i go i might have one last glimpse of this beam of light, if the fates were somehow to save me from my impending doom, i would hurry to the place my shaft of flowing hope most frequents and wait for its return, as i prepare to meet my unexpected but not undeserved end my dying wish is that this star of peace and serenity shall be seen unto me one last time.

THE PATIENT HAS BEEN RETURNED TO HIS CELL. WE ARE SORRY YOU HAD TO FIND OUT THIS WAY. HIS ILLUSIONS COME MORE OFTEN NOW BUT WE HAVEN'T LOST HOPE. IF YOU FEEL YOU MAY BE OF ANY HELP IN CURING HIM, FEEL FREE TO DROP BY. YOU HAVE MY SYMPATHY.

DR. I. X. ZARKOV,

RESIDENT DOCTOR, STATE REMEDIAL HOSPITAL

The place he picked for his rocks and geology that fall was far away—in Golden, Colorado, not far from Denver, in the rugged mountain country he'd always loved, the Colorado School of Mining. Not long after he got there, his ROTC advisor showed him an inter-departmental memorandum. The memorandum said that next year geology would no longer be offered as a major, and that all geology majors would have to major in geological engineering. It went on to say there would only be one introductory psychology course offered. He knew he would have to leave.

He began corresponding with the ROTC advisor at Kent State and with an ROTC advisor at Ohio State. He took all the philosophy and psychology courses he could in that one year and planned to transfer at the end of the school year. His interest in people and their motivations grew. His mind opened further. Why did people do certain things? Why did they react differently under different circumstances? What part did environment and background play in their actions? He found people were suddenly more interesting to him than rocks and he began to read as much psychology as he could get his hands on.

He was enjoying his ROTC program at Colorado. He was part of a counter-insurgency engineering unit and spent most of his ROTC time scaling mountains and doing outdoor survival testing. His letters home were filled with good humor. The return address was sometimes: SCHROEDER'S WILD WEST SHOW, PINCH PENNY, U.S.A. On especially happy days, the return address would be a picture of a smile. He never called his parents for money and began sending his mother ten dollars a month. He sent little gifts home: wooden pencil holders for his mother and beer mugs for his father. The pictures he sent home showed him against a backdrop of mountains wearing a cowboy hat, his grandfather's denim jacket, cowboy boots, and Levis. He had a problem with the boots and Levis, he explained. The boots wouldn't fit into the tight Levis. He told his mother one day happily that he had solved the tuck-the-boots-in problem: bell bottoms.

He wore his hair medium-length and, at one time, he and four others shaved their heads totally bald. It was a protest of sorts— some of the rock musicians who'd come in from Denver would be kidnapped by townies after the show and have their heads shaven.

When he shaved his head, Bill Shroeder considered it classic one-up-smanship. Earlier that year he had written his mother to send him his favorite pair of scissors so he could cut his own hair and avoid the three-dollar barbers.

He was opening his mind to new things: One of his best friends was black. He found something deep, eloquent, and moving in the funky down-home blues-rock sound of the Rolling Stones. He knew everything about the Stones. He played their songs six or seven hours a day. They symbolized to him a kind of hip, rugged individualism, a pop individualism that "took no shit from nobody." The attitude combined brute force with a gentleness of soul. He particularly admired Mick Jagger, the group leader. Mick, who Bill thought was "rugged," lived his own life on his own terms. He refused to compromise with the binding laws of society. He knocked his girlfriend up and then sang about it. He blew a whole generation's mind.

"I'll tell you what I want to be," Bill Schroeder told his friends, "I want to be Mick Jagger." A big poster of Mick went up above his bed. He began redefining his home environment. He had gone far away from home and now he rushed home for Thanksgiving and Christmas, staying around the house, talking to his parents seriously, throwing out his ideas, exploring theirs. For semester break, he took a trip with some of his friends to the Grand Canyon and the Navajo Indian reservations. He was fascinated by the Indians and appalled by their primitivism and poverty.

For spring break, he went to Guaymas, in Mexico, with a missionary who had worked in South America and with two conscientious objectors. He slept on the beach and spent long hours talking to the people. He couldn't believe the children, he told his friends. They looked like they were seven and eight and yet they were fourteen and fifteen years old and suffering from emaciation. He was deeply moved by the poverty he saw. He couldn't get the squalor he had seen out of his mind. He began seriously questioning his aims, his goals, his values. He concluded very firmly that the war in Vietnam was wrong. He concluded that the kind of poverty he had seen in Mexico and among the Indians—in a land of plenty—was immoral. He took an interest in the blacks, read Malcolm X, and became conscious of racism.

He came home that summer listening to the Stones more than

ever, attuned to the secret meaning of the beat. He read Joseph Heller's *Catch-22* and Yossarian struck a deep chord in him. In a sense, he thought, we are all Yossarians. In a sense, life was a series of Catch-22s. He urged his mother to read it.

Having gone as far away as he could the year before, he now picked Kent State over Ohio State because it was closer to home. He and Lou Cusella, who lived in Lorain two blocks from him, drove down together and decided to be roommates. He buckled down on his schoolwork. He changed his major to psychology. He sought out the best courses and the best teachers. He was committing himself and he demanded commitment in return. He withdrew from two courses because the professors' attitudes angered him. In one course on the first day the professor said: "I am not interested in seeing you individually. I am not interested in seeing you in class. I am interested only that you show up for your tests. I am not very interested that you pass them. And I am very much beyond the point where female pulchritude impresses me." In the other course, political science, the professor said: "You can come to the lectures if you want, but the lectures will be the same as the book, so there is no real need to."

He found himself more and more in conflict with ROTC. The mountain climbing of the engineering unit was gone. He was placed in an infantry unit at Kent and he learned combat. He formed a friendship with Captain Don Peters, his advisor and a Vietnam combat veteran, and the two talked often about life, the war, and values. They talked about the Vietnamese people and, Peters noted, "Bill couldn't get over the fact they were just like us." They talked about the Trials at Nuremberg, which Bill found himself favoring and opposing at the same time. "You get to the point," Bill told Peters, "where 99 percent of everything is gray." He listened to Peters' war stories critically, without relish, and Peters noted: "It bothered him that he might have to kill people someday."

The two discussed the theories of Mao Tse-tung and Che Guevara. "I think he wanted to understand the revolutionary movement," Peters said. He told Peters that he was taking a lot of kidding back at the house about being in ROTC. He ranked second in the ROTC academic program, which his housemates also ribbed him about. One of his mates had hung a large mural of Bill on his wall. There, in caricature, Bill was shown in his green ROTC uniform, his feet tangled, an upside-down peace symbol in place of a battle ribbon. Lou Cusella heard the kidding, too, and thought Bill took it to heart. Peters thought Bill's knowledge and curiosity were driving him to learn more and more about people and the world.

In February, Bill wrote his mother: "Me and ROTC are sort of coexisting at separate levels, but I don't have any worry about the future, I'll always be rolling along having a good life. I talk with the bossman [Peters] from time to time. We disagree a lot, but there's an intangible mutual respect." He was offered a ride to the November Moratorium in Washington but turned it down, he told his mother, because he didn't think the ROTC people would like it.

In April, with the knowledge of Captain Peters, he attended an anti-war conference at Case Western Reserve University in Cleveland. Peters liked him. When ROTC devoted a day to selling high-school seniors on its program, Peters picked Bill to help him. "It got me ten merits," Bill told his mother, "besides, we played pool a part of the day when there were no kids there." He liked Peters, too, but was afraid, fearing Peters was jotting notes on their conversations and passing them to superiors. He felt himself trapped. He didn't like ROTC, but needed it to complete the education he desperately wanted. There was a secret hope in his mind, too, that in the summer of his junior year, when he'd have to take his six-week summer training, the army doctors would find the painful knees unacceptable for army duty. He was home in late April and, while driving his mother to a shopping center, said: "Yesterday I learned three more ways to kill in ROTC. Did you know you can kill a man with two sticks and a wire? I don't know how long I can take it."

Sometime in the fall he heard of an area project in Ravenna designed to help retarded children. He surprised his roommates by taking part. Twice a week he drove ten miles to a little school where he played volleyball and checkers with the kids. He never talked about it with his friends. He went home one weekend and told his mother the goals he had envisioned once seemed hollow now. "Money isn't important anymore," he said, "there are other things in life much more important than that." He and his mother talked often and honestly. "He would throw ideas at me, watch them bounce off, and watch me agree with him." Bill often told Lou Cusella about his mother. He loved her deeply. He belonged to a record club and would star selections he thought she'd like.

He enjoyed the atmosphere at the old red-shingled house in Kent and enjoyed the guys he roomed with. Besides Lou Cusella, his housemates were Mike, a would-be writer; Bruce, a would-be artist and photographer; and Rich, Lou's debating partner. They all had good grades and spent much of their time studying. Lou remembers Bill's supreme self-confidence. "Mike was trying to write a book and it became a joke with Bill. 'How's the book today?' he'd ask, knowing full well that Mike was having trouble writing a few paragraphs each day. 'I can write better than he can,' Bill would say, and the funny thing was that it was true. Some of Bill's things were better than Mike's. Or, Bruce would take some of his artier pictures out and Bill would say, 'I can take better pictures than that, all it takes is imagination and I've got plenty of that.' And the pictures were better."

His mother, at this point in Bill's development, thought her son would probably wind up writing some day, if not for a living, then to supplement perhaps a teaching position. Bill seemed content. He had two girlfriends in nearby Elyria and a few more on campus. "I'm the emotional kind," Lou said, "and when I get hung-up on a girl, I get terribly depressed. Bill would laugh. He couldn't empathize very well with that type of thing."

He talked still, again and again, of Mick Jagger and the Rolling Stones. The poster he had had of Mick in Colorado now hung above his bed at Kent. "One day he came in," Lou said, "and told me there was nothing wrong with him wanting to be Mick Jagger. The Stones symbolized something to him he admired but could never really be and I think that's why he was so hung-up about them." He listened over and over again to a twelve-and-a-half-minute Rolling Stones cut called "Going Home." When *Rolling Stone*, the rock periodical, called "Going Home" the best Stones song ever done, Bill was jubilant. When Mick Jagger showed up on an American tour wearing an Uncle Sam hat, Bill thought "he is the coolest motherfucker in the world."

He had worked, since he got to Kent, at a variety of jobs, in a school cafeteria, at a hamburger stand, and at a Kent aluminum company. He worked there on an assembly line four hours a day, six days a week. He needed the money to live but found, at this vibrant point of his development, that the assembly line was holding him back. One day after he came home from work, he scrawled out a poem about a day in the life of Bill Schroeder at the plant:

Sunshine, blue skies, it's beautiful today.
But here I am at CPM pretending to earn my pay.
Within these walls of filthy stone, my life is such a bore
Cuz day after day I do the same old chore.
I know to you I might seem strange,
But how I wish for change, change, change.
It hurts so badly I wanna stay outside
But if I skip a day of work the boss will have my hide,
I'm not bitchin cause the work is so unclean oh yeah,
But it aint no fun pulling parts from a machine.
Now it's wrecking my brain, yeah, I'm going insane.
At quitting time my powdered body runs right out the door
My mind is like the products on the line I can't take no more.

During Christmas break, he and Lou Cusella drove to Florida in Bill's shiny Fiat. "We went down there for the Hollywood Rock Festival," Lou said. "It was a wild trip—we drove his car and I have a mental image of him with his long arms all over the little car opening and closing windows. He didn't want to drive his car because he babied it. He wanted me to drive. Well, I didn't want to drive either. He was usually accustomed to getting what he wanted and so was I. It was a major battle of wits to get him to drive.

"We drove down to Hollywood and found that the entire area had freaked out. They didn't want any longhairs down there for any festival. We tried to sleep in the car or on the beach and we couldn't. Cops would come around with their flashlights and say: 'We don't want your kind here.' We both felt: What in the world is happening to this country?

"Down in Hollywood we met a speed freak from Rhode Island named John. John said he had a groovy place to stay out in some swamp and asked if we wanted to go out there. We said sure. We walked for what must have been five or six miles through what seemed to me like the Okefenokee Swamp. When we finally got to the place, John collected some wood and tried to light a fire. He couldn't. It was Bill, good old Eagle Scout Bill, who finally got the fire going. We didn't stay there, the guy was driving us nuts with his chatter. We had to get out. I think we both realized then that we sympathized a lot with the kids and the freaks, but we just weren't a part, couldn't be a part of the thing, we were on different levels. Bill and I left the rock festival and we drove up north along the coastal highway.

"Somewhere around Pompano Beach we found a secluded forest and went in. We slept in the middle of the forest and built a campfire each night without the cops busting in. We called it our Jungle Fortress. We stayed there for about four, five days. Each morning we'd drive down to Fort Lauderdale and get some sun on the beach. It was great. Here it was seven o'clock in the morning and we were out on the sand and there was no one else out there. You could get all the sun you needed by noon while the fat cat in the Sheraton across the street was still asleep. Bill got a beautiful dark tan and I got sun poisoning.

"We started back earlier than we'd planned. We were tired, I guess, of the whole thing and I guess of each other. I guess Bill had had it up to his ears with Looie by that time. He told me that, too. We had a very honest relationship, but he said not to take it personally, he just got tired of people after a while."

The spring quarter at Kent was Bill's happiest. He'd stopped working at the aluminum plant, he'd earned enough money to get through the year, and he had all the courses, professors, and books he wanted. He was fascinated by the Pavlovian dog theory he had learned about. When his sister, Nancy, had a baby in Lawrence, Kansas, in April, he wrote her to say he'd send the baby some "goodies" as soon as he was working again. He said he was going to all the concerts and lectures he could attend. "The classes are beautiful," he wrote, "at last I'm getting a semblance of an education." On the weekend of April 23 he came home. He told his mother he had been spending some time at Lou's fraternity. He didn't want to join or anything, he said, but the Sigma Nus were interested in him and that meant free beer.

On Thursday night he listened to the President's speech announcing the move into Cambodia and thought it was "silly." "What is this thing going to be," he asked Lou, "an eternal war?" Friday night was a beautiful spring evening. "It was the kind of spring night Kent was supposed to be famous for," Lou said. "I had been drinking with some of my fraternity brothers earlier in the day and when I got to the house that night, all the guys were there. I said, 'Let's go downtown, it's a beautiful night.' It had been a hard, long winter—we had all studied and there wasn't much time left for chicks. Everybody agreed. We all went downtown.

"Bill and his buddy, Al, went downtown before the rest of us. By the time we got to Orville's, Bill and Al had picked up a couple chicks, so we split up. Later on, when the trouble started, I saw Bill and Al and the two chicks standing on the sidewalk, watching. When the rock throwing started, I knew the cops would come down with billyclubs to bust our noses and I went up to Bill and said, 'Listen, you better split, we're gonna get our noses broken.' I got back to the house around midnight and soon after that Bill and Al and the two chicks came in. They left with the chicks around three in the morning and Bill drove Al home to Akron. Bill stayed at Al's place in Akron that night."

Bill Schroeder spent Saturday with his friend Al in Akron, first at the Akron Reservoir, a favorite place of trees and quiet, where he and Al scrambled on Al's motorcycle. Then, later, at a place called the Draft House in Akron, a college hangout. About eleven-thirty, Bill heard on the radio that the ROTC building had been burned and that the National Guard had been called in. He came back to Kent immediately and got as close to the building as he could to see the damage. When he got back to the house, he told Lou he "couldn't believe it." The burning and the violence he had seen Friday night were "violence for the sake of violence." He said he hated the war, too, and could understand the symbolism ROTC stood for to some students, but that he didn't think rock throwing or burning would help end the war any sooner. He recognized, he said, that the peace marches didn't seem to be doing much good, but said he just couldn't condone violence as a means to end the war.

When Lou got up Sunday morning, a bright sunny day, and said he was going for a walk, Bill asked if he could go with him. Lou had a date. So Bill went to the Akron Reservoir with his friend Al again and scrambled with the motorcycle. That evening Lou got his date home minutes after the eight-o'clock curfew. "I was wearing a pair of denim bell bottoms," Lou said, "and my hair had grown down to the neck. About a block from home four sheriff's deputies with walkie-talkies stopped me. Three of them wanted to take me to jail. I just about got down on my hands and knees and begged them not to take me. The one guy in charge finally let me go. I guess he noticed the fear on my face. The guy said 'Go fast and walk the shadows.' I finally got to the house and all the guys were there. I told them it was the longest block I'd ever walked. Bill just shook his head and said it seemed like we were living in a police state. He didn't like the Guard on campus any more than I did and said he feared the Guard's presence would cause more trouble."

Soon after he spoke to Lou, Bill got a phone call from a friend he'd known from Lorain High School. The friend said he'd been out of town over the weekend and "missed all the fun." He told Bill he'd spent Sunday night confronting guardsmen. "That asshole," Bill said, "that stupid asshole."

Late Sunday night, as the helicopters hovered overhead and the sound of walkie-talkies and radios could be heard everywhere, he called his mother. "I'm all right," he told her, "nothing has happened to me." He said the burning of the ROTC building was "terrible" but that he understood the reasons. "They've got to end this war," he said. He told her he felt the presence of the Guard on campus was inflammatory. "It's hard to step outside without four or five cops coming down on you," he said. He said it was most important to him to finish the quarter successfully. He was disturbed about the future of ROTC at Kent. If the program was to be discontinued because of the burning, it meant he'd have to switch to a school that had an ROTC program. He told his mother he had just about decided to go to summer school and he told her not to worry.

The alarm clock in their little room went off at 7 a.m. Bill had asked Lou to wake him. He had sat on his own clock during the year, and though Lou's had fallen off the wall once and wasn't totally dependable, he felt it was better than his own. Lou shook him at seven o'clock and, half-awake, heard Bill get up about eight-twenty. Lou's debate partner, Rich, was in the shower, and Lou heard Bill go into the bathroom and flush the toilet seven or eight times. Each time the toilet was flushed, Rich was scalded by hot water. Lou remembered Bill laughing and Rich shrieking.

Bill dressed for class in his "scrub" bell-bottoms and denim jacket. He wore a purple flower and a yellow flower in each lapel of his jacket. He told Rich, who went to class with him, that the purple flower was his "purple heart." On the way across campus, he found a tear-gas canister and handed it to a guardsman.

He had a nine-o'clock experimental psychology class. "I had to cancel it," said Robert Fernie, an assistant professor. "The biology department had a liquid crystal research project in the same building, part of a Defense Department project, and we were afraid someone would try to bum the building down."

Shortly before noon, near the Commons, he met Gene Pekarik, a friend he'd gone to high school with. Pekarik told him of the previous night's trouble when, during a sit-down and its aftermath, two students were bayoneted by National Guardsmen. "Bill was repulsed by the fact people were getting hurt," Gene said.

"Are you going to the Commons?" Gene asked.

"Sure," Bill said, "let's go."

On the way over, he told Gene that during his ROTC class that morning, another student, discussing a hypothetical military operation, said the way to success was to "go in there and wipe them all out."

"What kind of mentality is that?" he asked Gene.

As they walked near the Commons toward Johnson Hall, Gene's dorm, several hundred feet from Blanket Hill, Gene said, "I hope there aren't any trigger-happy reactionaries with guns out there."

"Naw," Bill said, "lots of these guys don't even have clips in their guns."

He bumped into Captain Don Peters. "The Commons had a mudfight atmosphere about it," Peters said. "Bill was just hanging around, excited, curious, wanting to know what was going on."

Bill and Gene Pekarik watched the rally from Johnson Hall and the knoll by the dorm overlooking the Commons. "He wasn't just a participant and he wasn't just a bystander," Gene said. "He went there to observe." When they saw a student throw a stone at the National Guard jeep telling students to disperse, Bill said, "Christ, that's all they need!"

As the guardsmen advanced up the Commons in the direction of Johnson Hall throwing tear gas, the two got separated. "I ducked into the dorm. I looked around and there was no Bill."

No one who knew him saw him alive after that. At 12:14 p.m., when gunfire rang out, Bill Schroeder was walking to the rear of the guardsmen as they were going over Blanket Hill back toward the Commons. When the Guard suddenly turned and fired, he was a hundred feet behind them, a hundred feet from the flash of the guns. His friends say he was probably figuring it was smart to walk behind the Guard, that he wouldn't get hurt that way. The bullet that killed him struck him as he tried to throw himself to the ground. He hit the ground flat on his face. The bullet began as a graze, fracturing the seventh, sixth, fifth, and fourth ribs before it tore inside, perforating the upper left lobe of his left lung, and exited from the top of the shoulder. He died of massive internal hemorrhaging. He fell near the pine trees on the slope of Blanket Hill.

Other students saw him: "He was laying there all covered with blood. He didn't move. Somebody put him on a stretcher to the dormitory. We had to move him off that to the ambulance stretcher. Somebody took his shirt off. They were using it as a pillow under his back. The blood was soaking into the grass."

Gene Pekarik didn't see the shooting, but he ran to the area after the volley ended. He saw a girl he admired and knew slightly, Allison Krause. He was numb. His roommate ran up to him.

"Gene, you know who they shot, you know who they shot?"

"Yeah, they shot Allison."

"No, your buddy."

"Who?"

"Your buddy, the buddy you were with before."

"Bill, oh God, Bill."

He ran there and found a crowd of students around him. When the ambulance came, the attendants started for three girls who had fainted. "Get Bill," Gene screamed.

Bill Schroeder was the first victim to arrive at Robinson Memorial Hospital. He was barely conscious. He had no identification on him. They asked him in the emergency room what his name was. He gave a barely audible reply. They wrote down what they thought he said: WILLIAM SCHNEIDER. A few minutes later a doctor told a nurse to call the morgue and to notify William Schneider's parents because William Schneider was dead.

Lou Cusella, who had been near the scene of the shooting but who had not seen Bill Schroeder, went home in disbelief. *This has actually happened,* he thought, *this has actually happened.* Everyone was in the house except Bill and Mike. Bruce said not to worry because he thought he saw Bill and Mike near the Commons with Mike's girlfriend and Bill was probably over at the girlfriend's place with Mike at Glenmorris Apartments.

When, near three o'clock, Lou heard one of the dead had been identified as William Schneider, he feared the worst. A pessimist anyway, he thought of the names: Schneider and Schroeder, both Germanic, easy to confuse. He tried to call Glenmorris Apartments. The phone was dead.

At five o'clock, Mike called.

"How is everybody?"

"How are you and Bill?"

"Bill?"

He felt cold.

Minutes later, Gene Pekarik called to say he had seen Bill after he was shot. He didn't think the wound was serious and wondered if Bill was still in the hospital.

Lou called Robinson Memorial Hospital, and as he dialed he thought: *I have to write my own phone number down, because if it's Bill, I'll go berserk.*

"Has William Schneider been positively identified?"

"No, why?"

"Because I think he may be my roommate."

The man gave the phone to State Senator Robert Stockdale, also a Kent State instructor, who had been given the task that day of notifying relatives.

"Would you mind going down to the morgue?" Stockdale asked.

Would I mind?, Lou thought. *Would I mind?* The morgue?

A sheriff's department car picked him up minutes later. He had never sat in a police cruiser before. He was now on his way to the morgue. *It won't be so bad,* he thought, *you've seen him asleep on the bunk a hundred times.* The sheriff's deputies wore riot helmets. The car stopped at a red light and the people on the street lowered their faces against the glass to see the long-hair the deputies had in the car. The sheriff's deputies made small talk. Had he participated in the demonstration? No. "Well," a deputy said, "I talked to one of the guardsmen afterwards and he said those kids were all drugged up and just kept coming." *Drugs?* Lou thought. *Bill?* The morgue was on the outskirts of Ravenna, in the boondocks. *My grandparents live in the boondocks*, Lou thought, *and they're dying and their friends are dying. Why does it have to be here?* When the car stopped, a deputy told him he was sorry but regulations required that everyone who entered the morgue be searched. They frisked him.

Inside the door he met a coroner's assistant with white gloves. The man looked Italian. He looked like a nice guy. Lou said he had to go to the bathroom first.

"Wait a minute," a deputy told the coroner, "the boy wants to go to the bathroom."

Boy? Lou thought. *Boy? Am I five years old? Is this a dream?*

They made small talk with him while they prepared the body. He took a handkerchief out of his pocket because he had to have something to wring. On the wall was a collection of weapons that had been used in Portage County to commit suicide with.

"Was he wearing a belt that had peace symbols scrawled on it?"

The coroner nodded.

"Let me see him, let's get it over with." A deputy held his arm to support him. He shook it off. He thought, *I'm wearing my glasses, not my contacts, how close will I have to get to identify him, why didn't I wear my contacts?*

A shutter was opened on a glass pane. Behind the pane, a bright light focused on a body on a cart. For a second the coroner held his hand on the pane. *He is trying to block it from me*, Lou thought. He saw the profile, the light brown sideburns, the eyes; Bill open-mouthed.

"Oh, God, God, God, it's him, it's him." He heard himself speak with a voice he had never heard before. He sobbed uncontrollably. His body trembled. He felt his face twitch wildly in contortions and he remembered magazine pictures he had seen of faces like that: Malcolm X's relatives around him on a dance floor; Patrice Lumumba's family around him at the funeral.

After a while he went back to the house and about an hour later, when he felt able to speak, he called Senator Stockdale.

"It's him," he said.

"I kind of thought it was," Stockdale said. "Could you do me a favor? Could you notify the family?"

Me? Lou thought. *Why me? Haven't I done enough today? Won't this ever stop?*

After a silence, Stockdale said, "All right, I'll call them."

Lou Cusella sat in the little room with the big picture of Mick Jagger on the wall for a long time and cried. He was cold. He had on a Navy-blue windbreaker he had bought from Bill Schroeder for two dollars and a half the night before. He was obsessed with a mental picture of Bill's mother hearing about William Schneider and not knowing it was Bill. *Then, when the tide rolls out, they will find their son,* he thought.

He called Stockdale back to ask if he'd notified the family. Stockdale said he had.

"How did they take it?"

"Not too well," Stockdale said.

Not too well?

State Senator Robert Stockdale never called the family. At the little house on Missouri Street with the American flag on the door, Bill Schroeder's mother tried to call 603 Franklin Street every ten minutes after she'd heard of the shooting on the radio. She couldn't get through. They said the lines were dead. When she heard one of the dead identified as William Schneider, she was afraid. But surely, she thought, they would have notified her. When she heard a radio newsman spell the name out, she was still not reassured.

At four o'clock a rewriteman from the Cleveland *Plain Dealer* called and asked if the family had a picture of Bill Schroeder.

"Why do you want it?" she asked. The reporter said it was a mistake, he had called the wrong Schroeder.

When Lou Schroeder came home, she sent her husband across the street to a Lorain policeman mowing his lawn. She was near panic. Her husband talked to the policeman. Of course, it couldn't be. They would have notified them. But still, his wife was near tears, could he check?

At six o'clock, the rewriteman called back. He told her he had reliable information that her son, William Knox Schroeder, had been shot at Kent State.

Minutes later, as she began to lose control of herself, a Lorain police dispatcher called, telling her to call a number in Kent. She couldn't get through. The phones were still out. She called the chief operator and begged her. The operator said she would see what she could do.

The call went through fifteen minutes later. Robinson Memorial Hospital answered. She talked to a nurse, who hurriedly switched her to an administrator. The administrator was nervous. Hadn't State Senator Stockdale called her? She said no.

When she heard the word "expired," Bill Schroeder's mother collapsed.

The next day, under the effect of a tranquilizer, she got a call from the Kent Police Department.

"Don't you know your son is in the hospital?" a policeman asked.

"I know that my son is dead," she said.

"I know that too," the policeman said, "but I didn't want to be so blunt about it."

14

Jeff Miller

The words were scrawled on a piece of paper torn from a loose-leaf notebook, stuck onto the wall above his desk with a big wad of bubblegum:

Follow your dream—
You know what I mean?
—JEFFERSON AIRPLANE

He followed his dream to a parking lot behind the place called Blanket Hill. He knew what it meant. The dream was constant and well-defined and he committed himself to it. He was twenty years old. With pale face, long black hair, and a headband to keep the sweat out of his eyes, he looked like a caricature of Dustin Hoffman. He grew up in the Bronx and in the miniature-lawn suburbia of Long Island. Holden Caulfield could have been a friend of his. He drove a cab for a summer. He was a fan of the New York Mets. He collected baseball cards when he was a kid. He ate Wheaties, the breakfast of champions. He believed in higher education. He was shot to death by National Guardsmen in his sophomore year of college.

A picture taken moments before shows him with his right fist high, middle-finger extended. There is a look of calm on his face. "Jeff was just a kid," a friend said, "he was not a right-on radical."

The dream would not have accepted the puddle of blood that remained of Jeff Miller after they packed him off to the morgue. It did not tolerate battle helmets, combat boots, bayonets, and real bullets. He did not want to know how to maim and kill. He would have gone to jail or into exile to avoid learning those things. He believed that if a man learned how to kill, he was less than a man.

He dreamed of a land where there were no poor; where there was no suffering, no hypocrisy, no bigotry, no intolerance; where all men were equal; where freedom meant living life the way you *really* wanted to live it; where you didn't have to convert everything you learned into dollars and cents. He looked at the society around him, as his mind opened to experience, and he was afraid. It seemed to him that perhaps America was not the place for his dream; perhaps America did not want love and peace and brotherhood.

He saw his dream realized only once, fleetingly. It was a powerful and blinding insight. After three days of the world he envisioned, it was harder and harder for his mind to adjust to the real world around him. He kidded his friends and said he had turned in his American citizenship. He had become, he announced, a citizen of the Woodstock Nation. His friends said he was beautiful and in harmony with himself. Those who didn't understand said he had no purpose in life. He felt he had finally found his purpose: to be a troubleshooter for humanity.

Woodstock was the world he envisioned. He spent three days at the pop festival in Bethel, New York, with half a million of his "brothers and sisters." It was a deeply spiritual experience. He walked miles to get there; the roads were blocked with parked cars. He had a knapsack and a blanket. It was much more than a merry-go-round of heavy rock music and pretty girls. It was, for this short, impish boy, a personal world where there was no violence, no hostility, no aggression, no hassles. He lay in the sun and in the mud. He dipped into a pond. He lost himself in the grass and in the stars. He was not self-conscious. He spent some time in the medical tent helping those who had had too much sun or too much drugs. And he learned something about life and about himself. Jeff Miller was turning into a different human being, no longer the product of environment, upbringing, education. More a creature of his own making. "Something's happening here," he told his friends, "but you don't know what it is, do you?"

Jeff Miller, citizen of the Woodstock Nation, lived in a small off-campus apartment in Kent. Flowers were painted on the door.

The door was never locked. The lights were always on. Anyone was welcome to come and rap. Dirty knives and forks littered the sink. The table was covered with plastic plates, crumpled cigarettes, comic books, and a transistor radio. There was an ad for a toy machine-gun on his wall. Next to it was a handpainted sign: "IF YOU THINK THIS GUN LOOKS GOOD, WAIT UNTIL YOU HEAR IT!" On his bedroom wall, an army recruiting poster had been edited: "DO IT OR DIE!"

His barbells were in the living room, so were his drums, a stereo, and empty beer mugs. His motorcycle was in the basement with one of its wheels off. A properly displayed American flag was over his bed. A stack of rock records was lined on his dresser, next to a row of twenty-one books. Most of the books were about psychology, his major. Two or three were on conversational French. There was a copy of Salinger's *Catcher in the Rye*, a copy of Hemingway's *The Sun Also Rises*, and a copy of Hilton's *Lost Horizon*. There were no books about revolution.

Catcher in the Rye was well-worn. The scene where Holden Caulfield tries to erase a four-letter word from a wall was heavily underlined. In the margin Jeff Miller wrote: *"Great. That's what we all have to do."* There was a well-thumbed copy, too, of the latest *Playboy*.

Afterward, when his roommates collected his things, they found his wallet on his desk. There was no money in it. There were tickets worth fifteen rides on the Long Island Railroad between New York and Hicksville, two bank credit cards, an airline credit card, a library card from the Plainview-Old Bethpage Public Library. There was a draft card, too, indicating that Jeffrey Glenn Miller was 2-S. On the desk were a notebook, a copy of a statement issued by university president White on Sunday and, still in an envelope, not yet completed, an application form from the Selective Service System for status as a conscientious objector. Writing on the notebook indicated it was owned by "Jeff Miller and a dog named Lassie." Across the top he had written, "Rocky for President in '72."

His roommates found, too, taped to his door a note on a piece of toweling from the girl he had dated for three months:

Jeff, I was here with a bottle of apple wine and you missed it!

He lived with his roommates who shared his feelings, but the students in the neighboring apartments and houses hardly knew him. "I knew that someone named Miller lived back there, but I really didn't know him," said twenty-two-year-old junior Bob Rochester, of Cleveland, whose apartment was separated from Jeff's only by a small swimming pool. "I don't know if he was active on campus. As long as those things don't affect me, I didn't care. He had long hair, but no longer than most of the kids. Anyone who wants to look that way, I don't care. I might have gotten to know him if the pool had opened sooner."

Randy Rust, a twenty-one-year-old junior from Cleveland, said, "The guys in the house were all the same type. I would call them activists. They were always speaking out against things and girls would come and go from their house. I think he played the drums, but I'm not sure. All the fellows in this building used to play basketball out here, and we built this picnic table together. But those guys never joined us. They stayed in the house." Len Henzel, twenty-one, a graduate student in journalism, said, "That house was never a center of activity. They might have been left-leaning, but none of them were radicals."

Jeff was the baby of the family. He grew up with his brother, Russ, three years older, first in the Bronx and then at the friendly white-shingled home in Plainview, Long Island. "We're a bedroom for New York City," said a Plainview high-school teacher. "There are some thirty-five thousand residents, but little to provide a community of interests. Except the school district. I think the students, through their schools, their clubs, and teams, have more a sense of community than the adults."

Jeff's father, Bernard, a stout, middle-aged man with a mustache, is a linotype operator for the *New York Times*. His mother is a secretary at John F. Kennedy High School. They are separated. "I bought the house in Plainview about eight years ago," Bernard Miller said. "We had to get out of that old neighborhood. Thank God we did that because all the kids who grew up there went sour—dope, car theft, everything."

As a boy, Jeff loved sports but, because of his small size, was content to be a spectator often. "Jeff was very willing to always come out and play anything," a neighbor said. "The only trouble is that he was always the last man picked on the team. So when we played baseball, he was the pitcher a lot, pitching for both teams, you understand. And sometimes when we played football, he was the referee. But he never seemed to mind." He played tennis with Jacqueline Ribaudo, the girl from across the street. "He loved to play. He tried extra hard and he hated to lose. Sometimes he'd make believe he was Pancho Gonzales. 'Watch out,' he'd say, 'here comes one of Pancho's hundred-mile-an-hour serves.'"

Sidney Firestone, an English teacher at Plainview-Old Bethpage High School, remembers him: "His desk was right up front, almost touching mine. I got to know him well. He was well-liked, quiet, a little shy, self-conscious perhaps about being small for his age. He showed, with occasional flashes of subtle wit, a delightfully impish, casual sense of humor and genuine good nature. Modestly apprehensive about making it in my accelerated class, he worked at it assiduously when I urged him, and made it. He'd come in after school now and then to discuss his work or to just talk." Jeff's guidance counselor, Mrs. Alice Bukberg, said: "He was a wonderful, well-loved kid. Math was his strongest area. He was very eager to go to college. He was concerned about the state of the world but he was never a political activist." When he graduated from high school, an above-average B student, his hair was short and, he said, he thought he'd become an architect. His values were those of his upbringing. He wanted to raise a family sometime in the vague future. He wanted to make money. He wanted to succeed. "He was never a leader," said Jeff Weingarten, a boy who grew up with him. "He was influenced by people around him. It was part of his way of belonging."

In the fall of 1968 he went to Michigan State University where his brother, Russ, had been graduated. He decided to major in architecture. He wore blazers and button-down shirts and he rarely cut classes. He joined his brother's fraternity, Phi Kappa Tau. "He was a good pledge," a fraternity brother said. "He took a lot of crap. We had one guy in the house who I thought picked on him because he was Jewish, but he didn't seem to get rattled by it. I thought he must have had a lot of strong stuff inside because the more this guy picked on him, the more he smiled and laughed."

He was active in the beginning, but after a few months began to miss fraternity functions. "He was losing interest. He didn't want to have much to do with the activities," the fraternity brother said. "We'd have teas and go out on gin jugs and he didn't seem like he was having fun. Then, after a while, he stopped coming. One time we went out on a big gin jug. Everybody was having a great time and Jeff was there with a date. Then he got up and started leaving. I asked him what the hell the matter was and he said: 'I don't have time to play all these games.' He seemed mad as hell. I couldn't understand it. The occasional times when he'd come to meetings his hair was real long and he'd wear bell bottoms or old clothes. He became the House Radical. We started calling him a hippie and one time when somebody called him that he smiled and said maybe we were right, maybe that's what he was, a hippie."

A friend who knew him at Michigan State said, "He was going through all kinds of changes. He had convictions but he wasn't always consistent. He thought things were screwed up but he wasn't sure why and what he should do."

He began talking over and over again about the war. It assumed a central importance in his life. ("Lately his entire life, his every concern," his brother, Russ, would say, "was to end the war. He wasn't the kind of guy who would shout 'Let's go get them.'") He thought the war was immoral. He told his friends he thought America had become a militarist society. He said the war was doing nothing except making the businessmen richer. And, he said, he couldn't hurt his fellow man. "The army brainwashes you, it turns you into a murdering robot," he said. He said that if he was drafted, he would go to Canada. He felt that picking between Johnson and Nixon was "picking from the same batch of bad apples."

The Chicago Convention became a symbol in his mind. "The same thing was happening inside and outside. They used a gavel to beat people down inside and they used billy-clubs outside." His father said, "He was upset about the way the government was going, the viewpoints and expressions that were being made. He was particularly upset about Agnew. We talked about the war. He felt it was foolish for men to die over there." A friend, Michael Ohrenstein, said, "He was floundering, looking for something. He was very disillusioned about this country. He was peace-loving but he knew that when you get pushed too far, you have to take a stand." One of his Phi Tau fraternity brothers said, "He was a thousand miles away from us, I suppose. He was into peace—peace in the world and peace in his own mind."

He quit the fraternity—"All those guys wanted to do was make up stories about getting laid," he'd tell friends—and he switched his major to psychology. His values changed. He deemphasized clothes, rarely wearing anything other than bell bottoms and sweaters. He got a buckskin jacket. He said money was no longer important to him. "I want to be the best human being I can," he said. And, "What good is it building all kinds of fancy buildings when the people in them are screwed up?"

He became more and more attached to rock music. He would spend hours by his stereo, headphones on, listening to his favorite groups, the Jefferson Airplane and the Grateful Dead. Rock said something to him he couldn't verbalize. He studied the subculture, entertaining his friends with stories about the plaster casters, a group of teeny-boppers who made plaster casts of famous rock stars' penises. He followed the lives of his favorite groups. "McCartney didn't die," he said later, "the Beatles faded away." He saved concert ticket stubs. "Jeff could go see the crummiest group in the world," a friend said, "and if they had a good live guitar or a guy with a good set of drums, he'd be perfectly happy." He started playing the drums, practicing to the Airplane or the Dead. When his roommates begged him to stop, he said his middle name was Glenn and, being Glenn Miller, he had to perfect his art.

He went back to New York in the summer of 1969 and worked as a cab driver. "He got a kick out of it, he loved to talk to people," his father said. He told his friends picaresque, rambling, and, they suspected, often apocryphal stories about his adventures as "a hack in the jungle."

He told, too, of the poverty and misery he saw during his travels. He said he saw a man lying on the street twice in one day. He went up to a policeman and asked him to look at the man. The policeman said: "Oh, that's just another dead bum." When the policeman looked at the man, he was dead.

He went back to Michigan State in the fall and began to take an active part in anti-war demonstrations. He went to Washington, D.C., for the November Moratorium, and told his friends he got some of the same vibrations he'd felt at Woodstock, but that somehow it seemed different. He said he feared that out of total frustration, the movement was swinging toward violence. "What are we supposed to do," he said, "start shooting people to end the war? Are we supposed to become violent to attain peace? That's what Nixon says he's doing—killing all those people so we can have peace." He told his friends that during his stay in Washington, a group of Weathermen asked him if he wanted to take part in the demonstration against the South Vietnamese embassy. Jeff told them he wasn't interested. "He said he spent a lot of that weekend walking around," a friend said. "He liked some of the buildings. He said it was a shame all that architecture contained all those war rooms."

He transferred to Kent State in January. "He transferred to find himself," a Michigan State classmate said. "He thought he didn't learn much up here. He wanted to get away." His father said, "He seemed happy at Kent State."

He was trying to build himself up, using barbells. He spent many hours a week doing exercises. He got a motorcycle and drove the nearby rural roads. Once he drove fifty miles to an Amish settlement. He tried to talk to the Amish farmers but they wouldn't talk to him. He was disappointed. He kidded that he was Captain America and said *Easy Rider* could have been made in Ohio, too. He said that with his hair growing long, he got a "funny feeling" sometimes when he passed a pickup truck on a rural road. He took great interest in and followed closely the events at Altamont, California, where, during a Rolling Stones concert, a black man was stabbed to death by Hell's Angels. He hated the Angels and he feared what Altamont symbolized. "Maybe we can't even have any Woodstocks in peace any more," he said, "maybe we've gotten fucked up too."

In mid-March, he met a girl he liked very much. They took long walks and rode his motorcycle. She was blue-eyed and had long, flowing hair. He thought enough of her to tell his parents about her. She shared his love of rock and peace. ("I was happy he met the girl," his father said. "We were joking about it. We don't even know who she was.")

The week he was killed, he went to see Antonioni's *Zabriskie Point*. He liked and disliked the movie. He insisted that Mark, the movie's revolutionary hero, couldn't have shot the policeman because he believed too deeply in peace. He enjoyed the love-in in the desert and said he wanted to get out West, too, to see what it was like. He thought the movie's conclusion "too simple." Daria, the hero's girl friend, imagines herself blowing up her boss's house. "What good does blowing up do?" Jeff said. "You hurt a lot of people."

When President Nixon announced the move into Cambodia, Jeff said to a friend, "How long is this going to go on? How many more countries are we going to invade?" The move angered him, but he didn't attend the noon rally on the Commons Friday. During Friday night's disturbances, he was at home with his girlfriend.

Len Henzel, twenty-one, a journalism graduate student and a friend of one of his roommates, saw him Friday night:

"I went to their house after I demonstrated Friday and told them about it. Jeff said he had never taken part in that kind of a demonstration before and he wanted to come if anything started. He was in the crowd with me Saturday and he got a little tear gas. He was kind of shy and he stayed behind me Saturday night. He told me that if anything happened, he was going to run. He didn't want to get hurt. But he was more than an innocent curiosity-seeker. When he went out, he was putting his body there as a statement against what the U.S. was doing in Cambodia. And I would say he lacked the courage to go out into the front lines."

Sunday night he participated in the sit-in at Lincoln and Main. "The presence of the Guard infuriated him," said Larry, a friend whom police would try to link to the burning of the ROTC building. "He felt it was unnecessary. He felt we were the victims of the kind of politics he abhorred. He came back to the house Sunday night and said, 'If this keeps up, we're all going to become immune to tear gas.' He said he had participated because he was committing himself. He said the Guard tricked everybody and started moving into the crowd. He said a guardsman had swung at him with a bayonet and missed."

Early Monday morning he called home and talked to his mother. He told her he had participated in the demonstrations and said he would participate in another that noon. He said he was living up to his beliefs. "You either believe in some things or you don't," he said.

His mother begged him to be careful.

"Aww," he said, "don't worry."

He woke his roommates at eleven forty-five on Monday morning and asked if they wanted to go to the demonstration. They told him they weren't interested and went back to sleep.

Jerry Persky, twenty-one, a junior from South Euclid he had met earlier in the year, watched him die:

"Jeff didn't run. He just fell. He fell on his face. I didn't know if he was shot. I looked over toward him because I wanted to see what was going on. And I saw this blood just dripping down the street. I saw that he was bleeding to death and I started to scream."

Dick Woods, a four-year Marine Corps veteran, was also watching: "I just saw the blood. I thought he'd been hit with a rock. There was this one girl kneeling over him, screaming: 'They shot him! They shot him! They shot him!' over and over again."

"I ran into Taylor," Jerry Persky said, "and I grabbed a phone. I got the operator. She couldn't get through. I told her—keep ringing, keep trying, this kid is really in bad shape. When I ran back outside, there was this girl standing over Jeff, praying. She had beads on, rosary beads, and she was just grabbing them and crying and screaming. And there was this other kid and I said, 'Let's turn him over' and we turned him over and his one eye was way off. And I saw him kind of wink, twice, the eye twitching. A kid ran over and said, 'I'm first aid,' and he felt it, the pulse, and he didn't feel anything."

Jeff was wearing a red cowboy shirt, a red headband, boots, and denim bell bottoms. The headband, blown off his head, landed two feet from the body. The pool of blood streamed ten feet into the parking lot.

A bullet had struck him in the right side of the mouth, fracturing his lower teeth and lower jaw, severing the blood vessel supplying the tongue, lacerating the carotid artery. It shattered the base of the skull and cut the spinal chord.

The body was taken by ambulance to Robinson Memorial Hospital. Jeff Miller lay next to Allison Krause. "We knew him," Allison's boy friend, Barry Levine, said. "We'd been over to his place. Part of his face was gone. He wasn't covered up. I didn't recognize him."

Later that day his father flew from New York. Bernard Miller was shown the body they said was his son and he stared at it. For a few minutes he didn't recognize him because part of the face was gone.

On Wednesday twelve hundred students jammed into John F.

Kennedy High School's gymnasium in Plainview to hold a memorial service for the boy who was a citizen of the Woodstock Nation.

"Who killed Jeff?" Theodore Sorenson asked at the service. "It was not only the guardsmen or the escalation of this nation's war effort. Jeff was killed by those national leaders who have turned a deaf ear to legitimate dissent."

Jeff Weingarten, a student at Case Western Reserve University who grew up with Jeff and traded baseball cards with him, sobbed, as he said:

> How could they kill Jeff? Perhaps as a defense mechanism, resulting from his short stature, Jeff developed into one of the most likable and easy-going people I have ever known. Like many of us, he left for college confused, seeking answers and trying to legitimize his own existence. Now his search has ended. A National Guardsman's bullet has brought him the final reality. Dust to dust—another statistic—why should the world notice?
>
> It's ironic that Jeff gave his life for something he'll never find whether he truly believed in. College radicalism—they were all games he played trying to get a perspective on life.
>
> When you know a person as well as I knew Jeff, you can make predictions about his actions. Yes, he would demonstrate and might even hurl some verbal abuse, but no physical violence. What possible non-violent excuse could anyone offer in justification of a human life?
>
> I am not condemning either side. Let's just stop and think. To the Establishment: I agree that it's very hard not to squeeze a trigger if you feel threatened and especially if you do it in the name of so-called justice. But see how quickly you would squeeze if you knew your son or daughter was out there.
>
> To the radicals: Our country is founded on the principle of the right to dissent. But, if you call the deaths at Kent State a "tragedy" then you are not really in favor of a revolution. Deaths are expected in revolutions. . . .
>
> Jeff, friend, you as much as anybody typified the fact that we all march to the beat of a different drummer. Why didn't you tell me it was going to be a procession?
>
> Goodbye.

The students formed a march through the quiet residential streets of Plainview. The adults watched. A brunette barmaid at the Andirons Lounge on Old Country Road said: "It makes me furious. My daughter's in junior high school and she left for school this morning. I called later on, and they told me she was on the absentee list. They said—real casual—'She's probably over at Kennedy at the memorial service.' Here it is a school day and I don't even know where she is." A woman in a red-checked cape said: "I don't like this war, either, but I don't like this. They're children, and they should be in school." The students urged a young mother with a baby carriage to join them. "I'd like to," she said, "but I'm afraid it might wake the baby."

That night, the school board meeting at Jeff Miller's Plainview-Old Bethpage High School opened with a minute of silence. The meeting was called to consider a list of requests submitted by students in the district, asking the board to condemn American intervention in Southeast Asia. The board members refused. "Jeff was killed for practicing the beliefs and principles and freedom that he was taught right here in this school," said Steve Drucker, a friend of Jeff's from Kent State. "And you won't take a stand. After seeing you people here tonight, I am sick." As he spoke, an older man moved toward him and tried to take the microphone away. A scuffle broke out. The school fire bell began to ring. Several girls were led from the auditorium as police moved in to restore order.

The next day, a memorial service was held at the Riverside Memorial Chapel in Manhattan. Three thousand of Jeff's brothers and sisters circulated and sat on the asphalt outside. It was a chilly day; there was a brisk wind. They carried signs —a banner with the dove of peace on a blue background; a huge picture of Bobby Kennedy; a sign that said "Students unite!" One student carried a blown-up picture of Jeff Miller in the pool of blood. Across the picture was scrawled the word "Revenge!" A few carried flowers. A girl from the Columbia School of Journalism, taking movies, tried to focus the camera with tears in her eyes.

A police truck arrived with a load of barricades. The students passed the barricades over their heads to the front so that a space would be left for the hearse to leave. A student yelled, "Don't let them barricade you in." The crowd ignored him. Two boys and two girls came with flowers and candles but the wind was too strong and the candles went out. The wind caught a banner: "WE THE PEOPLE MOURN OUR BROTHERS AND SISTERS."

Inside the chapel, New York's Senator Charles Goodell was saying, "We pledge to do what we can to make this a meaningful death."

Hearing Goodell's words through a loudspeaker, a boy outside yelled, "Fuck the politicians!" A girl yelled, "Politicians go home!"

Dr. Benjamin Spock spoke at the service: "Young people are first of all realistic. They are willing to look at the terrible injustices that exist in the United States. They have the courage to act out their idealism. They put the rest of us to shame. To me, the most impressive thing of all this is that they cannot be intimidated. The more efforts there are at oppression, the more it opens young peoples' eyes. His death and the death of the other three at Kent State may be a blessing. This may do more to end the war in Vietnam than all the rest of us have been able to do in five years."

On the street, a minister with a bullhorn in hand said: "God grant us the wisdom to understand what we are doing to ourselves." A police walkie-talkie squawked near him.

Jeff's rabbi, Julius Goldberg, recalled the biblical tale of Aaron, who faced the tragic loss of his son. "And Aaron remained silent," the rabbi said. He recalled how the Bible described man's reaction to senseless, tragic loss. Students in Plainview, the rabbi said, paid tribute to Jeff with "the kind of silence that demands adults lower their voices and listen to what the young are saying. He was killed by a fusillade of bullets labeled fear, panic, mistrust, war to end wars. We must listen to Jeff's brothers and sisters. We must give peace a chance."

On the shoulders of six pallbearers, Jeff Miller's simple hardwood coffin was borne to the street where the long-haired, bell-bottomed mourners filled the pavement for a block on either side of the chapel.

As they saw the coffin, they raised their hands in the peace sign. There was an incredible stillness in the air. A tall black girl with an Afro haircut kneeled on the asphalt, holding the peace sign with one hand and a rosary in the other.

"What beautiful young people," Rabbi Goldberg said, "but where are the adults?"

"He'll probably become a martyr," Jeff's father said. "Maybe we adults are sick. Jeff was a war casualty, the same as if he was shot in Cambodia, or Vietnam, or Laos. And he didn't even have a gun."

His brothers and sisters crowded into the street behind the hearse. As it pulled off, their arms were still in the air, but the peace signs were gone, replaced by clenched fists, raised to the sky.

15

The Investigations

Afterwards, it seemed, there was the greatest interest in passing the buck.

Three major investigations were launched—by the U.S. Justice Department, by the Ohio State Patrol (for use by the Portage County Grand Jury) and, later, by the Presidential Commission on Campus Unrest.

Astoundingly, none of these investigations set out to grasp the most significant problem involved in the tragedy: the cause. It was one thing to assemble all the known facts of what took place at the moment the National Guard lifted and fired their rifles. It was another to attempt to trace the twisting circumstances that stretch deep into the very viscera of the society.

The FBI conducted a general inquiry and then turned its report over to Portage County prosecutor Ronald J. Kane. A Justice Department official flew to Ravenna in mid-June to tell Kane the department had no plans to call a federal grand jury. Meanwhile, Kane made it plain he was interested in identifying for prosecution those students who had participated in Monday's rally on the Commons. He kept a glossy photo of Jeff Miller, middle finger extended toward the guardsmen, in his desk drawer and showed the picture to visitors.

The Presidential Commission chairman, former Pennsylvania governor William Scranton, said he was not interested in placing blame. The commission, which Ohio newspapers referred to sometimes as the Kent State Commission, was, in fact, not mandated by the President to fix blame for the shooting. When its sole student member, Joseph Rhodes, twenty-two, of Harvard, said he wanted to find out why the Guard was called into Kent, Vice President Agnew asked for his resignation. Rhodes refused.

Critics argued that President Nixon had sent Governor Scranton earlier to the Middle East when he wanted to soothe both the Arabs and Israelis. Was Scranton appointed to head this commission on the same basis? Why was another commission needed anyway? Why hadn't the 1968 Kerner Commission findings and recommendations been applied? That commission had placed blame; it had blamed the National Guard for being jumpy, undisciplined and deadly. It had said M-1 rifles were of no positive use in a riot. It had said most of the things that could be said about the National Guard at Kent State two years before the fact.

Critics pointed out that only the Portage County Grand Jury seemed sure of returning any indictments. Could this Grand Jury consider indicting National Guardsmen who were themselves neighbors in the same county? Could this Grand Jury, made up of the residents of rural Portage County, objectively view the actions of long-haired, foul-mouthed, counterculture students? And more important, could this Grand Jury provide any insight that would prevent this from occurring again?

In the days immediately following the shooting, fact was a rare commodity. There were only well-publicized cries of justification, many from the office of Adjutant General Sylvester T. Del Corso.

The night of the shooting, which also happened to be the night before Ohio's crucial primary election, an election that would decide the political future of the governor who appointed him adjutant general, Del Corso called Alan Douglas, moderator of a popular Cleveland radio talk show heard throughout the state. A tape recording of the call recounts the following exchange:

Douglas: General, was indeed there a sniper and where was he positioned, if there was one?

Del Corso: Yes, a definite sniper on top of a building using a shotgun.

Douglas: Can you say what building it was, sir, does anyone know?

Del Corso: It was a building on the city property. I had the name of the building once but I don't recall it now. We have it in the record.

Douglas: Well, that would have been far away from the Commons, wouldn't it, sir? Was it a commercial building across the main street in Kent, Ohio?

Del Corso: We don't know exactly where the building was, but this was definitely confirmed with the police and how far it was I don't know, I don't recall.

Douglas: An old military man would tell you, General, it's at least 250 yards to the Commons from any of the buildings across Main Street.

Del Corso: Uh hum.

Douglas: And also those buildings are only two stories at the very most.

Del Corso: Ah, yes, well, as I say, I don't know exactly which building they were talking about, but, it was one of the ah, ah, I don't know whether it was a—It was an apartment building, that's what, and I just don't recall the name because I saw it this afternoon and, ah, we have it in the record but I don't know what it is.

The next day, to a reporter from the Columbus *Citizen Journal*, Del Corso denied ever saying there had been a sniper. That same afternoon he denied the denial to a Cleveland *Plain Dealer* reporter and once again maintained he knew of the presence of a sniper.

On May 12, a statement issued by the adjutant general's office in Columbus refurbished the sniper theory by reporting a bullet had hit a nearby apartment. "The angle was such," the statement said, "that the bullet had to have been fired from on top of a roof or from an elevated position."

Until mid-June, Del Corso continuously referred to the finding of an Akron physician, Dr. Joseph W. Ewing, that a bullet wound suffered by one of the students was "certainly not caused from a bullet from an M-1 rifle or from a .45 pistol." Using the Ewing medical opinion publicly, Del Corso strove, over and over again, to impress on the public consciousness the presence of a sniper. Dr. Ewing is a close friend of two of Del Corso's golfing partners.

Forensic pathologists in Detroit and Miami contradicted Dr. Ewing's findings and said it was "entirely possible" the student's wounds were caused by an M-1 rifle.

When Portage County coroner Dr. Robert E. Sybert said the four students were killed by military ammunition of the type carried by National Guardsmen, the adjutant general's office said petulantly: "We have no comment until we see the report and we can't even say if we will have a comment then."

In an unusually candid explanation of the shooting in late June, Del Corso said there was no order to fire and said "what happened is that someone instinctively fired because there was fear he was going to be overrun and killed."

"There could not have been an order like that," he said. "We had forty-two men injured by rocks, two had teeth knocked out. A major there on the hill got hit with a full paving brick. As they went by one of the dormitories, someone threw a parking meter from the roof. Didn't hit anyone, but a parking meter. Some kids carried sacks of stones. One fellow said he was afraid they were going to take his rifle away and kill him with his own gun.

"At the moment the firing started," he said, "the officers immediately hollered cease fire. Now in the excitement when someone yells 'cease fire' probably down on one end of the line they didn't hear the 'cease' but did hear the 'fire.' When you shout 'cease fire' the word 'fire' is accentuated.

"This is probably where some of the confusion came over the order to fire. I can't conceive of ever giving an order to commence firing. It is just inconceivable. If they did, it would have been wholesale slaughter.

"They fired almost instinctively. The thing I think we've got to look into, you've heard the expression that these people were 'trigger happy.' It is not so. I just wonder sometime, and this is a concern to a military commander in a situation like this, whether you train your troops to react instinctively to something in combat. Did we train them to react instinctively here? When the soldier is in combat he reaches the point where he instinctively opens fire. Has our training gone to the point here? Is this the thing that happened?"

His big concern, Del Corso said, was the outcry that he feared would demand the disarming of the Guard. "There's going to be tremendous pressure on the President, on everyone, to attempt to disarm the Guard. The accusations are going to be pretty wild. Let me tell you this. If there is a shooting next week or next year by someone else you're going to get the accusations that the troops are untrained. If it happens in five years you are going to get the accusations that they are untrained."

The General is aware of the National Advisory Commission on Civil Disorders report, also called the Kerner Commission report, which was highly critical of National Guard performance in the Detroit ghetto riot of 1967.

The report told of units firing upon buildings with .50-caliber machine guns in response to sniper rumors. A Guard sergeant standing at a roadblock was killed by his own men, who suddenly opened fire on a passing automobile. The report said the National Guard killed "seven and very likely nine" of the forty-three slain in the riot.

"Actual use of the rifle in riot control operations is generally inappropriate," the report said. "It is a lethal weapon with ammunition designed to kill at great distances. Rifle bullets ricochet. They may kill or maim innocent people."

General Del Corso had long advised his guardsmen that they were to have their weapons locked and loaded. Each state Guard commander devises his own standards for weapons use, relying either totally or in part on army procedures.

The National Guard Bureau in the Pentagon, the liaison between state and federal forces, does not have the authority to order a state Guard commander to follow specific regulations unless the state forces have been called to federal service. The Bureau suggests that all states follow the army orders.

The army manual for a unit in a domestic riot situation gives the following sequence:

1. Rifles slung, no bayonets, ammunition in pouches.

2. Rifles with bayonets fixed but sheathed, ammunition in pouches.

3. Rifles with bayonets fixed, ammunition in pouches.

4. Rifles with bayonets fixed, ammunition in magazine.

5. Rifles with bayonets fixed, ammunition in magazine, one round in chamber.

The Ohio National Guard is ordered to be ready at the fifth and final level when it arrives at the scene of a riot. The first four steps are ignored.

Similarly, the army manual suggests these "measures of force" for a commander in a riot situation:

1. Show of force.
2. Use of riot-control formations.
3. Employment of water.
4. Employment of tear gas.
5. Fire by selected marksmen.
6. Full fire power.

On May 4 at Kent State, there was no show of force, no use of riot-control formations, no employment of water, no fire by selected marksmen.

The Kerner Commission advised that other means should be developed to control domestic disorder because the National Guard had no deterrent between tear gas and bullets. It suggested the use of water, the development of non-lethal weapons, and better use of chemicals.

In August 1967 army regulations called for thirty-two hours of mandatory riot-control training a year for each guardsman. The Ohio Guard calls for sixteen hours of riot training. Of the two units on Blanket Hill, one had completed its sixteen hours, the other had completed fourteen.

On June 9, Assistant U.S. Attorney General Jerris Leonard said the FBI's investigation disclosed "no evidence" of a sniper. To some, Del Corso's reaction was predictable. The adjutant general's office issued another statement claiming Del Corso had never said there was a sniper. Later, the general said that the confusion over the sniper had originated from a radio news report in which he believed but which later turned out to be untrue.

As the investigations got under way, critics noted that the agencies seemed interested in seeking out a conspiracy, a band of radicals directed by some high potentate to set the Kent campus and city ablaze. There had to be outsiders and a small indigenous group that functioned as some mysterious and disciplined underground. To many students who got haircuts in the days after the shooting, the situation was paranoid and frantic. They feared talking on the telephone. When they sat in a restaurant they examined the patrons with a probing eye, speaking in muffled whispers. When they spoke with outsiders, Monday was always related in the third person, a vague unqualified third person.

The details of a raid on a Kent apartment the night of the shooting, its logic, and the significance derived from it by law-enforcement agencies concerned with conspiracy, magnified the abrasive aftermath. On the basis of a phone number found in Jeff Miller's pocket at the morgue, state highway patrolmen and Kent police raided the apartment where the telephone was located. ("Jeffrey Miller Had Their Phone Number" a story in the Kent *Daily Record* would say later.)

The search warrant was issued "to seek radio broadcasting equipment." Authorities felt, when they found the number in Miller's pocket and found the same number scrawled on the hands of some students who had been arrested, that they were confronted with a communications center organizing a conspiracy. Shortly after seven o'clock Monday night they surrounded the apartment. They burst through the door with guns drawn, put the six student occupants—two of them women—against a wall at gunpoint, and searched them and the apartment. They found nothing, except a letter from Yippie leader Abbie Hoffman to one of the kids. The letter was confiscated. Discovering no clandestine radio station, the police herded the students out onto the sidewalk, where they were promptly arrested for violation of the eight o'clock curfew. Trouble was, it was only 7:36 p.m., and one of the students was able to prove it. The charges against the six were dropped. The students have a false-arrest suit pending.

How did the authorities reach their "radical communications center" conclusion? After Friday night's disturbances, one of the apartment's dwellers, Howard Katz, a dedicated civil libertarian and a Kent student, set up a legal aid center. He called the campus radio station and asked that the number be aired and it was broadcast. With a close group of friends he distributed circulars advising students to call the legal aid center if help was needed. Hundreds of Kent State students wrote the number down "just in case." Besides Jeff Miller, Lou Cusella, the member of the Kent debating team, wrote it down "because when there are so many law enforcement authorities on campus, anything can happen."

Months after the shooting and the apartment raid, a high-level Ohio State Patrol investigator sat under an elm tree in front of the university administration building and referred to the legal aid center as a "revolutionary command center." He said his agency, doing the investigation for prosecutor Ronald Kane, was working to prove the disturbances were part of a national conspiracy directed by national radical figures.

"This thing was perfectly planned," the investigator said, dawdling with a thin, black cigar. "Orders were given, assignments were made, teams of rock throwers and name callers were assigned. We think everyone had a specific task."

Ron Kane, the controversial and personable prosecutor, said at one point he thought three hundred persons would be indicted for participation in the weekend disturbances, many of them for participation in the Monday rally. A high-ranking State Patrol source close to Kane said three hundred was a conservative estimate. As the Portage County prosecutor took charge of proceedings, many claimed they saw the personality of Ron Kane making a big difference in the leaning of the only agency seeking indictments.

A rugged individualist and a refreshing sort, Kane is known to be seeking a judgeship in the county. His outspokenness and no-nonsense demeanor carried him singlehandedly to the courthouse after the shooting with an injunction closing the school. He made his move while others wrung their hands.

When he got there he found the courthouse empty, evacuated because of a bomb threat. He found Judge Albert Caris, a man in his late seventies, the only person in the building, and got him to sign the necessary documents. "Good luck, Ron," the old judge called after him as he left to face the wrath of Governor Rhodes. In Columbus they wanted him to hold the injunction and keep the school open. When the governor's office found that he was about to order everyone off campus, John M. McElroy, the governor's aide, said: "What do you think you are, a little czar?"

A few weeks after the shooting, Kane staged, for the benefit of the news media, what many consider Ohio's P. T. Barnum show of the year, a law-enforcement burlesque. The day following the tragedy, "Big Ron," using a California Court of Appeals decision which the American Civil Liberties Union was to claim was unconstitutional, ordered a search of the university dormitories. "School officials have a duty," Kane said, "to supervise the activities of students in order to promote the welfare of other students and to promote the educational aura of the premises under their control." In less Byzantine tongue, Kane explained that his dormitory search was legal because, at the time of the search, his injunction had already closed the university and the university administration had rescinded its room contract with students.

Therefore, explained Kane, it was very simple: The students no longer had legal possession of the rooms even though all their possessions were in those rooms.

Benson Wolman, the director of the Ohio Civil Liberties Union, immediately attacked Kane's action and called it "a gross violation of constitutional rights." He said, "It was made without warrants supported by probable cause, which is the constitutional standard. General searches are prohibited by the Constitution. The police participating in the searches will be liable in some type of legal proceeding."

But Ron Kane wasn't the kind of prosecutor to let the warning stop him. Less than two weeks after the shooting, he exhibited the fruits of his dormitory quest. There, neatly laid out on three tables in the rear of the Kent State University Gymnasium, was the Kane exposition, a better show than the Mobobrious Pit could ever provide; sixty knives, fifty guns, drugs of all types, some of them in medicine bottles. Weapons such as a twenty-gauge shotgun, a machete, and bayonets were displayed along with BB guns and starter pistols. Drugs displayed included marijuana, barbiturates, amphetamines, and cold capsules. There were several hypodermic syringes.

Asked what relevance the exhibit had to his investigation, Kane said: "The display of these materials indicates many of the students were obviously not coming to school to get an education." State Patrol Captain C. C. Hayth, assisting with the investigation, chimed in: "It's about time the parents of these kids begin to see what's going on here."

But what did it all have to do with the shooting? Kane was asked.

"Draw your own conclusions," he said.

Shortly after his exhibit, it was discovered the hypodermic needles belonged to a diabetic. Several guns shown, it developed, were cap pistols. It also came to light that Kane made sure no faculty members were admitted into the display. Captain Hayth stood by a door and made sure only newsmen entered. "I'm surprised he [Kane] didn't have his German shepherd there to snarl at us," one faculty member said. Kane explained that faculty members weren't admitted "so they wouldn't interfere with the news media taking pictures." A faculty spokesman, Dr. Lewis Fried, said: "All it did was aggravate a bad situation. The invasion of privacy was bad enough, but to use the events here for political gain was immoral."

"We knew there were diabetic syringes and harmless pills in that display," said Captain Hayth. "The prosecutor and I got a number of calls about the search. This prompted Mr. Kane and I to get the stuff for the benefit of the news media. But it went the other way. The damn news media made fun of it."

To make matters worse, a Kent State campus policeman was soon charged with stealing thirty dollars during the dormitory search and was fired from the university police force.

Said one statehouse columnist:

> It was the absurd event of the year. And yet, despite the fact that a massive search failed to turn up any valid evidence that the ordinary Kent student was on the verge of violent rebellion, most of the Ohio press picked up the hysterical cries of the county prosecutor and screeched, through the use of pictures and over-blown headlines, the disputable fact that the shakedown had turned up an arsenal. Also, the discovery of knives on a coeducational campus hardly is a sign that a massive revolution is in the offing. Anyone who has spent a minute talking with a contemporary coed would soon discover they carry knives not to overthrow the government but rather to protect themselves against molesters as they walk to and from classes at night. A search of 1,000 homes in peaceful and comfortable suburbs probably would have turned up a much more impressive arsenal. How many suburbanites keep a pistol or a rifle in their homes? How many keep cleaning fluid in closets? How many hunting knives could be turned up in suburbia?

The Justice Department entered the investigation the day of the shooting, in answer to a request from Governor Rhodes to FBI director J. Edgar Hoover. (Senator Stephen M. Young would claim months later that there were "hundreds" of incognito FBI agents on the Kent campus, which Hoover would call a "barefaced lie.") Attorney General John Mitchell appointed Jerris Leonard, assistant attorney general in charge of the department's civil rights division, to head the investigation. The appointment came a day after Mitchell met in Washington with twelve students from his own law school.

The students told Mitchell they wanted to form a Student Commission to probe the Kent State shooting under the auspices of the Justice Department. "Students will believe us, not you," one student told him. Mitchell said he would take their proposal under serious consideration. "He doesn't realize that normal, average people are being pushed to violence," a student said. "He focused on the violence as reaction to authority." Mitchell said privately he was "sickened and saddened" by the shooting at Kent State. When the students asked him why he didn't say so publicly, Mitchell said such a statement would prejudice the rights of any individual indicted as a result of the federal investigation.

When he appointed Leonard to head the investigation, Mitchell took the occasion to remind law-enforcement officers to "keep your cool, use only such minimum force as is required to protect the safety of the general public, the bystanders, and yourselves."

On May 12 Leonard said it had not yet been decided whether a federal Grand Jury would be convened to seek indictments in connection with the incident. On May 20 U.S. Attorney Robert Krupansky said in Cleveland that Leonard was determining whether any of the slain students' civil rights had been violated. On June 26, after a three-hour meeting with Leonard, Ron Kane said Leonard told him the Justice Department had no plans to schedule a Grand Jury investigation, but preferred that the Portage County Grand Jury handle the investigation and the charges.

The FBI's investigation, meanwhile, had run into controversy. In late May, Charles G. Cusick, special agent in charge of the FBI's Cleveland office, told reporters in an unusual move that the bureau had linked a Kent State sophomore to the burning of the ROTC building. It was headline-making front-page news.

Next day, agents searched the youth's campus apartment, seeking "clothing, explosive materials, devices utilized in the use of such materials, and other items which could be used for such purposes." They found none of these things, however. They did find a Jerry Rubin poster and an SDS pamphlet which they confiscated. The student said agents came to his home and took him downtown before telling him what they wanted to talk to him about. "The first thing they said to me was, 'You know you could get ten to twenty for this.' They grilled me for four hours. They showed me pictures of myself at the demonstration Saturday but I wasn't doing anything in the pictures. Finally, they let me go." Despite Cusick's headline-making announcement to the media, the youth was released and was not linked to the burning of the building.

Contacted by newsmen, Cusick was rude: "I'm not about to talk to you about this case. I don't want to have anything to do with you guys. Talk to the district attorney."

Robert Jones, an assistant U.S. attorney who had never been indisposed to publicity before, was adamant. He would not talk. No, he would not even sit down with reporters. There had been talk about his boss, U.S. Attorney Robert Krupansky, getting a coveted federal judgeship. No one was going to say anything. There were too many things at stake. Most of them personal.

The FBI investigation was also criticized when university professors discovered agents were probing into their classroom teachings and political beliefs. One graduate student questioned by the FBI said: "They tried like hell to get me to say something about my sociology prof." According to some students, a few professors in the English and sociology departments were singled out. Said Susan Kew of Westlake, a prosperous Cleveland suburb, "The agents came here and asked me if my sociology prof ever discussed making a molotov cocktail. I thought they were out of their minds. And then after we got to talking, they asked me six times if I was a member of SDS. I told them six times I was not."

The students were questioned after university registrar Donald Halter gave class lists to the agents. University vice president Louis Harris, after learning of the nature of the agents' inquiries, said the university would cooperate with the FBI only if ordered to do so by the court. Dr. William I. Gordon, assistant professor of speech, said the probe was a violation of the right of free expression in the classroom. "This kind of probe," he said, "may bring the death of social studies at the university and the destruction of the liberal education aspects of higher education."

As the FBI investigation garnered criticism, Portage County prosecutor Ronald Kane achieved more headlines. This time he denied that it was his office that leaked a Justice Department memo, but reporters were sure that the document came from his office.

There was confusion around the meaning of the memo, which stated that the "shootings were not necessary and not in order." One report said that information contained in the report, supposedly a summary of the FBI's 7,500-page report, was sent to Kane on his request for an outline of options and alternatives to bring before the Grand Jury. If this was the case, the memo, signed by Jerris Leonard, certainly did not read that way.

It made these points:

No guardsmen had been hurt by flying rocks at the moment of the shooting. None was in danger of losing his life.

The troops did not run out of tear gas. They could have controlled the crowd by making arrests.

Statements by the men who fired revealed that one shot at a student who was making an obscene gesture. Another fired at a student preparing to throw a rock. Still another was reported to shout hysterically, "I shot two teen-agers! I shot two teen-agers!"

Most surprising was the listing of six guardsmen in the memorandum who could be held criminally responsible.

Some of the conclusions in the leaked report were puzzling. For instance, even though there was no overwhelming rain of rocks showered on the guardsmen at the time of the shooting, several witnesses do mention one or two rocks and a piece of tree limb that were hurled at the troops on the hill. The Justice Department memo affords no reason or cause for the Guard to turn and fire into the students.

When the story broke Ron Kane found himself again in the midst of controversy. The Justice Department rebuked him; he had betrayed a trust. "I'm sick," Kane said, after denying ever having seen the memo. "I haven't received it in the mail yet."

The report caused a temporary sensation. Students had a hard time believing it and those facing possible prosecution took heart. The National Guard was stunned. "That sounds far-fetched," General

Del Corso said upon reading the article. "A lot of guardsmen up there were hurt by rocks and other objects thrown at them."

"We don't understand this," said another Guard officer. "I personally know that a list of forty-six guardsmen who were injured—many of them on that hill—was turned over to the FBI. They know what happened. This thing just doesn't ring right."

The buck was passed with expertise:

By the adjutant general, who first laid it at the hands of a nonexistent sniper, and then spoke of the dangers his men faced that day.

By the State Patrol, to a radical communications center.

By the Justice Department, to an ambitious county prosecutor.

By the prosecutor, to a rural Grand Jury.

"You are never going to get the true story in full perspective," said a dejected Robert White. "You'll take your choice, depending on your bias or the way a certain report is constructed."

In some ways, the aftermath was as sad, the implications as grave, as the volley itself.

16

Afterward

The university conducted a "referendum of crisis" through the mail. Of 5,399 students who voted: 78 percent supported a voluntary ROTC program; 63 percent opposed President Nixon's decision sending troops into Cambodia; 47 percent favored total and immediate withdrawal from Vietnam; 54 percent supported Nixon's policy of increased Vietnamization and gradual American withdrawal; 86 percent opposed an increase of American combat forces in Indochina; 68 percent supported the Hatfield-McGovern amendment cutting off war appropriations after June of 1971.

The Kent Student Medical Fund, a non-profit corporation, was organized to raise money for the medical expenses of the injured. Michael Pierce, a senior at the school, said nearly $100,000 was needed to help the injured students.

Of the nine students wounded that day at Kent State, two were in such condition that doctors feared they would be permanently disabled. Dean Kahler, a twenty-year-old freshman, was hit in the shoulder by a bullet that spun through his body to his stomach, grazing his spine and leaving him paralyzed from the waist down. According to Pierce, the medical bill for Kahler for the first two months of his convalescence was nearly $40,000.

Tom Grace, a sophomore from Syracuse, New York, was hit in the left foot. The bullet mashed the bone and left him disabled. An infection set in and his hospital bills reached $14,000 in the weeks after the shooting.

The others, to various degrees, were luckier. Douglas Wrentmore was hit in the knee, the bullet breaking his tibia. Alan Canfora, Tom Grace's roommate, was struck in the wrist. Donald MacKenzie was about two hundred yards away from the Guard when a bullet hit him in the neck, narrowly missing his spinal cord. It exited from his cheek, smashing his left jaw and leaving a hole in his cheek. Robert Stamps, nineteen years old, was shot in the buttocks.

Jim Russell was hit twice, both grazing wounds. A shot cut his right knee and tore his trousers. More serious was a bullet fragment or a piece of buckshot that lodged between his skin and skull. John Cleary, who lay wounded on the cover of *Life* magazine, took a round in the stomach which opened a gaping wound. Joe Lewis, an eighteen-year-old freshman, was shot in the left hip and yelled: "Oh, my God, they shot me!" The wounded were the most disbelieving.

A letter from General Del Corso to his men was published in *On Guard*, a National Guard newsletter:

> You have been spat upon, struck at, insulted, ridiculed, and threatened many times while on duty. Some of you were injured by rocks, pipes, and railroad spikes thrown by militant demonstrators. I am sure that you are all gaining considerable personal satisfaction from the widespread support of the Ohio National Guard by the general public. You men have served the State well. You can be proud of yourselves, and proud that you are members of the Ohio National Guard, just as I am proud to have served with you.

The Kent City Council passed an emergency ordinance prohibiting the desecration of the American or Ohio flag. Republican councilman Dal Hardesty drew up the resolution as a result, he said, of the disturbances on campus. The punishment set was no less than $100 and not more than $1,000 and no less than thirty days to a year in jail. Hardesty explained that his motion was prompted by the fact that a student burned an American flag the day of the shooting and the municipal court dismissed the case because there was no city ordinance prohibiting it. The new law went into effect immediately.

The Portage County chapter of the Red Cross said that the absence of students from the campus caused a blood shortage in its bank. "The Red Cross has always counted on the more than three hundred pints of blood donated by the students during May," a spokesman said.

A group of state legislators came to Kent to discuss campus unrest. A WKNT radio editorial said, "The legislative hearing was interesting because of what wasn't said. We noted two things. First, the vast majority of testimony did not speak to the topic of what legislators should or should not do. Second, very few students, concerned or otherwise, came to testify, to have their views heard by the very men who will determine budgets, laws, and so on. There was total lack of communication."

Rolling Stone, the West Coast rock periodical, said six students were killed at Kent State and that two of the deaths were covered up.

The university announced "Newsrap," a specially programmed telephone-connection hookup that played tapes of the latest news concerning the university. The purpose: to dispel rumors.

A police parade in Kent was canceled because the officers "worked too much overtime and further participation in activities would put undue hardship on the officers involved." Kent chief Roy Thompson added that he feared demonstrators would try to disrupt the parade.

LeRoy Holmes, a Kent State junior, flew to Jackson State College in Mississippi to establish relations with students there and set up a mutual Kent-Jackson Medical Fund.

A group of students set up a fund to help pay some of the damage done to downtown businesses during Friday's disturbance. Called the Student Fund for Kent Damages, it was formed in a series of meetings between psychology-department faculty members and graduate students.

Trash cans in downtown Kent were repainted. On Earth Day, April 22, students had painted the cans with peace symbols, doves, V-signs, and slogans. The new paint job was ordered by Mayor Satrom. The color pattern, as the students saw it: whitewash.

A study conducted by the Urban Research Corporation, a Chicago-based concern, said the deaths of the four Kent State students rather than the move into Cambodia caused the breadth and intensity of protests on the nation's campuses. "In spite of Cambodia, without the Kent State deaths, there would have been no student strike," said John Naismitt, corporation president.

A community-relations study was issued by a joint town and campus group. Among its recommendations: that Kent city police should be involved in meetings which include students and townspeople. "A better understanding of police and their problems is needed now," the study said.

A WKNT radio newscast, May 19: "The rumor mill has started again that there are more deaths as a result of the shootings over two weeks ago. Please dispel all rumors. There are only two students left in Robinson Memorial Hospital today and both are reported in fair condition."

In Youngstown, an eighteen-year-old Kent State student stole three American flags from a police display. "I hate America," the boy said. He was sentenced to ten days in jail and was ordered to write the Pledge of Allegiance five hundred times. Said the judge, "It's time people began appreciating this country."

A resolution praising Mayor Satrom was passed in Kent City Council. The resolution expressed "deep, profound appreciation and thanks to the mayor for his faithful devotion above and beyond the call of duty during the emergency."

At a press conference Mayor Satrom said, "I wouldn't hesitate to call in the Guard again. I'd never send them onto a campus without loaded weapons."

University alumni donations doubled in 1970 from the previous year. Many pledges were made after May 4. "We weren't doing too badly before the tragedy," said Robert Toll, university director of development, "and we've done not too badly since."

Mayor Satrom ordered city policemen to stop working as off-duty guards in Water Street bars.

ROTC Captain Don Peters announced that, due to student criticism of the cadet program, cadets would no longer drill on the Commons, but at a location shielded from the general student body.

Mayor Satrom asked council to ban all live entertainment in downtown Kent in the future. "Remember May 4," he said. "That should convince you."

Councilman Dal Hardesty proposed a petition banning all rock concerts in Kent. "I'm not proposing this action as a cure for all the evils here," he said, "but it is one corrective measure which can be applied with or without the university's sanction."

A young evangelist drew standing-room crowds at the Ravenna Assembly of God Church. His sermon: "Rock and Roll: The Devil's Diversion." The climax came when a group of listeners destroyed a mound of rock albums on a center stage.

Mayday, the campus underground publication, handed out identification cards:

This is to certify that

_____

(typed name)
IS A CARD CARRYING NO GOOD, DIRTY
HIPPIE, PINKO, COMMIE, BASTARD, FREAK PERVERT.

_____

(authorized signature)

A group of Kent State faculty and students formed a university-in-exile at Oberlin College and listed these demands:

1. A new governing body for the university comprised proportionately of administrators, faculty, students, and non-academic personnel.
2. Abolishment of all military and war research on campus.
3. Severance of all ties by the university with the military.
4. Disarmament of the campus police.
5. Amnesty by the university for all those participating in the May 1-May 4 demonstrations.
6. Announcement by the university that no university funds would be used to pay for the burned down ROTC building.
7. Opening, for the public, of all campus police records.

Kent police chief Roy Thompson, in a Rotary Club speech, said American Civil Liberties Union lawyers defending students were "pinkos and reds."

General Del Corso said he feared more students and even college administrators would be killed in campus violence. "I don't think we've seen the end of violence on campus," he said. "I'm afraid before this thing is over more students and administrators will get killed. There just isn't any such thing as a peaceful demonstration any more. They seem to think that crime on the campus is okay but not crime on the street. We can't have a double standard."

Ad on a Taylor Hall bulletin board: "Young man who doesn't love it desires to leave it. Rednecks, here is your chance." Contributions were requested.

Kent resident Mrs. Phebe Harrison, eighty-three, who stumped the nation in the mid-fifties arguing prohibition, said, "If the bars had been closed, Kent wouldn't have had trouble in May."

Leonard Vogt, a bearded, long-haired graduate student, was brutally beaten while walking with two women companions on South Franklin Street. He was verbally abused by four men who then yelled, "Get the hippie!" He was knocked to the ground and stomped in the head and body. One of the girls ran screaming into a nearby bar and was told, "So what? What are you fussing about?" Witnesses described the assailants as "construction-worker types." Vogt was shown a copy of the police report. It described his attackers as "four hippies."

Trevor Rees, a member of the Kent faculty since 1946 and for years the university's head football coach, suggested in a letter to Mayor Satrom that he begin a program to make the town dry. He said that both the university and the town had gained "extremely bad reputations" as a result of the "liquor-induced disturbances."

Edward Petrella, a bar owner, said, "After the events of May 4, we have received the first concrete proposal for remedial change from a university representative. Mr. Trevor Rees says that 'the tragedy stems in some respect from students emerging from bars on North Water Street.' We have heard again and again how students are selfish, naive, and shortsighted. If Mr. Rees' proposal is representative of the ideas to which students are exposed, maybe their ideas aren't so peculiar. If some students get drunk, dry up the town. If some students get into accidents, take all the cars away. If students need more sleep, let's make the eleven o'clock curfew permanent. Wow."

University officials voiced concern that when the university's insurance policy expires in 1973, the university will "pay through the nose."

One hundred American flags were stolen from graves in the Rootstown Township Cemetery, outside Kent. Portage County sheriff's deputies said a group of "longhairs" was seen leaving the cemetery, waving the flags.

Judy Haberek, columnist for the *Record Courier*, wrote, "With recent events in Kent, there has been a steady increase of right-wing Wallaceite thinking because of the great backlash of opinion surrounding the shootings. Moderates in the area must be warned not to succumb to the vigilante type thinking growing in the area."

Mayday, the underground publication, wrote, "Recently on weekends we have been treated to the sight of four to six policemen standing on North Water Street preventing young people from gathering on the sidewalk, alone or in groups. When asked, police officials indicate they are under pressure from local citizens to take action."

General Del Corso reported that the mail received by his office was running fifteen to one in approval of National Guard performance during campus disturbances in Ohio. Del Corso said his office had received 7,000 pieces of mail commending the Guard in its confrontation with Kent State students. He said only 433 letters were critical. The volume of mail was greater than at any time in the 182-year history of the Guard. Many approving letters, the general said, came from students.

Mayday wrote, "For your protection and the protection of others, don't give the FBI any information. It may be used in future indictments for the ROTC building or for general vandalism. The FBI will try to intimidate you by saying that it will go on your record that you didn't cooperate. This is bullshit. Agents may promise you a writ of immunity or say they just want the student side of the story. More bullshit. Your side of the story may lead to your own indictment."

A Lou Harris poll published in midsummer showed that only 11 percent of the nation's college students thought resorting to violence an effective technique in bringing about change in the system, while 65 percent thought working to elect better public officials was the answer.

The faculty senate passed a resolution that a public-address system be established on the Kent campus that would reach all extremes on campus. It would be available to the administrative staff on a daily basis for information that might be pertinent to the campus.

Marie Nussbaumer, a *Record Courier* columnist, wrote, "Among other things, we millions of Americans have been called the silent majority. It seems that as if by silent command, we are showing our love for our country. The sudden surge of patriotism is refreshing. It's good to see Old Glory flying proudly again in front of my home."

Twelve young people, aged fifteen to eighteen, were arrested for trespassing after they moved into an empty and unlocked house. "They were hippies from California and Colorado," the owner said. "They just moved in when the students left because of the disturbances." Said one of the young people, "There was no sign saying we couldn't live there."

The cover of *Mayday* showed three long-haired girls. One, in 1966, holding a flower. One, in 1968, holding a peace sign. One, in 1970, holding a raised fist.

Sign on a bulletin board in the Student Union: "THANKS DICK NIXON FOR BRINGING US TOGETHER."

For the first time in its history the university's summer enrollment decreased 6 percent from the previous year.

After June 30, when the city subsidy of $1,500 a month ran out, the City of Kent was without ambulance service. "We will have to call on ambulances from other cities, but we will not rely on this for any length of time," said Mayor Satrom.

Saul Daniels, former editor of the *Kent Stater*, said, "Everything just broke loose after May 4. For instance, we stopped at a gas station on the Pennsylvania Turnpike. We were having the oil changed and we were talking to the fellow. He said that orders came down from the corporate headquarters not to hire college students this summer and they said they were really hurting because they needed help and they had dependable kids who'd worked for them before, but they couldn't hire them. This is an example of that kind of thing. College students are bad, you can't have college students working for you."

Said *Mayday*, the underground newspaper, "Reports have reached us that having a Kent decal on your car might not be the safest thing. We have learned of at least one car that had every window smashed out in an Ohio town. Its only crime was the Kent decal. And there are cases of people being stopped, searched, and questioned because of that decal. On the other hand we have also heard some interesting friendships have been made around the country because of the decal."

Robert C. Dix, publisher of the *Record Courier* and chairman of the university board of trustees, wrote in a column, "The Soap Box Derby here truly became international this year for the BBC had a team photographing it for British television. The team didn't come here just for this event. It came to the community to do a sort of documentary on the town, proving to the corporation's great audience that Kent is a fine, vibrant community and not just the place where May 4th occurred."

The university's Lab Band, a jazz-Dixieland group, raised enough money in town to go to Europe for a concert in Switzerland. "The fact that the community gave the money needed for the trip," said the *Record Courier*, "in light of what happened, was much more important than the trip itself."

Kent councilmen passed a resolution asking the state liquor department not to grant any more liquor licenses for the area. Leading the motion was councilman and university public-relations director James Bruss who said, "There is no justification for any more licenses granted near the university."

Living in an apartment on the east side of Kent, four students were quoted in a lengthy newspaper account of the shooting. Their names were mentioned. Their landlord gave them two days to get out.

A National Socialist White People's Party was founded in nearby Cuyahoga Falls. It claimed that the events at Kent State were part of a Jewish conspiracy and said the fact that three of the dead were Jewish was proof of the conspiracy.

Mayday wrote, "The Ohio State Patrol, conducting its own investigation into the shooting, is into an apparent heavy intimidation trip. In at least one case they used a lie detector on a student who was unaware that he did not have to take the test. And even though you do not have to go with them, they imply that your refusal is an admission of your guilt."

An English professor discovered a proclamation which was issued in 1649 by the Magistrates of Portsmouth, New Hampshire, and reprinted it: "For as much as the wearing of long hair, after the manner of ruffians and barbarous Indians has begun to invade New England, we, the magistrates, so declare and manifest our dislikes and devastations against the wearing of such long hair as a thing uncivil and unmanly whereby men do deform themselves and do corrupt good manners."

The Rev. Billy Graham announced a fall appearance at the university.

Police radio report, July 9: "Dynamite taken from construction site on 1-80." The report was unverified.

At the international film festival at Cannes, France, Michael Wadleigh, the producer of the film *Woodstock*, a former Kent resident, dedicated his movie to the four students killed. "The deaths of the four students and Woodstock are complementary," he said.

General Del Corso said, "There's going to be tremendous pressure on the President, on everyone, to disarm the Guard. There is going to be tremendous pressure because here they have the focal point. Four students were killed and four were wounded and accusations are going to be pretty wild to get the point across.

"Let me tell you this. If there's a shooting next week or next year by someone else you're going to get the accusations again that the troops are untrained. If it happens in five years you are going to get the accusations they are untrained. It happens all the time.

"The question I'm worried about is this: Are we going to have security or aren't we going to have security? Are we going to have protection? We can't disarm the police. We can't disarm the Guard. We don't want to be called to these situations, but who is going to do it? We don't want the citizens to arm themselves. Then it will be wholesale slaughter."

Southern evangelist Wade Clemons came to the area and attracted big crowds. "The signs are all around us," he said. "War and campus unrest are both signs. The Bible says they are signs of the second coming of Christ."

On July 13, his first press conference since the shooting, Governor Rhodes said he would call in the Highway Patrol and the National Guard at any future campus disturbance "if I'm asked to do so by the university president."

Craig Morgan, the incoming student body president, an ROTC cadet, said, "Things are going to happen on the campuses again. Students are frustrated and tired of being slapped around and gassed and killed. But my message is to be cool. Violence won't work. Let's not destroy the system. Let's take it over peacefully."

"There is no doubt about it," said a city politics watcher, "LeRoy Satrom's prestige has gone sky high as a result of his decision to call in the Guard."

A rock festival was held in nearby Newton Falls, attended mostly by Kent students. Members of the International Society for Krishna Consciousness beat their drums. "I understand the people around here are a little conservative," one rock singer said, "so watch it with your stuff." There were eighteen cases of drug overdose.

Mayday wrote, "We have been unable to verify rumors of a Cuban submarine with Eldridge Cleaver aboard that has reportedly been sighted in the Cuyahoga River."

Corky, vice president of the Chosen Few motorcycle gang, reflecting on the shooting: "We'll make bullets equal to gold, then no one will be shot."

Without any announcement the university removed the victory bell from the Commons. A group of students crowded around workmen as they dismantled the bell. An impromptu protest began.

A week later the bell was returned to the concrete structure. Students painted the structure black and rang the bell with heads bowed.

About the Authors

Joe Eszterhas was twenty-five years old and had been with the Cleveland *Plain Dealer* for three years when he co-wrote this book. In 1968 he received the Cleveland Press Club Award and the Ohio Associated Press Award for his coverage of the Silver Bridge disaster. In 1969 he wrote the *Life* magazine account of the My Lai massacre; in 1970 he received the Associated Press Award for his six-part series. He was a senior editor at *Rolling Stone* magazine from 1971 to 1975. He has written screenplays for several major Hollywood movies, including *Basic Instinct* in 1992, and has written several other nonfiction books, including *Hollywood Animal*, an autobiography, and *Crossbearer: A Memoir of Faith*.

Michael D. Roberts was thirty years old and had been with the Cleveland *Plain Dealer* for seven years when he co-wrote this book. In 1966 he received the Ohio Associated Press Award for exposing a forged Rembrandt painting. He reported on assignment from Vietnam, the Middle East, and the newspaper's Washington Bureau. He joined *Cleveland Magazine* in 1972 and served as editor for 17 years. He works in public relations and regularly writes for several publications.